Karlton E. Hester, Ph.D.
Herbert Gussman Director of "Jazz" Studies, Cornell University

FROM AFRICA
TO AFROCENTRIC INNOVATIONS
SOME CALL "JAZZ"

Volume 3: The Creation of Free, Fusion and Reconstructive Modern Styles (1950-2000; Chapters 9-12)

Hesteria Records & Publishing Company

Areas of Scholarship:
1. Music / Musicology /2. Africana Studies /3. History
4. Sociology /5. Humanities /6. Biography

ISBN 1586840-54-1

Published by:
Hesteria® Records & Publishing Company

Co-distributed by:
African American
Innovators, LLC
P.O. Box 4613
Ithaca,
New York 14852, USA
T (610) 361-0166
F (610) 361-0165
E-mail:
orders@aainnovators.com

Global Publications
State University of New York
at Binghamton
Binghamton,
New York, 13902-6000, USA
T (607) 777-4495 or 6104
F (607) 777-6132
E-mail:
pmorewed@binghamton.edu

Printed in the United States

To the Memory of My Parents,

Clara Briggs and Daniel Webster Hester

Contents

IX
Innovators Emerging
Between 1950–1960

My cheeks started bulging out. I didn't
get any physical pain from it, but all of
a sudden, I looked like a frog whenever
I played. I hadn't always played like
that. . . It was technically incorrect for
playing with a symphony orchestra; but
for what I wanted, it was perfectly
correct.

—Dizzy Gillespie

Continued Resistance to African-American Freedom

Although art often reflects the environment in
which it resides, it can also provide a social pabulum
enabling people to deflect controversial,
embarrassing, or uncomfortable conditions. On the
surface, "cool jazz" and other musical styles that
evolved during the 1950s were less volatile than

bebop. Nonetheless, the "strange fruit" Billie Holiday sang about continued to be a reality with which African Americans had to deal. The death of Emmett Till in 1955 reminded us that imperious, sanguineous, and pandemoniac behavior was still very much a part of the American way of life.

Emmett Till was a fourteen-year-old African-American boy from Chicago who was unaccustomed to the racist apartheid practiced in the deep South when he visited his uncle Mose Wright (a preacher) in Money, Mississippi. Emmett had graduated from an integrated school where he felt comfortable with friends of all races.

While on vacation in Mississippi one Sunday in August, while Wright delivered his sermon from the pulpit, Emmett slipped away with his young cousins from church and drove down the road to a grocery store that catered primarily to an African-American clientele. Emmett was dressed in dress slacks, wore a tie, and was a handsome young man. A twenty-one-year-old European-American woman named Carolyn Bryant, who was working as a clerk in the store, later testified that Emmett whistled at her. Mose said his sons told him that Emmett merely told the woman that she was pretty.[1]

Regardless of the exact nature of the verbal exchange that day, Carolyn's husband (Roy Bryant) and his friend, J. W. Moses, forcefully abducted Emmett from the Wright's home later that week and told him, "Boy, you ain't never goin' to see the sun come up again."[2] The men then took Till at gunpoint to a barn in nearby Sunflower County and proceeded to bludgeon the boy with heavy clubs for an extended period of time before tying his dead, distorted body to a cotton gin exhaust fan (weighing almost a hundred pounds) and submerging him in the Tallahatchie River. When a seventeen-year-old fisherman discovered Emmett Till and the local authorities recovered the body, his head was no longer recognizable as human.

Bryant and Milam then ordered the Wrights to bury young Bo (Emmett) three hours after the body was found, telling them, "Don't let the sun go down and that body is out of the ground." He had not even been embalmed. Mrs. Wright shipped the body to Till's mother in Chicago instead. He was the third African-American boy to be murdered in the area within three months. Mamie Till, Bo's mother, refused to allow the undertaker to alter the young Till's appearance for the funeral. She wanted the world to see what had been done to her only son. Reportedly hundreds of thousands of people marched past the open casket in Chicago at A. A. Rayner & Sons Funeral Home.

The trial began Monday, September 19, in Sumner, Mississippi. A surprise witness, Willie Reed was brought forth. He was an eighteen-year-old boy who had heard Till's screams and had positively identified Milam. The Leflore County sheriff, George Smith, testified that one of the defendants admitted abducting Till. Mose Wright also identified the alleged murderers, yet the all-European-American jury found both Bryant and Milam innocent after only an hour and seven minutes. One juror said, "If we hadn't stopped to drink pop, it wouldn't have taken that long."[3] Later, the entire Sumner County bar admitted that sufficient evidence had been presented to convict the pair. Jurors also later confessed that all members of the panel knew the pair was guilty. The African-American community was outraged. The American Jewish Committee sent a seven-page memo from its Paris office to New York stating, "Europe's reaction to the trial and the verdict in Sumner, Mississippi, was swift, violent and universal. There was total and unqualified condemnation of the court proceedings, of the weakness of the prosecution, the behavior of the jury and the judge, and at the verdict for acquittal."[4]

Changes

Many musicians in the late 1940s and early 1950s tailored new styles for themselves that served to express their ideas within the limits of their own technique, temperament, and personal musical aspirations. Miles Davis began moving in his own direction and found a slower, cooler "jazz" more natural for his particular brand of genius to develop. Parker remained a part of his musical world, but Miles was then in control of his own musical destiny. In his autobiography, Miles gives the reader a glimpse of this transition.

> Nineteen fifty-three began all right with me making a record for Prestige with Sonny Rollins (who had gotten out of jail), Bird (who appeared on the album as "Charlie Chan"), Walter Bishop, Percy Heath, and Philly Joe Jones on drums (who I was hanging with a lot at the time). Bird had an exclusive contract with Mercury (I think he had left Verve by then), so he had to use a pseudonym on record. Bird had given up shooting heroin because since Red Rodney had been busted and sent back

to prison at Lexington, Bird thought the police were watching him. In place of his normal big dosages of heroine, now he was drinking an enormous amount of alcohol. I remember him drinking a quart of vodka at the rehearsal, so by the time the engineer was running the tape for the session, Bird was fucked up out of his mind.

It was like having *two* leaders at the session. Bird treated me like I was his son, or a member of *his* band. But this was *my* date and so I had to get him straight. It was difficult, because he was always on my back about one thing or another. I got so angry with him that I told him off, told him that I had never done that to him on one of his recording sessions. Told him that I had always been professional on his shit. And do you know what that motherfucker said to me? He told me some shit like, "All right, Lily Pons . . . to produce beauty, we must suffer pain—from the oyster comes the pearl." He said that to me in that fucked-up, fake British accent. Then, the motherfucker fell asleep. I got so mad all over again that I started fucking up. Ira Gitler, who was producing the record for Bob Weinstock, came out of the booth and told me *I* wasn't playing shit. At this point, I was so fed up that I started packing up my horn to leave when Bird said to me, "Miles, what are

you doing?" So I told him what Ira had
said, and Bird said, "Ah, come on Miles,
let's play some music." And so we
played some real good stuff after that.[5]

The idea of a "producer" in innovative African-
American music is an interesting phenomenon.
During most of the time producers have been
associated with "Black" music, they have rarely been
knowledgeable about the music they are "producing;
they merely have access to the money needed to
cover the costs involved in a recording session.
Stravinsky, Bernstein, or Cage never had producers
calling the shots in their recording sessions. In a
racist society where African Americans are
systematically ostracized from the American
economic infrastructure, the "plantation" and
carpetbagger mentalities inherited from the slave
and reconstruction eras persists in the formation of
the numerous "middleman" occupations that
traditionally leech off the labor of creative African-
American musicians. Because their positions go
unchallenged (because musicians need work and
have few alternatives beyond the modern "plantation
store"), people like Ira Gitler become very arrogant
and deluded in regards to their professional
relevance to the music created. The music evolves
regardless of whether Gitler is involved, but the
musical direction would be severely altered if Miles
and Bird had actually left the session.

Hard bop produced a sound that was more
aggressive, darker, simpler melodically, and slower
paced harmonically than bebop. The drums are more
freely expressive. The hard bop pianist places even
greater emphasis on the right hand than bop
pianists do. On the West Coast, music became more

reserved, less experimental, and more mellow; "cool" rather than "hot" in musical disposition. The social environment in America during that period included the baby boom and an intensified emphasis on structure and social conformity. It was generally a more conservative (and male-dominated) decade than the 1940s. Women gradually disappeared from the workforce in post–World War II years and disappeared from the big bands with whom they played during the 1930s and 1940s. The film *Rosie the Riveter* and other documentaries covering women's roles in American society during those eras clearly portray the social tendencies. Such documentation addressed the styles and forms of propaganda that persuaded American society that women should be confined to the home, taking care of their family's domestic responsibilities. *Rosie the Riveter* also sheds light on the economic elements that served as the catalyst for this movement toward sexist indoctrination.

Art forms are not constantly stable but, rather, are continuously evolving, changing, and reflecting the world in which they exist. The essence of spontaneous art forms is missed when too much attention is focused strictly on analyzing chord progressions or searching for formulaic devices. In focusing exclusively on such an approach, other crucial factors involving personal expression and intuitiveness are eliminated. Miles talks about Bird's approach to music:

> Bird would play the melody he wanted. The other musicians had to remember what he played. He was real spontaneous, went on his instinct. He didn't conform to Western ways of

> musical group interplay by organizing
> everything. Bird was a great improviser
> and that's where he thought great
> music came from and what great
> musicians were about. His concept was
> "fuck what's written down." Play what
> you know and play that well and
> everything will come together—just the
> opposite of Western concept of notated
> music.[6]

Miles and Bird were the members of the first
generation of African-American innovators to develop
their music largely outside the African-American
cultural milieu. When "jazz" moved downtown into a
sometimes-hostile setting out of financial necessity,
more impersonal presentation styles or terse aspects
of the music emerged, displaying levels of musical
and social defiance as a result. The confidence and
independence that bebop produced enabled modern
musicians to withstand negative consequences of
their sociocultural transition.

Harlem produced a phenomenal array of
cultural manifestations despite economic
disadvantages. In the typical urban American
setting, an area like Harlem is economically destined
to be a slum where cheap labor is exploited when
needed by the more affluent citizens in an area, then
discarded after the labor is deemed no longer
necessary. Slums are not supposed to produce art
forms that influence and modify the entire world.
Although it has struggled against shortages of
money, security, and political respect, early
twentieth-century Harlem has always successfully
resisted becoming a slum. Instead it became a
community that fostered powerful twentieth-century

music, culture, and political thought that influenced social behavior throughout the globe. The Apollo, the Harlem Globetrotters, Marcus Garvey, and other names wielded influence far beyond the United States borders.

European composers began to abandon functional tonality near the end of the nineteenth century. From Richard Wagner's *Prelude to Tristan and Isolde* (1859) (where the listener's awareness of a single nuclear tonal center is reoriented) to more radical adjustments made by the composers of the second Viennese School (Anton von Webern, Alban Berg, and Arnold Schoenberg), efforts aimed toward migrating further from tonal concepts were explored. One method involved devising systems (twelve-tone and serial composition) where no one tone within a set of tones serves as a gravitational tonic.

In the early 1950s, George Russell, Buddy Collette, Gunther Schuller, Jimmy Giuffre, and others used serial techniques in their "jazz" compositions. The Modern Jazz Quartet began to compose and perform music that incorporated instruments such as flutes, cellos, violins, and other instruments usually associated with European chamber music in some of their pioneering work. Gunther Schuller coined the term "third stream jazz" to describe the stylistic movement launched by the Modern Jazz Quartet that fused elements of European "classical" music and "jazz." The quartet (featuring pianist John Lewis [b. 1920], vibraphonist Milt Jackson [1923-1999], bassist Percy Heath [b. 1923], and drummer Kenny Clarke [1914–85] was formed from members of the Dizzy Gillespie Big Band. They moved from Gillespie's big band bebop style to a more restrained and subtle sound associated with "cool jazz" of the 1950s. Of all the musicians who followed the third stream "jazz" line of innovation, the Modern Jazz Quartet came closest to moving beyond a fusion of styles, while still managing to sound less circumspect and self-conscious than most other Third Stream experiments. Other innovators (John Coltrane, for instance) realized that the blues and other modern forms of African-American music had always been styles that "used all twelve tones," but preferred organizing their musical systems in a more intuitive compositional manner.

Mal Waldron developed a style that merged the Silver and Monk approaches to hard bop with his own lyricism. Many hard bop players came to New York from Philadelphia and Detroit.

Among the important hard bop innovators were Sonny Rollins (tenor sax), John Coltrane (tenor/soprano sax), Horace Silver (piano), Cannonball Adderley (alto sax), Art Blakey (drums), Clifford Brown (trumpet), and Wes Montgomery (guitar).

Miles Davis and "Cool Jazz"

Miles Davis began performing professionally during the summer of 1944 while still a teenager in his hometown of St. Louis. When the Billy Eckstine band came to town with Charlie Parker, Gene Ammons, Lucky Thompson, Art Blakey, and other illustrious members, Miles had the good fortune to substitute for one of it's ailing trumpet players. When he later arrived in New York City he replaced Dizzy Gillespie in a band he and Charlie Parker shared. He eventually developed a midrange style that was technically less demanding that Gillespie's, but served as a catalyzing nexus for some of the most innovative music and musicians of the second half of the 20th century.

Davis attended casual sessions in Gil Evan's basement apartment where he collaborated with Evans, John Lewis, Gerry Mulligan, and others to produce music at a slower tempo with relaxed solos that were technically much more accessible for most musicians than bebop. Although the era of "cool jazz" eventually began to take root on the West coast and with a specific set of players (including Lennie Tristano and Lee Konitz), the term was most probably coined when Miles organized his historic session, in collaboration with Gil Evans and Gerry Mulligan, to produce the album *Birth of the Cool* (1949–50). The orchestration of "cool jazz" was sometimes different from that of bebop because it occasionally used an augmented instrumentation that included the tuba and French horn, producing unusual timbres. It stood apart from the big band sound because there were generally no homogenous sections.

The main advocates of the "cool" movement were Miles Davis, Stan Getz, Lee Konitz, and Gerry Mulligan. With Miles, the early "quasi-modal" experiments ("Milestones," "So What!" "Flamenco Sketches") were subjected to a gradual process of development into a mature experimental style such as that heard on the album *Nefertiti*, in free fission experiments like *Pangaea*; and even on fusion albums like *TuTu*.

Some "cool" musicians were influenced by Lennie Tristano and Claude Thornhill. The movement along that stylistic line flourished primarily on the West Coast, where several important groups of European-American musicians congregated in Los Angeles. Some "cool jazz" musicians used bop as its principal structure. Much of the resulting music often adopted a more transparent, Lester Young–influenced style, while conspicuously avoiding obvious characteristics of Charlie Parker's style. Emphasis was often directed toward arranging and composing and less on individual virtuosity. Some talented artists of the "West Coast" style eventually redirected their interest in innovative "jazz" experimentation toward more lucrative commercial "jazz" (Buddy Collette, Quincy Jones, and Oliver Nelson were involved in music for television and film, for example). Film scores also provided a creative outlet and attracted many capable "jazz" musicians on the West Coast because it provided steady and comfortable income. This was a practical move that was useful in popularizing the "cool jazz" movement.

"Deception" (recorded March 9, 1950) was composed and arranged by Davis. The instrumentation for the date included Davis (trumpet), J. J. Johnson (trombone), Gunther Schuller (French horn), John Barber (tuba), Lee Konitz (alto saxophone), G. Mulligan (baritone saxophone), Al McKibbon (bass), Max Roach (drums), and Kenny Hagood (vocals). Miles, Evans, and Mulligan explored a mixture of styles, all of which focused upon seeking freedom and new approaches to conceptual unity. The discovery of a new musical sensitivity within the Miles Davis Nonet marked the beginning of a series of experiments with timbre and orchestration for the iconoclastic trumpeter.

Over the next few decades Davis led a series of innovative groups which included many illustrious young innovators of the "jazz" world. His remarkable sextet in 1957 introduced John Coltrane to a broader audience. Later collaborations with Gil Evans produced such albums as *Porgy and Bess* and *Sketches of Spain*, expanding the *Birth of the Cool* idea into a full orchestral setting. Davis' 1959 album "Kind of Blue" was the recording that popularized quasi-modal improvisation in the 1960s, but later in his career he incorporated electronic music, mixing elements of rock, funk, salsa, blues, and "quasi-modal jazz" into his works. His vanguard performances and recordings as leader of experimental groups set the style for subsequent fusion and "jazz"-rock styled experiments. Miles' music attracted young prodigious "jazz" musicians who were willing to explore new musical territories. *Sketches of Spain* and *Flamenco Sketches*, both based upon Latin American themes, were excursions involving movement away from restrictive changes. Miles and Gil Evans both realized that African-American and Latin American music merged well (just as Dizzy Gillespie realized).

Davis was well grounded in the bebop style, and later led highly successful groups in the hard bop tradition. In his next phase, Miles Davis evolved a compositional approach that allowed the improviser greater freedom to focus on improvised melodies. Compared to the harmonic frameworks of his original "cool" and hard bop tunes, the number of chord changes were reduced drastically in the subsequent styles. Shifting the emphasis toward melody rather than chord changes was related to the compositional approach Ornette Coleman had introduced earlier. Now, Davis and his sidemen like Coleman began to realize that greater coherence between themes, phrases, and motives could be achieved in this more vertically oriented free fashion.

Beginning with the album "Kind of Blue," Miles began to break the limitations of modern compositions by breaking with the harmonic progression. The term "modal jazz" was applied to this approach, although the musicians rarely confined themselves to the notes of a particular mode. On "So What," Davis stays the closest to the Dorian mode in his cohesive melodic improvisation, which interjects only a few contradictory embellishments to this set of pitches. John Coltrane, in contrast, stretches the "modal" framework suggested by the pitch sets established by the bass melody. The term "modal" does adequately identify the emphasis Davis placed on his horizontal approach to improvisation and composition. The ensemble from this period, often called Miles' Classic Sextet (which included Cannonball Adderley on alto sax, Paul Chambers on bass, and James Cobb on drums and combined the trumpet of Miles Davis with the tenor sax of Coltrane) stretched the suggested modal areas rhythmically and melodically.

In compositions like "So What" Davis and his ensemble demonstrate a "quasi-modal" approach through a relatively static harmonic underpinning involving only a couple of chord changes over a thirty-two-measure cycle. The formal framework is the same as that of the popular song (AABA) but substitutes a single "quasi-modal" pitch set for the usual type of harmonic progression that might accompany each eight-measure phrase. Cannonball Adderley and John Coltrane, who were members of the Davis ensemble during the beginning of the trumpeter's "quasi-modal" experiments, continued to expand along that horizontal direction throughout remainder of their careers. Davis used fewer notes than he played in bebop, caressing the details of individual notes, rhythms, and phrases. This stood out as much as the new compositional process did during a musical period when other musicians were still striving to achieve technical prowess through the fast-paced technical virtuosity and elemental derivatives of bebop.

The length of the composition and its formal structure also eventually became relatively free of preconception in Miles' new approach. Each player had some degree of control over the length of time spent on each harmonic area of the musical construct. In the composition "Flamenco Sketches," Davis signals a new mode by falling silent and letting the bassist lead into the next tonal "modal" area. When aiming to advance to the next modal area, Coltrane signaled this by increasing the number of notes per beat and intensifying the rhythmic and dynamic strata. Adderley begins to embellish the "modal" notes in his melody just before leading the rhythm section into the next "mode."

The seeds for free "jazz" did not begin with "quasi-modal jazz," or with the experiments of Ornette Coleman or Lennie Tristano. It was instead a cumulative evolutionary and revolutionary process that dated back to the dawn of "jazz." This gradual process included the innovations of drummer Zutty Singleton, one of the earliest precursors of varied meters. The innovations in bass playing initiated by Jimmy Blanton and Leroy ("Slam") Stewart freed the bass from a functional role that set the course for the modern requirements of a freer style of bass playing. Thus, the bass became the foundation for spontaneous composition and improvisation. The enormous experimental progression of early pianists included Earl Hines, Teddy Wilson, Art Tatum, Thelonious Monk, and Bud Powell, all of who contributed to the evolutionary movement away from the stride piano style.

The 1950s musical explorations involved a continued expansion upon the modern "jazz" language. Parker developed his solos on compositions such as "Embraceable You" (recorded October 28, 1947) from motives he developed systematically throughout his improvisation, providing organic coherence. Before bebop, Coleman Hawkins, often regarded as primarily a vertical improviser (he outlines chord changes in shaping his solo), demonstrated how lyrical a harmonic approach could become in his classic recording of "Body and Soul." John Lewis and the other members of the Modern Jazz Quartet placed heavy restraints upon their music and combined African-American approaches with European styles to produce what has been called Third Stream or "classical jazz." Dave Brubeck emphasized meter while he, like the Modern Jazz Quartet, diminished the intensity and vitality of the music bebop unleashed. The search for freedom had always remained at the root of the "jazz" tradition, and "jazz" continued to move in an evolutionary fashion in the 1950s.

There were other "cool jazz" and post-bop directions taken during the 1950s. Claude Thornhill, sometimes referred to as the father of the "cool" style big band, influenced Stan Kenton. Kenton became one of the most reknown big band "jazz" arrangers due to his work on college campuses across America. Marian McPartland and Billy Taylor also spread the word about "jazz" to mass America over the next few decades as their musical messages were broadcasted over the radio. From the early 1940s, the Nat King Cole Trio moved from humble beginnings in small nightclubs in Hollywood and New York City to become an international success. Nathaniel Adams "Nat King" Cole (1917–65) was also a featured actor and performer in film, television, and radio. Between 1956 and 1957 he was the only African American in the country hosting his own variety show on network television.[7]

Although Lennie Tristano modeled his personal approach after Art Tatum's piano style, Tristano's music lacked the rhythmic drive and sophistication of bop innovators. In many ways Tristano's melodies were more predictable and less abstract than bebop, yet he avoided the musical complacency to which many "cool" tunes seemed to succumb. Tristano demonstrated yet another fresh and original set of ideas that were carried over into the 1950s.

The success of the "cool" style of Miles Davis, the Dave Brubeck Quartet, The Modern Jazz Quartet, and others during the 1950s might be due to the fact that "cool jazz" involved more easy listening than bebop. Perhaps many people enjoyed it because it did not challenge their ears to the degree bop did. Nevertheless, the music of Miles Davis from this period provides the perfect archetypes for both "cool" and "modal" stylistic approaches during the 1950s. Miles continued to explore new musical forms and revolt against conventional and conservative ideas. Innovative African-American music has always been progressive. Wayne Shorter once described Miles in unusual terms:

> To sum up Miles, I like to call him right now an original Batman. He was a crusader for justice and for value. He'd be Miles Dewey Davis III by day, the

son of Dr. Davis, and at night in the nightclubs he's in lizard skin suits with dark shades and he's doing his Batman—fighting for truth and justice. But Batman had to be a dual personality too, like he knew the criminal mind. So Miles, whatever he did that was not criminal but like short-tempered or he cursed everybody out, and when he was younger he'd hit somebody, or like they say Miles treated some woman really bad, or something like that. . . . I would say that Bruce Wayne, the guy that played Batman, he was capable of doing that too, that's why he was such a good Batman.[8]

Miles Davis indeed introduced the definitive cool style to the world, but his career encompassed a much broader range of innovative directions. After his sextet featuring, Coltrane and Cannonball Adderley separated, Davis formed another incredible ensemble (this time a quintet) with Wayne Shorter, Tony Williams, Herbie Hancock, and Ron Carter during the 1960s. He later experimented with jazz/rock/fusion at the beginning of the 1970 before retreating into a self-imposed exile in 1975. By the 1980s Miles was again experimenting on the "jazz" scene. He never ceased seeking new sounds and directions.

Louis Jordan and Sonny Rollins

Louis Jordan was a world-renowned alto saxophonist, vocalist, and bandleader born in Brinkley, Arkansas, on July 8, 1908. After moving to New York City, he eventually joined forces with drummer Chick Webb's band. Jordan gained prominence in the world of rhythm-and-blues in the Big Apple. Webb featured Jordan as both a vocalist and saxophone soloist between 1936 and 1938.

The "jump band" was a small swing band that developed between the late 1930s and early 1950s. It generally featured two or three soloists in front of a swinging rhythm section. It was appealing to the African-American cabaret audiences because it retained the sexual and nuptial humor of the music from old "Black" vaudeville shows.

In 1938 Jordan ventured out to form his own "jump band," playing and recording with many of the giants of the music industry, such as Bing Crosby (1944), Ella Fitzgerald (1945 and 1949), Louis Armstrong (1950), and various other artists. During these years his combo enjoyed a steady rise to national and international fame. His combo, known as the "Timpani Five," released many successful singles in the forties such as "Knock Me a Kiss," "Gonna Move to the Outskirts of Town," and "Choo Choo Ch' Boogie" (which sold over a million copies). Jordan broke into show business with his unique combination of visual showmanship, superb musicianship, a strong accent on humor, and a delightfully original and rhythmic vocal style. Jordan's vocal technique often incorporated an alternation between head and chest voice ("falsetto break") related to styles found in vocal music in various regions of Africa, south of the Sahara. He organized a big band for a tour in the fall of 1951 and occasionally augmented his combo for theater dates, but Jordan was primarily a small combo performer by preference. Though Louis Jordan's music remained closer to "jazz," he is generally considered to be the progenitor of rhythm-and-blues.

Theodore Walter Rollins is a "jazz" improviser and composer of significant skill who has always generated a powerful and ascetic tenor saxophone style that seems closely related to his personal lifestyle. Sonny Rollins was born in New York in 1930. Both his brother and sister played musical instruments, and Sonny started his musical studies on piano. He took up the saxophone after being influenced by the sound of Louis Jordan.

In addition to Jordan's hard-swinging influence on Rollins, the younger saxophonist was also fortunate enough to live in the same neighborhood with Coleman Hawkins, Thelonious Monk, and Bud Powell. Hawkins and Monk befriended Rollins and showed him things about bebop music. Of course, Sonny Rollins also came under the spell of Charlie Parker. He recorded his first record for the Capital label, *St. Louis Blues*, in 1948 with Babs Gonzales.

The following year he went into the studio with Bud Powell and Fats Navarro. In 1950 he joined drummer Ike Day in Chicago, an infrequently recorded musician who Rollins considers one of the greatest drummers of all time.[9] Miles Davis, who already developed a considerable reputation at the time, heard the tenor saxophonist in a club in Harlem one night after Rollins returned to New York. Their first recordings together were released on the Prestige record label in 1951. By the end of that year Rollins recorded his first album as a leader. He did not record again with Miles over the next couple years, but performed on recording sessions with Thelonious Monk, Charlie Parker (on tenor), and the Modern Jazz Quartet.

Rollins made important recordings with Miles Davis in 1954. His composition "Oleo," recorded during this period, became a "jazz" standard. After this productive musical phase, and during the height of a battle between critics over whether he or Coltrane was the "best" tenor player of the day, Rollins took the first of many long sabbaticals from public performance. It is interesting that *Down Beat* and other magazines continue to debate the "value" of musicians with their "Readers Polls" and "Critics' Polls" but have never considered the perspectives of the musicians themselves important enough to warrant the founding of a "Musicians' Poll." This neglect is quite an instructive barometer in calculating the levels of arrogance, disrespect, and delusion that Miles, Coltrane, Rollins, and other professional artists encountered in a racist society. Many artists suffer at the hand of the critic, regardless of race, but the levels of pompousness and irrationality found in early literature devoted to African-American music can be startling and embarrassing.

Rollins used the mid-1950s to kick his heroine addiction and returned to the scene in 1955 joining the Clifford Brown–Max Roach Quintet (replacing tenor saxophonist Harold Land, who returned to California). Rollins said, "Clifford was a profound influence on my personal life. He showed me that it was possible to live a good clean life, and still be a good jazz musician."[10] Rollins was playing better than ever in the Brown-Roach ensemble, but then Clifford Brown was killed, on June 26, 1956, in

an automobile accident. Donald Byrd briefly took
over the trumpet position and was followed by Kenny
Dorham. Parker died the year before, and Max Roach
left the group the following year. Rollins still
managed to record some of the work for which he is
best known, such as "Misterioso" (with Thelonious
Monk) and his own "Saxophone Colossus" (with
pianist Tommy Flanagan and bassist Doug Watkins).

In 1957 Rollins recorded "Way Out West" with
Max Roach in a pianoless setting. Ray Brown was on
bass and Shelly Manne was the drummer. Rollins'
willingness to take a popular song of any kind as an
improvisational vehicle has become his trademark.
In expressing his feelings about music he said:

> I think eventually that there won't be
> jazz any more or classical music, but
> one big music, in which everyone can
> play what he feels. What they call the
> third stream is a beginning at that, but
> the writers haven't left these people
> alone to work their problems out for
> themselves. They aren't ready to be
> analyzed yet. Of course, the real
> beginning of that attempt is Duke
> Ellington. Monk is an extension of
> Duke, I think, and Duke is the unsung
> giant of American music. I spoke to
> someone recently who had seen
> Ellington and Duke said that he had
> heard some of my records and liked the
> way I played. Can you imagine how I
> felt about Ellington saying something
> like that? I've recorded as many of his
> songs as I could. Perhaps he heard one
> of those.[11]

John Coltrane and Other New Approaches to Spontaneous Composition

With the conceptual and technical consolidation of the approaches of Lester Young and Coleman Hawkins with the influence Charlie Parker, the stage was set for a new order of saxophone evolution in the fifties. Dexter Gordon combined elements of Hawkins, Young, and Parker; while Sonny Stitt combined Young and Parker influences to create a synergistic style that served as one of the forerunners of hard bop. It was John Coltrane and Sonny Rollins, however, who ushered in the most influential and distinctive prototypes for "jazz" tenor saxophone after the Young-Hawkins-Parker tradition.

Rollins followed Young's influence more closely. His style emphasized melodic and thematic improvisation, but also involved a big, full sound (characteristic of Hawkins) and an impelling rhythmically driven melodic approach (a Parker trait). Coltrane seem to take more cues from Hawkins. From the beginning of his career, Trane was inclined to employ a systematic and sophisticated harmonic approach (as did Hawkins). His tone quality was centered and had an almost brittle edge that produced a timbre close to the sound quality of the alto sax (which was related to the sound Young and Parker produced). Coltrane's employed a more impetuous rhythmic freedom, involving uneven grouping of notes (a tendency found in works of both Parker and Young).

Both the Rollins and Coltrane style involved many gradual modifications. Initial influences attributed to Young and Hawkins were blurred at times before resurfacing periodically during their various stylistic periods of development. Coltrane was also instrumental in the resurgence of the soprano saxophone. Coltrane's long progression of musical achievements are heard on over a hundred LP and CD recordings and include pivotal performances such as "Kind of Blue" (with Miles Davis), his own "Giant Steps," "A Love Supreme," and "Selflessness" later in his career. Rollins' skills and inventiveness are displayed in the albums "Strode Rode," "Saxophone Colossus," and "The Freedom Suite." A few of the musicians displaying the influence of both Rollins and Coltrane are Dexter Gordon, Charlie Rouse, Joe Farrell, Jimmy Heath, Johnny Griffin, George Coleman, Benny Golson, Joe Henderson, Sam Rivers, Yusef Lateef, Wayne Shorter, Frank Foster, David Murray, Branford Marsalis, and Pharoah Sanders.

Charlie Parker innovations also found counterparts in the late fifties and early sixties in the work of Ornette Coleman and Eric Dolphy. Coleman revolutionized the approach to small group improvisation while challenging the tonal and harmonic regularities of the hard bop and "cool" schools of "jazz." Coleman is credited with the founding of the "Free Jazz" school. Dolphy pushed the borderlines of harmony and tonal textures, while bringing the bass clarinet and flute to new heights in the modern "jazz" milieu. Along with the pioneering work of flutists such as Wayman Carver, Buddy Collette, and Herbie Mann, Dolphy's work on flute was paramount in the evolution of the flute into a genuine "jazz" instrument.

A synthesis of the styles generated by the new saxophone dynasty (Coltrane-Rollins-Coleman) set the musical agenda for the primary approaches in "jazz" extant until the end of the twentieth century. Musicians such as Julius Hemphill, Dewey Redman, Branford Marsalis, Oliver Lake, Joshua Redman, Bobby Watson, David Murray, and Arthur Blythe can trace their approaches back to these three saxophonists. But the single most influential saxophonist after Charlie Parker was John Coltrane.

John William Coltrane was born in Hamlet, North Carolina, on the equinox, September 23, 1926. His mother, Alice Blair, and his father, John R. Coltrane, were both minister's children and amateur musicians.

When Coltrane was twelve, he began studying the E-flat alto horn (a brass wind instrument) with Reverend Steele, who formed a community band. He later changed to the clarinet. His mother soon bought him a used alto saxophone for his birthday. "Jazz" composer/performer Benny Golson recalls Coltrane's "exquisite sound" around that time as "even bigger than Johnny Hodges's."[12] In addition to Hodges, it was Lester Young and Coleman Hawkins who made the biggest impression on the young Coltrane.

"Any time you play your horn, it helps you," Coltrane said regarding his stay with Earl Bostic in 1952. His move to the group led by Johnny Hodges in 1953 was a more productive one. "We played honest music in this band," he recalled, "it was my education to the older generation."[13]

Following his productive musical association with Bostic, Coltrane continued to develop a sound knowledge of earlier "jazz" forms. He performed with the Dizzy Gillespie Big Band and was among the few carefully selected sidemen asked to play with Gillespie's new combo when the big band broke up at the end of 1950. Gillespie's ensemble included vibraphonist Milt Jackson, alto saxophonist Jimmy Heath, bassist Percy Heath, drummer Specs Wright, and Fred Strong on conga drums.

In September 1955 Sonny Rollins disappeared from the "jazz" scene "like he said he would," and Miles could not track him down. In trying to find a replacement for him, Davis tried John Gilmore (who was playing with Sun Ra at the time) but he didn't fit Miles' needs. Philly Joe Jones recommended Coltrane, with whom both Miles and Rollins had performed at the Audubon a few years prior. Miles felt that Sonny had "blown him [Coltrane] away that night," so Miles was not extremely excited about Coltrane as a prospect. Much to his surprise, however, Coltrane "had gotten a lot better" in the interim.[14]

Miles and Coltrane did not get along at first. Frustrated, Coltrane left for home only to accept another invitation to rejoin Davis' band later the same year. While Miles produced some of his best work with pianist Red Garland, bassist Paul Chambers, drummer Philly Joe Jones, and, later, alto saxophonist Julian "Cannonball" Adderley, it was Coltrane who most radically shaped his style. Gradually Coltrane's style became more confident and progressively more assertive, while his now distinguished full tone acquired a hard resilient sound. Some "jazz" historians feel that the period of "Cannonball" Adderley's association with Miles and Coltrane marked Davis' creative peak.[15]

Although Miles and Coltrane utilized contrasting musical approaches to performance, they shared important general mutual aspirations and worked along similar lines to achieve their objectives. During his bebop days, Davis' technique was criticized as suspect; perhaps due to this criticism, Miles always tended to incorporate a high level of simplicity into his post-bop stylistic approaches. The severance of his solos from standard bop and hard bop chord changes upon which earlier songs were built facilitated his aims, and this initiated the transition into "quasi-modal" and other musical explorations Davis later codified. While Coltrane, on the other hand, continued to emphasize the harmonic functions and potentialities of a given composition, he too began to focus his improvisation upon scales and horizontal dimensions. The resulting "quasi-modal" approach to improvisation was the most significant innovation to occur in "jazz" since bebop. Miles recognized Coltrane's value to this line of development and appreciated fully the gravity of this historic encounter: "The group I had with Coltrane made me and him a legend... put me on the map in the music world, with all those great albums we made for Prestige and later Columbia Records...[It] made all of us stars."[16]

Musicians who played in the big bands of the 1930s and 1940s were typically showcased only when they were considered advanced enough to take feature solos. Jam sessions were established so musicians could have more informal solo time to display or ameliorate their improvisational skills. Performers were also invited to sit in with groups in the clubs for a similar pedagogical purpose. The need to increase solo time was one of many factors that caused established bebop directions. As the recording industry eventually replaced the 78 rpm record with 33 1/3 LP recordings, "jazz" musicians could then play longer solos without having to worry about more restricted time constraints.

Unlike the bebop era, hard bop produced a large number of excellent tenor saxophone players. Just as the trumpet had been the predominant force in early "jazz," Sonny Rollins and John Coltrane made the tenor sax a dominant hard bop force. Their radical stylistic characteristics influenced rhythm sections as well as front-line "jazz" instrumentalists. The late fifties found Rollins employing themes with bi-tonal implications, where the piano was omitted to provide maximum freedom of improvisational interpretation of the harmonic structures. Coltrane's approach was equally exploratory as he continued to discover material that served as a springboard for a significant portion of his later development.

Although tremendous musical growth was achieved, Coltrane was not sufficiently satisfied. He recorded the album *Mating Call* with Tadd Dameron on November 30, 1956, and a third album with Paul Chambers, in addition to his work with Davis. After performing with Miles throughout 1955 and 1956, Coltrane decided to return home to "woodshed" and to resolve personal problems. He managed to quit his drug habit during this break.

Upon returning to New York, Coltrane joined Thelonious Monk and his highly innovative quartet. This proved to be a challenge that would permanently alter Coltrane's approach to music, as his recordings made in 1957 demonstrate. As Coltrane affirms, his conceptual, technical, and creative authority increased dramatically during his collaboration with Monk.

> In 1955, I joined Miles on a regular
> basis and worked with him 'til the

middle of 1957. I went with Thelonious Monk for the remainder of that year.

Working with Monk brought me close to a musical architect of the highest order. I felt I learned from him in every way—through the senses, theoretically, technically. I would talk to Monk about musical problems, and he would sit at the piano and show me the answers just by playing them. I could watch him play and find out the things I wanted to know. Also, I could see a lot of things that I didn't know about at all.

Monk was one of the first to show me how to make two or three notes at one time on tenor. (John Glenn, a tenor man in Philly, also showed me how to do this. He can play a triad and move notes inside it—like passing tones!) It's done by false fingering and adjusting your lip. If everything goes right, you can get triads. Monk just looked at my horn and "felt" the mechanics of what had to be done to get this effect.

I think Monk is one of the true greats of all time. He's a real musical thinker— there're not many like him. I feel myself fortunate to have had the opportunity to work with him. If a guy needs a little spark, a boost, he can just be around Monk, and Monk will give it to him.[17]

In contrast to Miles's quintet, Monk's music was more difficult conceptually and based upon densely constructed chords that were innovative, exciting, and in defiance of traditional song form and blues formats to which Coltrane had grown accustomed. Even Monk's approach to performance presentation was iconoclastic. After ending a piano solo, the leader would often leave his piano bench for more than a half hour, leaving Coltrane to solo alone as Monk ventured out on an uninhibited spiraling and lurching dance to the music. Of course Monk's repertoire also contained some pieces that adhered to traditional song form and blues formats, such as "Ruby, My Dear" (song form), "Straight, No Chaser" (blues), and others.

As Coltrane expanded his harmonic conception in Monk's band, he also gained independence from restrictions imposed by chords dictated by the keyboard and traditional stratified functions of the rhythm section. He began to explore the principles of multiphonics on the tenor saxophone. "[Monk] also got me into the habit of playing long solos on his pieces, playing the same piece for a long time to find new conceptions for solos. It got so I would go as far as possible on one phrase until I ran out of ideas. The harmonies got to be an obsession for me. Sometimes I'd think I was making music through the wrong end of a magnifying glass."[18]

Coltrane's music from his late stylistic periods often had religious titles: "A Love Supreme," "Ascension," "Om," "Crescent," "The Father and the Son, and the Holy Ghost," "Ogunde," "Meditations," "Amen," "Ascent," and others. His thinking, much as that of Sun Ra, also focused on cosmic principals and outer space: "Infinity," "Interstellar Space," "Sun Ship," "Cosmos," "Out of This World," etc.

Coltrane influenced his musical colleague Cannonball Adderley, and Adderly affected Coltrane's thinking. Adderley developed a personal modern style even before joining Miles and Coltrane in the Classic Miles Davis Sextet. Independently of the direction Parker carved out, Adderley developed a virtuoso musical language of his own, grounded in a soulful saxophone style that grew from his association with Miles and Trane. While not the revolutionary artist Coltrane ended up becoming, Cannonball was one of the first altoists since Parker to carve out an independent personal style that retained the technical and expressive qualities of bop, but with the knowledge of a newer generation directed along a slightly different path. While admitting that Benny Carter was another important influence, Adderley apparently worked out his style without falling under the spell of Parker.[19] While most musicians seem to understand the value of Adderley's musical contribution, he has generally been underrated by the listening public.

Ornette Coleman

Ornette Coleman was born in Fort Worth, Texas, in 1930. He bought his first alto saxophone at fourteen after being inspired by his cousin, James Jordan, who was a saxophonist. Unable to afford lessons, he taught himself music from a piano book. The anomalies formed through this self instruction would eventually lead Coleman into a quandary. Taking his own approach to music later got him fired, beat up, and thrown out of places in which he performed.

Ornette was chased out of Natchez, Mississippi, because the local police did not like his skin color, long hair, and beard. After finding work in a rhythm-and-blues band in New Orleans with Clarence Samuels, he was invited to meet some men in Baton Rouge. The trip was a pusillanimous and brutal trap in which Coleman lost several teeth and his tenor saxophone. The local crowd apparently didn't like the attention "their" women gave traveling musicians. Coleman's next job was on a tour to California with Pee Wee Crayton. By the time the band reached Los Angeles Crayton was paying Ornette *not* to perform. The saxophonist returned to Texas. Coleman never forgot the racism he encountered in those early days: "Because of being a Negro, I've been in certain places and had certain kinds of sadness that would never bother you, that you could never conceive. Do you think some sadness surpasses a reason why you don't have to be sad?"

Coleman mentioned one European-American man who said to him, "I got enough money to burn a wet elephant but I ain't gonna give it away," and offered Coleman three dollars a performance, which began at 9 PM and ended at 1 AM. Coleman said:

> I thought that as long as they were white, they all had the same thing in common, to control and rule you. . . . During intermission, I'd have to go in the back and sit down like I was a porter. One night a drunken woman came right up in front of me and raised her dress over her head, and I was

frightened. . . . People in Texas, they're so wealthy, it's still like slavery. You had to be a servant. You had to be something to somebody to make some money. . . . The Texan thought I was just a mixed up, complexed Negro.[20]

Coleman left Texas to return to California, where he was married. He worked odd jobs as a stock clerk and elevator operator, while continuing to study theory on his own. Trumpeter Don Cherry and bassist Don Payne heard Coleman at a session in Los Angeles and were impressed with his music. They suggested he take his material to Lester Koenig, owner of the Contemporary record label in Los Angeles. Coleman's collaboration with Koenig resulted in his successful debut recordings with that label. Koenig's interest in Coleman's music thus launched the career that would have a tremendous impact on music in the second half of the twentieth century. Coleman became the harbinger of the direction music would take when he made his vision clear in 1958: "Music will be a lot freer. The pattern for a tune, for instance, will be forgotten and the tune itself will be the pattern."[21] Two albums were recorded for Contemporary Records. The first, *The Music of Ornette Coleman: Something Else* (Contemporary S7551, 1958), featured Coleman on alto saxophone, Don Cherry on trumpet, Walter Norris on piano, Don Payne on bass, and Billy Higgins on drums. The second album Coleman recorded before leaving Los Angeles bound for New York was *The New Music of Ornette Coleman: Tomorrow is the Question*, featuring Ornette, Cherry, Red Mitchell and Percy Heath alternating on bass, and Shelly Mann on drums.

Percy Heath, bassist for the Modern Jazz Quartet, heard Coleman one night and later brought his fellow band member (and pianist) John Lewis to hear him. Upon John Lewis's recommendation, Nesuhi Ertegun recorded the first Ornette Coleman records for the Atlantic record label and paid for his scholarship to the Lenox School of Music. Coleman used the advance payment against his royalties for those two albums to move to New York. His Harmolodic approach to spontaneous composition was beginning to take shape when Coleman appeared at the Five Spot Cafe in 1959 for his first extended engagement. His group now consisted of Don Cherry (trumpet), Charlie Haden (bass), and Billy Higgins (drums).

Many of his compositions have programmatic titles. Though his debut at New York City's Five Spot Cafe was essentially triumphant, Coleman's skills and concepts were not yet fully matured. Detractors ridiculed him, accusing him of lacking a basic knowledge of harmony. Others raved about his revolutionary sound. Critics did not like his plastic alto, the same kind Charlie Parker had played earlier. Coleman wanted a new Selmer alto saxophone but had only enough money for either a used Selmer or a new plastic alto. Coleman liked the sound of the plastic horn and bought it.

Coleman's experimentation with collective improvisation involved a significant advancement in liberating the melody from preset chord changes. Many hard bop performers aligned their melodic improvisations closely to preset chord structures, while Coleman devised a conceptual methodology that allowed musicians more autonomy. This freedom applied whether an artist was constructing solo improvisations or playing accompaniment.

Cecil Taylor

Although Cecil Taylor always attracted an esoteric audience of fans and curious spectators, this clientele was often not of the type or size that club owners desired. It was conducive to neither selling drinks nor creating the typical bar room ambiance (ripe for conversation, selling drinks, sexual advances, etc.) because Taylor's audience generally listened and didn't want to be disturbed. His was not background music. Taylor's music filled a musical void. He suggests: "The thing that makes jazz so interesting is that each man is his own academy. . . . If he's really going to be persuasive, he learns about other academies, but the idea is that he must have that special thing. And sometimes you don't even know what it is."[22]

If developing a unique and individual voice within a rich tradition of musical innovation and experimentation is adequate criteria for "jazz," then Cecil Taylor is one of those few artists summarily qualified as a unique "jazz" innovator. "You need everything you can get," Duke Ellington once said. "You need the conservatory with an ear to what's happening in the streets."[23] In the 1970 publication of the book *Jazz People* by Valerie Wilmer, the author describes Taylor as "a genius whose work is the jazz, or black, equivalent of straight composers like Bartok."

Whether or not we are inclined to accept maladroit comparisons of artists, clearly Taylor has chosen to view the world strictly through his own eyes. Among initiated innovators of African-American music, it is understood that uncompromising artistic approaches inevitably lead to the creation of unparalleled artistic expression. Anything from Taylor's discography (that spans five decades) demonstrates that he has always maintained his own musical personality, and his music is grounded in solid preparation.

From the beginning of his career, musicians knew that they had to find new ways of thinking about music when performing with Taylor. Drummer Sunny Murray remembered the difficult time he had adjusting to the music Taylor and saxophonist Jimmy Lyons were playing when he worked with them in Europe. He said, "With Cecil, I had to originate a ·complete new direction on the drums because he was playing different then; he wasn't playing so rhythmically."[24] Preconceived notions about musical style and performance are innocuous in the realm of exploration that Taylor visits.

Born in Long Island City in 1929, Cecil Taylor's uncle interested him at an early age in stride pianists like Fats Waller. His mother grew up with Sonny Greer (one of Duke Ellington's drummers), but Taylor's influences were wide ranging. Cecil graduated from the New England Conservatory of Music in Boston before returning to New York. He attempted to launch a career at a time when work for pianists in clubs was scarce. Wilmer mentions the bitter irony that the roughest of Taylor's difficult times landed him in a restaurant as a dishwasher where his own records were played regularly along with those of Ornette Coleman and John Coltrane's.

Adroit practicing quickly led Taylor out of this dire situation into the controversial role of an uncompromising pianist, experimentalist, and composer who, along with Ornette Coleman, Albert Ayler (1936–70), and other innovators, split the international "jazz" community evenly between (1) those who recognized the significance of innovative artists' contributions to the evolution of American musical tradition and (2) those who insisted upon clinging to well-worn standards of days long past. As with most things of authentic quality and lasting value, however, each of the African-American innovators eventually received just recognition. Ayler did not live long enough to witness the benefit of the eventual appreciation for his musical contribution, but both Taylor and Coleman received the prestigious MacArthur "Genius" Award for their work and have continually expanding audiences for their music.

Record companies had little confidence in Cecil Taylor's music during the 1950s, nonetheless. One of Taylor's recordings with John Coltrane made for the United Artists label during 1958 was not released with his name attached, but instead bore the title *Coltrane Time* (October 13, 1958). Coltrane was well established on the Milestones label at the time and had enjoyed a motivating stint with Thelonious Monk at Five Spot. This was only the third record date for Taylor after a decade of harsh criticism. Despite the misleading attribution, the album stands as an important document for both Cecil Taylor and John Coltrane. The Taylor/Coltrane collaboration proved that six months before Ornette Coleman's first recording session, the prevailing musical rules were broken and new standards being set in "jazz."

Cecil Taylor did not get his first steady engagement at the Five Spot in New York until 1957 following his first album recording, "Jazz Advance." His music in the fifties conflicted sharply with previous "jazz" dialects and traditions. It was dismissed (along with the music of Coltrane and Coleman) as "anti-jazz." It was not music that contained the particular variety of "swing" to which people had become accustomed before the 1950s. A more elastic musical force, that was more difficult to pin down, propelled Taylor's music. Ekkehard Jost attempts to describe the "energy" that often served as a foundation for phases of Taylor's compositions in his book *Free Jazz*.

> As time went on, Taylor compensated the "stagnating" motion (also found in Brubeck's music) by a kind of playing whose dynamic impetus arose not from off-beat phrasing but from combining the parameters of time, intensity and pitch, this term is frequently misused as a meaningless catchword for anything that suggests "power." Let's look closer at this term. Energy is not the equivalent to intensity (measured in decibels) as some of my jazz practitioner countrymen, champions of a misunderstood freedom in jazz, often assume. Energy is, more than anything else, a variable of time. It creates motion or results from motion; it means a process in which the dynamic level is just over *one* variable, and by no means a constant. We need not continue analogies to physics here. Suffice it to say that the kinetic impulses emanating from Cecil Taylor's music are based on the rise and fall of energy.[25]

The most salient elements of a musician's compositional process is often best described by the artist who creates it. Cecil Taylor's unique method of describing his music prepares the listener for hearing it. In the liner notes to his album *Unit Structures* (recorded May 19, 1966), Taylor chooses to describe his composition "Anacrusis to Plain" in this metaphorical fashion: "Joint energy disposal in parts of singular feedings. A recharge; group chain reaction. Acceleration result succession of multiple time compression areas. Sliding elision/beat here is physical commitment to earth force. Rude insistence of tough meeting at vertical centers. Time strata thru panels joined sequence a continuum (movements) across nerve centers. Total immersion."

Listening to the music the composer describes is the only way to understand his description of it. In the same set of composer's notes he comments on "Swing":

> The way—cleansed pearl—many nights passed in isolation darkly what works similar effort. The point of view not to be considered—finally an area of action is created logic in adjustment-end material accumulation dottering fidelity to family breeding class/unaccountable time unseen action resultant produce: overlay reaction 2nd murmurs shape/hunger satiated on plain of absolute; self universal compass/language of silent kings-embodiment-ancestral region hero's plain, a "Gilgamesh" to wine lilacs mania on either side. As high relief fancied time or magic struck winds to

play and enscribe tzuringas moan-to
meaning;   hariecha   we
propagate/foreign   images   converge
upon   consciousness: mind
converses/with additional reason the
mind color gives/overruled political
chatisement moments appeased to
survive (in)/life of choice within
esthetic curve. Creative energy force =
swing motor reaction exchange/fused
pulse expands measured activity
relating series of events.

Taylor forces the listener to understand that
music is not about a simple description that makes
the audience feel comfortable. Music is about many
things. Spontaneous composition often involves
many layers of thought and emotional expression.
Musical inspiration or purpose could never be as
prosaic as many program notes generally suggests.

Cecil Taylor's approach to performance is
often interdisciplinary and has often included dance
and poetry with music. A collaborative performance
was presented at an outdoor concert presented by
the Guggenheim Museum in New York on September
17, 1994, with Taylor on piano and featured
dancer/choreographer Min Tanaka (with whom Cecil
has worked for over ten years). More recently, the
press for his landmark performance at Lincoln
Center enthusiastically acclaimed the virtuoso
pianist. Cecil Taylor's mastery of his own musical
domain and dialect has now been witnessed
throughout the world for several decades, and much
of his solo and ensemble music is preserved on
scores of record albums. A few performances can be
viewed on video recordings as well.

Sun Ra

Sun Ra was a visionary composer who realized that discipline; creativity and unity formed the foundation over which freedom is constructed. He realized that any group or ensemble must have a designated leader regardless of the degree of freedom the music involved. His musicians performed and expressed their ideas within the context of Sun Ra's philosophical focus, aesthetic values, artistic conceptions, and with the leader's sense of compositional proportion well in mind. The consequence of Sun Ra's brand of stewardship was the production of musical performances devoid of self-centered expression and egoistic competition between individual artists.

Many younger musicians who came through the Arkestra perhaps could not conform to such conditions for long; but the seasoned veterans who remained with Sun Ra throughout their careers understood the social, political, spiritual, and musical implications involved in Sun Ra's philosophical approach. African retentions within American culture are found in African-American religious practices and magical beliefs.[26] Sun Ra continued to combine metaphysical forces with his cosmic brand of innovative music.

Sun Ra, one of the most individual composer/pianists in twentieth-century America and leader of the first "free" big band on planet earth, was born in Birmingham, Alabama, in 1914. He admits to having used the names Sonny Lee and Herman "Sonny" Blount at times. When asked about his date of birth he replies, "Actually I don't have an age." When pressed he continues, "Well, really around 1055 or so, I didn't just arrive on this planet you know. I have been around for quite some time. I'm not of any generation, because if I was, I couldn't play the music I am playing."[27] As a follower of numerology and astrology, he refers to his astrological sign, Gemini, in the month of May, but resisted being pinned down to a specific day because of "controversial aspects" involved. "I arrived on this planet on a very important day, it's been pinpointed by wisemen, astrologers as a very important date. I arrived at the exact moment of a very controversial arrival so that's the only reason I don't talk about it. . . . It was controversial because, Well, it's the way the stars were set at that moment. In a position where a spiritual being can arrive at that particular point" (Rusch 1978 b:4).

Sun Ra's music was always experimental and had a unique ecumenical core. Electronics were incorporated into his Arkestra before any other "jazz" musicians began to experiment with them. Sun Ra's music is unique because of its diversity and the emphasis placed upon sound, traditional or otherwise. He said "I remember things—images and scenes and feelings. I never felt like I was part of this planet. I felt that all this was a dream, that it wasn't real. And suffering. . . . I just couldn't connect."[28] He continues: "I came from somewhere else, but it [the Creator's voice] reached me through the maze and dullness of human existence. It could still reach me because I am pure and sincere. . . . I came from somewhere else, where I was part of something that is so wonderful that there are no words to express it."

Sun Ra recalled keeping the protection and education he received from the creator secret from his parents, who owned a restaurant business. In elementary school he studied solfeggio and his mother bought him a piano when he was around eight years old. Violinist William Gray, a friend, would bring European "classical" music and church music for him to read. Sun Ra said he could perform this music effortlessly because "I could hear so I could read." Most musicians in the Western world approach music in the opposite fashion, with reading being the supreme priority and initial element in the sequence of learning. Sun Ra's understanding of the connection between spontaneous composition and prayer were apparent at an early age. "Everyday I composed something for the Creator. I first started around eleven years old and that's what I was playing. I wouldn't even play for my family. I played just for the Creator."[29]

As a child he listened to Fletcher Henderson records at home and attended theaters regularly with his parents. He also went to blues concerts featuring Bessie Smith, Mamie Smith, Butterbeans, and others. When he was fifteen another friend, trumpeter Bill Martin, encouraged Sun Ra to begin to arrange music, thus motivating him to transcribe "Yeah Man," by Horace Henderson, from a Fletcher Henderson record. This became the first arrangement for his new band composed of fellow students. At this time Sun Ra was also performing professionally with John Tuggle "Fess" Whatley, his band director, while still attending junior high school. His sight-reading skills made him a pianist in demand, playing for both "exclusively White" gatherings and African-American social clubs around Birmingham. Sun Ra was proud of the fact that he was the only student in Whatley's band, which was otherwise comprised of teachers.

Sun Ra's band director arranged a tour that took them from Florida to Chicago. He joined the musicians' union on December 15, 1934, and performed during the Christmas season, (under the name "Sonny Blount") with this band at Chicago's Savoy Ballroom. Later, "Herman S. Blount" was awarded a scholarship to the State Agricultural and Mechanical Institute for Negroes in Normal, Alabama (currently Alabama A & M University) in September, 1935. He was attracted to the teacher's training course because "in that you majored in everything." According to interviews he gave later, Sun Ra left college "as a result of an extra-terrestrial experience." "They said they needed somebody of my kind, my kind of mind and spirit. . . . They were from Saturn, I presume. . . . But I was aware of one being. It always stood on my left-hand side. I really couldn't turn my head fully to see. I could just see the image."[30]

Sun Ra's compositions dating back to the mid-1950s demonstrate both his broad traditional roots and his free "jazz" style. He was a charismatic, knowledgeable, and demanding leader who sought band members who were well disciplined, open-minded and humble. Nightclub owners often complained when his band showed up in "red Egyptian fezzes."[31] The fact that people were listening so intensely that they forgot to buy drinks didn't please these owners either. John Gilmore and Art Hoyle were playing with Sun Ra's quintet at this time. Hoyle talks about a job in Chicago on North Broadway Street during this period. "I heard Sun Ra play some of his most astonishing piano on that job. . . . Because of the less structured situation, he played more, and really played some outstanding things. . . . I was shocked that he could play like that. I had never heard him play in those kinds of veins . . . on regular standard tunes."[32]

The band performed five nights a week (and an afternoon every week); nevertheless, an intensive rehearsal schedule (five hours daily) was still maintained. Sun Ra focused on technical details during these rehearsal sessions: dynamics, articulation, stylistic interpretation, and the like.

Sun Ra always encouraged his musicians to experiment. The bassist Richard Evans (another band member) recalls Sun Ra's musical control over his ensemble: "He was a good programmer of people. He would actually control you, but make you think you were doing it yourself." Music was worked out both by ear and through notation. Evans once asked Sun Ra "Well, what are the chord changes?" He replied, "Whatever you want them to be." At the end of the process Evans realized, "This man is bringing stuff out in me that I didn't know I had."[33] Trombonist Julian Priester, in regards to his early days with Sun Ra, adds:

> He'd set up only the slightest thing going with the band and then he'd suddenly be pointing to me to solo. And I'd get up but I wouldn't know what was going on! I wouldn't know where I was in terms of a harmonic framework, I'd just have to listen to what was going on in back of me with the band—which was liable to be just about anything— and I'd have to work from that. I'd have to measure things instantly and start playing. . . . What he was doing was teaching me to be free. . . . It was a lot of knowledge.[34]

Saturn records was established around the end of 1956 by a group of Sun Ra followers who issued the earliest recorded LP's and 45 rpm's. *Super-Sonic Jazz* was the first issue. The details regarding many Saturn recordings are purposely obscure. In 1957 Sun Ra enclosed a small book of notes with one of his earliest albums, *Jazz by Sun Ra, Vol. 1.* Sun Ra took the time to explain the purpose of his music on this first recording. (This album has been reissued as *Sun Song* on the Delmark label: DD-411.) He wrote:

THE AIM OF MY COMPOSITION:

All of my compositions are meant to depict happiness combined with beauty in a free manner. Happiness, as well as *pleasure* and *beauty*, has many degrees of existence; *my aim is to express these degrees in sounds which can be understood by the entire world.* All of my music is tested for effect. By effect I mean mental impression. The mental impression I intend to convey is that of being alive, vitally alive. The real aim of this music is to co-ordinate the minds of peoples into an intelligent reach for a better world, and an intelligent approach to the living future. By peoples I mean all of the people of different nations who are living today.

Performance opportunities began to decline around 1960, the year the Arkestra accepted an engagement at a nightclub in Montreal. "I left

Chicago when a friend of mine said he felt I should because the people weren't listening."[35] They eventually moved on to Quebec City before returning to Chicago at the end of the year. John Gilmore, Marshall, Pat Patrick, and Ronnie Boykins moved to New York with Sun Ra soon after their return to Chicago. Ornette Coleman and Cecil Taylor had arrived a year earlier. The band did not appear publicly in New York during 1961 but continued to rehearse and record. Sun Ra's Arkestra was hired for its first performances in New York in 1963. Gene Harris hired the ensemble to perform at The Playhouse at 131 MacDougal Street in Greenwich Village, where Ferrell ("Pharoah") Sanders was working as a waiter.

Sun Ra added to the musical controversy started by Taylor and Coleman, and soon influential musicians like Coltrane and Dolphy joined this evolution in the direction of free experimentation. The atmosphere was often hostile, and the musicians were ostracized from many mainstream musical venues. John Gilmore was among the most loyal of Sun Ra's band members. He was offered a position in Miles Davis's ensemble and other prestigious bands, but remained with Sun Ra despite his towering status on tenor saxophone. There were times of frustration, however, as Gilmore remembers:

> It was getting kind of frustrating. I'd been walking around New York, and I wasn't working anywhere, and half the cats were out there playing my ideas. I said, what is this? Here I am not working, and they're stealing my ideas. . . . So Lee Morgan knew me and

recommended me to Art Blakey. I was
just frustrated at the time, and I had to
make some kind of move. I couldn't see
myself getting myself anything
anywhere. All I could see was these
cats imitating me, and I didn't have a
quarter in my pocket.[36]

Some of the musicians Gilmore mentioned
having had a indelible influence on are Sonny
Rollins, Charles Lloyd, Pharoah Sanders, Roland
Kirk, and John Coltrane. Coltrane confirms that
Gilmore had a strong influence during the early
1960s when he was, yet again, modifying his
approach to music.

During 1964-65, Gilmore was with the edition
of the Jazz Messengers that included Curtis Fuller
on trombone, John Hicks on piano, Gary Bartz on
alto saxophone, trumpeter Lee Morgan, and Art
Blakey on drums. He continued to live in the
Arkestra's house with Sun Ra and the other
members. Pharoah Sanders replaced him whenever
he was on the road with Blakey. John Gilmore was
present on March 28, 1965, for the benefit concert
for the Black Arts Repertory Theater/School when
the Impulse album "The New Wave In Jazz" was
recorded. John Coltrane, Archie Shepp, Albert Ayler,
Grachan Moncur III, Charles Tolliver, Sun Ra, and
Betty Carter were recorded on that date. According
to LeRoi Jones, Sun Ra and Betty Carter were
omitted from the eventual release due to undisclosed
reasons that were apparently known only by the a &
r (artist and repertoire) man for the date. Later in his
career, John Gilmore also worked and recorded with
Babatunde Olatunji, Freddie Hubbard, McCoy Tyner,
Paul Bley, Andrew Hill, Elmo Hope, and Chick Corea.

Gilmore was sixty-three when he died on August 20, 1995. He was a pioneer who helped define the fierce, screaming sound of the avant-garde saxophone. He defined his style as "playing rhythmically and melodically at the same time."[37] Gilmore also played bass clarinet and drums with Sun Ra. He was the ensemble's most outstanding soloist and took charge of the Arkestra after the leader's death in 1993.

Sun Ra had a measurable impact on the AACM (Association for the Advancement of Creative Musicians) during its early years of development. There is a related philosophical underpinning that can be discerned in the theatrical presentation of the Art Ensemble of Chicago, an attitude involving unbridled experimentation with strong elements of traditional African-American history and culture. Sun Ra sums up the function of his music by saying: "I'm actually painting pictures of infinity with my music, and that's why a lot of people can't understand it. And when I say so, a lot of people don't believe me. But if they would listen to this and to other types of music, they'll find that this has something else in it, something from another world."[38]

Charles Mingus

Charles Mingus was a modern "jazz" musician who felt his particular brand of music should be unrestricted yet disciplined melodically, rhythmically, harmonically, and formally. He was one of the most celebrated composer-arrangers of the modern "jazz" era. He was a bassist and bandleader of extraordinary power and enduring musical influence. Mingus and his musical associates studied the experiments of other genres and traditions and applied them to their own natural approach to spontaneous composition. His music was not always cheerful or entertaining in ways that much earlier "jazz" forms were; instead he explored a wide range of moods and emotions in his various "workshops."

Mingus was born in Nogales, Arizona, in 1922 and grew up in Los Angeles. He studied piano, trombone, cello, and solfeggio[39] by the time he was sixteen. Mingus' ambitions were directed toward developing his skill on cello in the European "classical" tradition, but those aspirations waned when he learned that "Black" cellists had no future in symphony orchestras during this time. He then switched to bass and continued to advance his musical knowledge. Mingus participated in the sanctified settings of the Pentecostal and Holiness churches, began studying the works of nineteenth-century European composers, and performed in big band "jazz" settings. He also studied bass for five years with H. Rheinschagen of the New York Philharmonic.

Mingus' professional career began in the early forties. He performed with Louis Armstrong for two years, spent another two years with Lionel Hampton, and performed in bands led by Duke Ellington, Kid Ory, Red Norvo, Charlie Parker, Billy Taylor, Art Tatum, Stan Getz, Bud Powell, and other great musicians. By the early fifties he had founded his own recording label (Debut Records), becoming one of the early pioneers of such efforts among "jazz" musicians. In 1951 Mingus recorded his first album on that label while celebrating his thirty-ninth birthday. Three other "jazz" musicians founded their independent record labels the same year: Dizzy Gillespie (Dee Gee), Lennie Tristano (Jazz Records), and Woody Herman (Mars).[40] One of Debut's most important releases was *Jazz at Massey Hall*, a live recording of a Canadian concert in Toronto's Massey Hall in 1953. This date featured Charlie Parker, Dizzy Gillespie, Bud Powell, Max Roach, and Mingus in a performance that reunited Parker and Gillespie for the first time in many years.

Mingus organized his first workshop during 1954 and continued to explore related experimental formats until his death in January 1979. A sample of Mingus' work during the 1950s is preserved on his album for the Jazztone Society label entitled *Jazz Experiment with Charles Mingus and his Modernists* (originally released in 1955). John LaPorta plays alto saxophone and clarinet; Teo Macero is featured on tenor saxophone; Quincy Jones is heard on trumpet; Jack Wiley plays cello; and the drummer for the session is Clem DeRosa. Mingus is both pianist and bassist on the date. "What Is This Thing Called Love" and other compositions on this album contain music that, like the composer, is rarely static. Colorful counterpoint and timbre are combined to create interesting moods within the context of structured freedom. Both the loose form (which allows such freedom) and the general propensity toward uninhibited swinging became trademarks of Mingus' performances and compositional style. This feature remains constant in both Mingus' small group settings and his extended orchestral works of the sixties and seventies. In each such musical situation, the listener may perceive a balance of musical emotion with ample room for intellectual exploration.

Mingus developed his varied, and frequently complex, compositions with a succession of ensembles, each called the Charles Mingus Jazz Workshop. Mingus' workshops were experimental "conservatories" for prodigiously endowed artists such as Eric Dolphy, Rahsaan Roland Kirk, Clifford Jordan, George Adams, Dannie Richmond, Hameit Bluiett, Yusef Lateef, John Handy, Jackie McLean, Booker Ervin, Ricky Ford, and Don Pullen. The workshops exemplify Mingus' eclecticism and his willingness to explore new modes and styles of artistic communication. His respect for the process of musical genesis gained him the admiration of musicians, but perhaps cost him varying degrees of popularity among those audiences he was forced to admonish (usually for making noise) during his performances. His temper was not always spent on his audiences, however, as authors Wayne Ernstice and Paul Rubin point out:

> Dubbed "the university of Mingus" by his sidemen, the workshop provided an intense and exacting training ground, characterized by long hours of rehearsal and punctuated by the frequent eruptions of Mingus' volcanic personality. As a bandleader, Mingus was notoriously short-tempered with sloppy or superficial playing. During rehearsals, and even on-stage, he was known to stop a number in midstream to chastise a band member; he commonly warned, "Respect the melody" and "Play in tune." Sometimes in concert he would order his

musicians to start a piece all over again.[41]

Mingus was at the height of his musical development during the early part of the 1960s and then fell into obscurity. His 1959 recording of his bitterly comical and highly polemic composition *Original Faubus Fables*, and his disagreement with Columbia Records over the sales figures for his recordings, left the company unable to renew their contract with him. The lyrics for his composition did not sit well with some listeners or industry executives:

Oh Lord, don't let them shoot us
Oh Lord, don't let them stab us
Oh Lord, don't let them tar and feather us
Oh Lord, no more swastikas!
Oh Lord, no more Ku Klux Klan!

Name me someone ridiculous
[response] Governor Faubus
Why is he sick and ridiculous?
[response] He won't permit integrated schools
Then he's a fool
Boo! Nazi Fascist supremacists/Boo! Ku Klux Klan!

Name me a handful that's ridiculous
Faubus, Rockefeller, Eisenhower
Why are they so sick and ridiculous?
Two, four, six, eight
They brain wash and teach you to hate.

Other Charles Mingus small-group recordings were collected under the title *Pithecanthropus*

Erectus in the fifties (Atlantic Records 1956-61). In the mid-1950s and early 1960s, Mingus introduced a number of innovative compositional and improvisational techniques involving structured freedom in which the employment of functional tonality is noticeably minimal. His 1960 recording of "What Love" (from *Stormy Weather*) is an extended composition in which the other instruments drop out well into the development of the piece, leaving Mingus and bass clarinetist Eric Dolphy to begin a collectively improvised dialogue in which both instruments come close to duplicating the inflections of impassioned speech. Mingus' free counterpoint with Dolphy's improvised melodies involves an extension of bass technique beyond all traditional functions exercised before his time.

Mingus departed the United States on a European tour in 1964 in which he visited Scandinavia, Germany, Belgium, and France. The tour featured one of his most exciting workshops. Musicians in his ensemble included Johnny Coles (b. 1926, trumpet), Eric Dolphy (flute, bass clarinet, and alto saxophone), Clifford Jordan (1931—93, tenor saxophone), Jaki Byard (b. 1922, piano), Dannie Richmond (1935–88, drums), and Mingus on double bass. By the conclusion of the tour, Dolphy was offered solo gigs in Paris and began to travel around Europe to Holland, Sweden, and Berlin on his own. Dolphy died alone in his hotel room on June 29, 1964, nine days after his thirty-sixth birthday. He was planning to marry Joyce Mordecai from New York within a few weeks. When Dolphy was admitted into the hospital, European medical personnel assumed he was a "jazz" musician on drugs and failed to treat his diabetes. Dolphy never used drugs. An autopsy revealed his extremely high sugar levels.[42]

Charles Mingus was grief stricken and dropped everything to attend the funeral in Los Angeles on July 9. Dolphy had managed to record his most intriguing bass-clarinet solos on that final tour, where he evolves the art of "vocalizing" instrumental "jazz" in some of the most unusual, evocative, expressively coherent, and animated musical discussion on record. The exchanges are at once confidential raillery and the impassioned yearning of friends separated by an indomitable force. The passion involved is of a type uncommon in Western music. These musical "discussions" are preserved on recordings of the April 26, 1964, concert at Wuppertal Town Hall, West Faubus, and on the Enja recording *Mingus in Europe*, volume 1.[43] When audiences for "jazz" gradually decreased during the 1960s, Charles Mingus fell into obscurity and did not record for several years (between 1966 and 1970). Mingus lived a reclusive existence during this period but returned during the 1970s with some of his best-recorded works for large instrumental ensembles in the "jazz" repertoire.

In his autobiography, *Beneath the Underdog* (first published in 1971), Mingus presents a poignant indictment of racial discrimination, as well as frank (and often revealing) descriptions of his excursions into his own musical mind and personal affairs. It provides an extraordinary glance into the lives of both artists and their fans in frank language and with meritorious clarity.

As cited previously, the hard bop style that prevailed as the dominant "jazz" tendency from the mid-1950s into the following decade emphasized melodic lines that conform to chord structures, a particular kind swing feeling, and the use of a twelve-bar or thirty-two-bar form. Drummers remained timekeepers. Mingus, along with Ornette Coleman, Cecil Taylor, and other music innovators, was among the first musicians to challenge these restrictive conventions beginning in the mid-fifties.

As a composer, Mingus experimented with variable tempi, alternating meters, polyrhythms, utilized rubato, ametrical structures, and experimented with free collective improvisation. His elevated stature as a composer and bandleader often overshadows his significant contribution as a bassist. As one of the founders of modern bass playing, Mingus extended the range of the instrument from the traditions established by Walter Page, Jimmy Blanton, Slam Stewart, and Oscar Pettiford into the present era.

Two "Jazz" Harpists in the 1950s

Dorothy Ashby (1932–1986)

Composer Dorothy Ashby, an accomplished pianist, was self-taught on the harp. She began playing in Detroit in the early fifties, the beginning of what she refers to as the "golden years" of "jazz" in that city. Ashby created a style on the harp that was unprecedented in its authenticity and supple versatility. Traditionally an awkward instrument in music because of its chromatic limitations, the harp would seem an unlikely candidate for "jazz," where one rarely finds music that is simply diatonic. The harp's strings are arranged diatonically and chromatic changes require the movement of one or more of seven pedals, each of which has three notched positions. Ashby overcame this limitation and developed a lyrical and rhythmic voice on the harp that has been equated with the guitar playing of Wes Montgomery.[44] Her father, Wiley Thompson, was a "jazz" guitarist. Her husband is also a musician and composer. Ashby says,

> I played the things that I heard and played along with my father, who taught me more about harmony and melodic construction than I learned in all my years of high school, college, and private study, and sacrificed more time and money than the family could afford for my musical training and instruments . . .

> When musicians would come to rehearse with my father, I would get a chance to chord along with the adults, and they thought that was a big thing. I thought it was quite wonderful, too, because I was so young at the time. And from there, I guess my interest was always primarily jazz. My father had perhaps other aspirations for me. He didn't want me to wind up in clubs and suffer the hard times so many of them encountered. The excellence with which they played had nothing to do with the bucks they made.

> When I changed to harp, I just tried to transfer the things that I had heard and the things that I wanted to do as a jazz player to the harp. Nobody had ever

told me these things shouldn't be done,
or were not usually done on the harp,
because I didn't hear it any other way.
The only thing I was interested in doing
was playing jazz on the harp.[45]

        The Dorothy Ashby Trio toured (with her
husband, the band's drummer) throughout the
sixties. By the end of the decade Ashby became
increasingly involved with writing and presenting
musicals that dealt with African-American concerns.
Her husband established an African-American
theater company (the Ashby Players of Detroit), and
Dorothy wrote scores and lyrics and performed with
the events. In the early seventies the Ashbys moved
to California, where Dorothy established herself
firmly in the Los Angeles studio scene.
        Dorothy Ashby was not the first harpist to
play "jazz". Caspar Reardon is considered to be the
first "jazz" harpist, and Adele Girard was the first
woman to play the harp in "jazz." The distinguishing
quality that Ashby's harp playing brings to "jazz" are
described by Ira Gitler in the liner notes to Ashby's
1961 album *Soft Winds* (Jazzland Records): "Her
feeling for time and ability to construct melodic
guitar-like lines mark her as the most accomplished
modern jazz harpist." After the release of her album
The Fantastic Jazz Harp of Dorothy Ashby in 1962,
Ashby was given *Down Beat's* Critic's and Reader's
Awards as best harpist. A reviewer of the music said,
"This isn't just novelty, though that is what you
expect. The harp has a clean jazz voice with a
resonance and syncopation that turn familiar jazz
phrasing inside out."[46] Few recognized the inherent
difficulties and unique power and skill involved in

creating the music that Ashby executed so flawlessly and effortlessly. She remains relatively unrewarded for her innovative contribution. Because the number of professional harpists performing authentic "jazz" was and is negligible, "people don't know what you're doing," she says. "Nobody else knows enough to know that nobody else is doing it."[47]

Corky Hale

Corky Hale (harp/piano/organ/flute/piccolo/cello) heard Dorothy Ashby performing in a Detroit club in the early fifties before she realized that there was another harpist exploring "jazz." Hale's primary instrument is the piano. "It's very frustrating to me," she admits, "very frustrating, in that people mostly think of me as a harpist and mainly call upon me because I do something on the harp." "Dorothy is very wonderful," Hale thinks. "I don't want to say that Dorothy and I are the only jazz harpists, but Dorothy and I are the only ones that can go in with a group, sit down, and improvise a tune like a piano player."

In the fifties, Hale was working in the recording studios, clubs, and TV in Hollywood when her career began. She appeared with various all-woman bands and appeared on the 1954 recording session *Cats vs. Chicks*. She performed with Ray Anthony, Harry James, Freddy Martin, Dave Rose, and others. Leonard Feather said in *The Encyclopedia of Jazz*, (in response to her 1954 album with vocalist Kitty White) that she had an "exceptionally modern approach to the harp."

Hale spoke of the brief period she spent with Ada Leonard and Ina Ray Hutton: "Ada was terribly sophisticated, and boy, I was scared to death of her. And, of course, Phil Spitalny called and asked me to go on the road with his all-girl band. I didn't join Phil, and I didn't last very long with Ada or Ina."[48] In a Hal Holly profile titled "Corky, the All-Girl Harpist, Won't Talk on Gal Bands" (*Down Beat*, June 4, 1952, p. 4), Hale discusses her experiences with the all-woman bands. Corky, who considered herself a "sort of well-bred little Jewish girl from northern Illinois" at the beginning of her career, said:

> It's like this. . . . If a girl is a good musician she doesn't want to work in an all-girl band because it implies she is working in it because she is a girl. A girl doesn't feel successful as a musician unless she can work with guys—just like one of them. She wants to feel she's been hired not because she's a girl but because she can play the job.
>
> I've always been in a man's world. I've always been in a man's job. Along with that, strangely enough, I always did all those womanly things. After work, at two in the morning, it was very common for maybe sixteen, seventeen guys in the band to come to my apartment and I would cook up an enormous breakfast.

Art Blakey (1919—1990)

Art Blakey (drummer and band leader) made it clear that drums were very expressive and versatile instruments. Like Gene Krupa, Blakey was instrumental in liberating the drums from a purely time-keeping role to that of a front-line instrument. Blakey, originally a pianist, never studied drums formally, but he absorbed the "jazz" drumming tradition by listening and studying the music of Baby Dodds, Big Sid Catlett, Chick Webb, Kenny Clarke, and other great musicians. In 1939 he played in Fletcher Henderson's orchestra, then joined pianist Mary Lou Williams's first big band. In a career that spanned half a century, Blakey's performance and recording credits also include appearances with Errol Garner, Charlie Parker, Dizzy Gillespie, Bud Powell, Thelonious Monk, Miles Davis, and the Billy Eckstine Orchestra.

After 1944 Blakey remained an integral part of Billy Eckstine's big band until it broke up in 1947. He visited Africa during the forties, spending several months in Nigeria and Ghana. He worked constantly when he returned to the United States with Lucky Millinder, Buddy DeFranco, and other bandleaders. He also led his own small combos. Art Blakey's Jazz Messengers later became one of the most important "schools" in modern "jazz."

The earlier African-American "jazz school" involved on-the-job training in the oral/aural tradition with a person who had mastered the evolutionary styles. The master musician (and designated teacher) usually acquired his or her knowledge through a similar process. The Jazz Messengers were the epitome of such a process in modern "jazz," just as the Ellington, Basie, and Eckstine bands had been in earlier eras.

The Jazz Messengers were a series of ensembles that trained young musicians for more than four decades. In Blakey's bands, players learned the meaning of communal balance, precision, style, musicianship, and individual expression. Messengers were trained to bring joy and excitement to an audience through their improvisational and ensemble performance skills. Alumni from Art Blakey's Jazz Messengers include (on trumpet) Clifford Brown, Lee Morgan, Kenny Dorham, Donald Byrd, Freddie Hubbard, Wynton Marsalis, and Terence Blanchard; (on piano) Horace Silver, Bobby Timmons, Ray Bryant, and Joanne Brackeen; (on reeds) Jackie McLean, Hank Mobley, Johnny Griffin, Benny Golson, Wayne Shorter, and Billy Harper; and (on trombone) Julian Priester and Curtis Fuller. Other recent "graduates" include the Harper Brothers, Branford Marsalis, and many other "Young Lions."

Born in Pittsburgh, Blakey's impact on "jazz" drumming is as notable as his contributions as a leader. Despite his explosive presence and emotional range on the drums, Blakey considered himself first and foremost an accompanist for his ensembles. He understood the power and importance of the drum: "The drums, they can move mountains, tell messages, everything! Whatever the drum says, you got to do it man. They're the pulse of everything. If the pulse isn't there, it's dead. That's my concept of playing drums. If people are out there, I'm going to get them. That's what happens in Africa and other societies. The rhythms make music meaningful. Listen to Stravinsky's *Firebird Suite*. See how militant he is with the drums? It tears you up."[49]

Phineas Newborn (1931–1989)

Pianist Phineas Newborn was born in Whiteville, Tennessee. His father was a bandleader in Memphis, so Phineas learned to play tenor saxophone, French horn, trumpet, baritone horn, vibraphone, and other instruments by the time he was a teen. Calvin Newborn, his brother, can be heard on guitar on many of Phineas' recordings.

When he emerged on the scene in the 1950s, Newborn's piano technique was often ranked with that of Art Tatum and Oscar Peterson by colleagues, fans, and critics. While Bud Powell was considered the driving force on piano during the bebop era, Newborn etched out a piano style "so unique as to make any attempt at copying it seem almost cliché."[50] His career often oscillated between highly productive periods of excellent recordings and periods of self-imposed obscurity. The world in which he was forced to perform involved too much pressure and too many negative experiences for a humble, introspective, and extremely sensitive artist. Pianist James Williams recalls, "I think I actually heard Junior play in person before I heard his recordings. When I heard him and went to the record store the next day, they didn't have any of his albums. I ordered every record they had listed in the category. I didn't know which ones were considered to be the classics . . . but I figured anyone who plays with that kind of emotional depth and expressiveness, anytime they touch the piano it is going to be something worth hearing."[51]

Critics who knew little about Newborn's personal life speculated that he "went into a decline as a consequence of emotional illness." Contrary to comments such as these, as expressed by Leonard

Feather in *The Encyclopedia of Jazz in the Sixties*,
Newborn spoke of a different reason for his obscurity
and reticence. In a radio interview on National Public
Radio in the early 1980s (after insisting that his
name should be pronounced like the word *"finest"*—
with a long *i*), Newborn told of an incident that took
place at a club in the South after his performance
one evening. He had just finished playing when an
attractive European-American woman in a red dress
approached him and said some friends wanted to
talk to him outside. He followed her out and was
assaulted and beaten savagely by a gang of
European-American men until he was unconscious.
When he got out of the hospital he went to his
mother's house and didn't touch the piano again for
a long period. His mother gradually coaxed him into
playing again, but it was never to be the same.

Summary

The lyrics of blues singers were usually
personal commentaries about intimate topics spoken
to a close second party or shared with the general
listeners ("Baby Please Don't Go," "I'm Wild About
You Baby," "Lightnin' Don't Feel Well," etc.). In the
swing era some of the intimacy of the personal song
was retained, but vocals with slightly more general
commentaries also became common ("Moonlight in
Vermont," "That's the Stuff You Gotta Watch," "When
a Woman Loves a Man," etc.). A similar degree of
change can be measured from listening to the way
individual notes are caressed and savored by the
swing soloist (Lester Young, for instance), while the
bebop player treated notes more as a multitude of
distant stars organized into magnificent galactic

systems by triumphant strokes of a wise, but impersonal, magician's musical wand.

It may be that bebop was more distanced, inaccessible and curt in musical demeanor partly due to the diminished word usage in connection with that style. Swing lyrics often had an original set of lyrics, even if the songs eventually became best known as instrumental arrangements. The instrumental players usually knew the words to the songs they interpreted, and they worked closely with vocalists in the communal big band settings. Rather than working within the structure of traditional ensembles and exploring its traditional language, bebop pioneers preferred the combo and created a new musical system. This approach involved casting old melodies away and using functional harmony in revolutionary ways to expand the medium to new extremes. Instrumentalists during the 1940s needed to reform the concept of "jazz" for themselves.

Emphasis was on virtuosity and a complete technical knowledge of the conventional functions of music. This set of esoteric knowledge transmitted orally and aurally, deprived musicians on the fringe of the culture access to methods of decoding the new modern "jazz" language. Consequently, the number of bop innovators is far lower than both the number of names commonly associated with swing and other earlier periods. The list of hard bop musicians who emerged during the 1950s form a larger set of practitioners. Even those few bebop musicians who learned the language thoroughly could not all develop the level of fluency and virtuosity that Parker, Gillespie, or Bud Powell produced, thus a yet smaller inner circle of hyper-esoteric bop innovators stood elevated far beyond their peers.

Despite the early stereotypes that relocated all "jazz" to either the secular domain or, worse, to the realm of "the devil's music," many innovators began to dedicate a portion of their music to sacred domains. Duke Ellington's concerts of sacred music began on September 16, 1965, at Grace Cathedral Church of San Francisco. The second concert occurred on January 19, 1968, in New York at the Cathedral of St. John the Divine, while the final performance was at Westminister Abbey in London on October 24, 1973. In 1957 the Ward singers were persuaded to bring their gospel singing to the Newport Jazz Festival to demonstrate the aesthetic affinity between African-American sacred and secular musical traditions. After Mahalia Jackson sang at the same festival the following year, gospel music took its place next to "jazz" and blues annually at the festival.

Mary Lou Williams wrote three "jazz" Masses. Her hymn, "St. Martin de Porres" (Black Christ of the Andes) as well as two other smaller sacred works ("Anima Christi" and "Praise the Lord") are samples of her interest in and dedication to spiritual music. An ordained Catholic priest named Clarence Rivers (b. 1931) is credited with introducing "jazz" and other African-American music into the Catholic religious services. David Baker (b. 1931) has written music for Catholic and Lutheran services including *The Beatitudes* for chorus, narrator, dancers, and symphony orchestra, and *A Modern Jazz Oratorio*.[52]

Negative stereotypes of African-American "jazz" musicians and sociopathic behavior continued nonetheless. Norman Mailer, in his 1957 essay "The White Negro," suggested the complex notion that the attitudes of the "hipster" and "philosophical psychopath," found during the 1950s within the

European-American population, was an infatuation with the "Negro" that stemmed from a protest against European Americans' fear of integration. Mailer also felt this rebellion against mainstream America was also somehow due to "White" anxiety over the sexual superiority of African-American males. Mailer's mythological theories were closely related to related myths that "motivated the lynching and castration of thousands (maybe millions) of black men since the first slave was delivered to Virginia in 1619."[53] Nelson George discusses the effect of Mailers delusions further:

> Yet in perpetuating the romance of blackness, supporting the notion that black jazzmen, for example, were in touch with some primal, sexual energy, Mailer was guilty of stereotyping blacks as the rednecks and social mainstreamers his white Negroes opposed. While liberals hailed and debated Mailer's provocative rhetoric, many working-class white teens were already living out the ideas Mailer articulated, infatuated as they were with black style and culture. But Mailer saw jazz as the crucial element in this new modern white personality; he had no real idea of what most Negroes, or their white teenage fans, were recording or buying.
>
> If Mailer had done a little more homework, he might have cited first the white R&B deejays, and then a kid named Elvis Aaron Presley. Elvis had

been recording professionally for three years by the time "The White Negro" was published, and it may be that Mailer's musings were at least in part inspired by the white public's perception of this country boy. Elvis's immersion in black culture, both the blues and gospel, was as deep as his white Mississippi background would allow. Aside from the music he heard on black radio (Memphis's WDIA and Nashville's WLAC were favorites), Elvis also utilized now obscure bits of black culture to create the style look so integral to his mystique. Even before he'd made his first record, Elvis was wearing one of black America's favorite products, Royal Crown Pomade hair grease, used by hepcats to create the shiny, slick hairstyles of the day. The famous rockabilly cut, a style also sported by more flamboyant hipsters, was clearly his interpretation of the black "process," where blacks had their hair straightened and curled into curious shapes. Some charge that the process hairstyle was a black attempt to look white. So, in a typical pop music example of cross-cultural collision, there was Elvis adapting black styles from blacks adapting white looks.[54]

At the end of the twentieth century, are contemporary art forms dominated by the notion that what will sell determines what will be presented? How can such cycle be broken if music that is considered too abstract or experimental is never heard by general audiences—live or otherwise? Musical styles are as different or conforming as the individual personalities of the people in the societies from which they emerge. If people have an opportunity to hear a cross-section of music, then there will always be an audience for an infinite variety of musical styles—past and present.

---

[1] George E. Curry, "Killed for Whistling at a White Woman," *Emerge Newsmagazine,* August 1995, pp. 24–32.

[2] Ibid., p. 30.

[3] Ibid., p. 32.

[4] As cited in ibid.

[5] Miles Davis with Quincy Troupe, *Miles: The Autobiography* (New York: Simon and Schuster, 1989), p. 161.

[6] Ibid. p. 89.

[7] William Barlow and Cheryl Finley, *From Swing to Soul: An Illustrated History of African American Popular Music from 1930 to 1960* (Washington, D.C.: Elliot and Clark Publishing, 1994), pp. 113–14.

[8] Krystian Brodacki, "The Original Batman: Wayne Shorter Remembers Miles Davis," *Jazz Forum,* January 1992, p. 28.

[9] Joe Goldberg, *Jazz Masters of the Fifties,* p. 91.

[10] Ibid. p. 94.

[11] As quoted in ibid., p. 105.

[12] J. C. Thomas, *Chasin the Trane* (Garden City, New York: Doubleday, 1975), pp. 34–35.

[13] Ira Gitler, "Trane on the Track," *Down Beat*, October 16, 1958, p. 16.

[14] Davis, *Miles*, pp. 194–95.

[15] Mark Gridley, *Jazz Styles: History and Analysis*, 2d ed. (Englewood Cliffs, N.J.: Prentice Hall, 1985), p. 213.

[16] Ibid., p. 147.

[17] "Coltrane On Coltrane," p. 17.

[18] *Chasin the Trane'*, p. 90.

[19] According to the liner notes on this LP—"*Portrait of Cannonball*" on Riverside.

[20] Goldberg, *Jazz Masters of the Fifties*, p. 233.

[21] Liner notes to *The Music of Ornette Coleman: Something Else*, Contemporary S7551 (1958).

[22] Introduction to article on Taylor in Valerie Wilmer, *Jazz People*.

[23] Valerie Wilmer, *As Serious as Your Life: The Story of the New Jazz* (London: Serpent's Tail, 1992), p. 52.

[24] Ibid. p. 161.

[25] Ekkehard Jost, *Free Jazz* (Graz, Austria: Universal Edition, 1974), pp. 69–70.

[26] Joseph E. Holloway, ed., *Africanisms in American Culture* (Bloomington: Indiana University Press, 1991), p. 99.

[27] Phil Schaap, *Sun Ra: The Sequel*, WKCR Program Guide, WKCR Radio, Columbia University, New York, March 1989, V(6), p. 28.

[28] Ira Steingroot, "Sun Ra's Magic Kingdom," *Reality Hackers*, Winter 1988, p. 50.

[29] Phil Schaap, "An Interview with Sun Ra," WKCR Program Guide, WKCR Radio, Columbia University, New York, March 1989, V(5), p. 26.

[30] Allan S. Chase, "Sun Ra: Musical Change and Musical Meaning in the Life and Work of a Jazz

Composer" (Unpublished thesis, Tufts University, 1992), p. 48.

[31] Graham Lock, "Big John's Special," *Wire*, no. 82/83 (December 1990/January 1991): 22.

[32] Chase, "Sun Ra."

[33] Ibid., p. 91.

[34] Eugene Chadbourne, "Wandering Spirit Song, Pepo's Interview," *Coda*, December 1974, pp. 4–5.

[35] Ibid., p. 151.

[36] John DiLiberto, "John Gilmore: Three Decades in the Sun's Shadow," *Downbeat*, May 1984, p. 28.

[37] *Allegro: Associated Musicians of Greater New York*, Local 802, A.F. of M., October 1995.

[38] Wilmer, *As Serious as Your Life*, p. 74.

[39] The musical science of pitch and key relationships.

[40] Brian Priestley, *Mingus: A Critical Biography* (New York: Da Capo, 1983), p. 46.

[41] *Jazz Spoken Here*, pp. 213–15.

[42] Ibid.

[43] The flute and bass duet on a theme by Eric called "Starting" is a classic recording.

[44] Orrin Keepnews made the comparison in complimenting Ashby on her playing.

[45] Sally Placksin, *Jazz Women* (London: Pluto Press, 1985), pp. 239–40.

[46] Robert Ostermann, "Records in Review," *The National Observer*, undated clipping, courtesy Dorothy Ashby.

[47] *Jazz Women*, p. 239.

[48] Ibid., pp. 243–46.

[49] Liner notes to *Art Blakey and the Jazz Messengers: In My Prime*, vol. 1, Muse Records TI-301 (1979).

[50] Mitchell Seidel, "Truth, Justice and the Blues," *Down Beat*, March 1994.

[51] Ibid., p. 26.

[52] Southern, *The Music of Black Americans*, p. 491.
[53] Nelson George, *The Death of Rhythm* (New York: Pantheon, 1988), pp. 107–8
[54] Ibid., p. 61–62.

X
Innovators Emerging between 1960 and 1970

The cooler or more intellectual forms mean reversion back to the original African. It's like modern painting and sculpture. The same thing with bop-Charlie Parker, Dizzy Gillespie and those people-that was in the direction of Africa.

—Duke Ellington

Evolution of Innovative Music for 1960s Audiences

By 1960 African Americans had become a highly unique people. Separated from their homeland for a long period of time, the connecting elements binding African Americans to Africa had grossly diminished. They were generally not accepted as first-class citizens in America. Nevertheless, there were some unexpected advantages to this alienation. Taking advantage of unprecedented musical freedom, African-American innovators drew upon their African heritage freely, unbound by Old World traditions. European music could be exploited in similar fashion. The lack of a single binding tradition encouraged a cultural, social, and aesthetic freedom that few other people in the world enjoyed. As marginalized people, African Americans were free to create new celebrations, social customs, dialects, and modes of musical expression. Evolution, invention, and experimentation became survival traits. The evolution of "jazz" reflects such tendencies.

The distancing of the innovative forms of "jazz" music from the African-American mainstream community that occurred at the dawn of modern "jazz" was not necessarily a consequence of artistic experimentation becoming too extreme. The experimental proclivities present during the 1960s reflected the changes that occurred in the broader world. Many experimental musicians, as well as other African-American citizens involved in the "Black Pride" movement, were interested in the perpetuation of both African and African-American music and cultural traditions. More African Americans traveled to the African continent and embarked upon careful studies of African culture and history. Through musical experimentation, musicians began to demonstrate the inherent compatibility that exists between various forms of African and African-American musical forms. Nigerian master drummer Babatunde Olatunji worked with a number of master "jazz" musicians in New York. Sun Ra's concerts displayed a synthesis of various concepts while reflecting the natural evolution of many African-American styles. Sun Ra also demonstrated that music from several stylistic eras can be merged. Randy Weston, Dollar Brand, and other musicians contributed to this evolving notion as well.[1]

One set of reasons African-American "jazz" musicians inadvertently distanced themselves from their old audiences after the swing era was the location of performance venues. When bebop musicians emerged on 52nd Street in New York, they performed for a new integrated audience. This new setting was primarily composed of European American patrons. Modern "jazz" musicians generally performed outside the African-American community after "jazz" moved downtown from Harlem. At the same time, the innovative artists during the 1960s continued to evolve farther from European and popular musical structures, aesthetics, and limitations.

When bebop and hard bebop musicians mastered the required skills, they were highly cognizant of the caliber and value of their music. An artist gained respect in the African-American community for his or her personalized artistic contribution as well as for the technical mastery of a particular musical style. Disappointments came when "Black" artists realized that the broader American society would remain unappreciative of their music regardless of its artistic merit.

Listening to some of the live recordings of performances such as Charlie Parker's "Embraceable You" (*Bird at St. Nick's*),[2] where an apathetic, rude, and noisy drinking crowd is often much louder than the music being performed, gives the listener a clue as to the typical situation with which musicians were confronted during bebop.

In contrast, listening to Betty Carter's live performance of "By the Bend of the River" (at a birthday party at the Village Vanguard) or "Ego" on her first album Betty Carter (Bet-Car MK 1001) displays an eager and responsive African-American audience. The audience is actively engaging Carter's music in a communal fashion. Another supportive audience can be heard on performances in Japan of John Coltrane's "Meditation Part I" from *Live in Japan*. Coltrane's album has an excited audience that rivals the enthusiasm of an audience at a rock concert in America. Sun Ra's "For the Sunrise" from his album *Live in Montreux* also displays an extremely enthusiastic European crowd of a type that would be atypical for his Arkestra's performances in the United States during the time in which the performance was recorded.

The club experiences that Charlie Parker, Miles Davis, John Coltrane, Charles Mingus, and other African-American artists ordinarily endured not only produced a frustrating or debilitating situation for African-American artists, but also restricted the range of musical elements that could be explored. Bass solos were often completely lost during live bebop performances, so it was difficult for Parker to pursue his interest in strings in settings in which he typically performed. Musicians were obliged to perform at particular levels of amplitude, and in a dynamic fashion aggressive enough to rise above the general noise level of a nightclub. This, of course was a restrictive adaptation.

Movement away from the big-band format challenged the modern "jazz" artist in ways related to those ragtime pianists confronted during the early period of their development. Back then, musicians were required to produce a sound on the piano that retained all the salient features of the brass bands and other small ensembles that were heard in the barrelhouse environments. Later, "jig bands" and "jig piano" led to the "syncopated songs" that eventually became ragtime in the late nineteenth century.

The modern artists were becoming more self-consciously aware of their musical work. In modern "jazz" individual musical efforts were more exposed than they had been during the era of the big swing bands. Solos became longer, and music was documented for posterity more frequently. Modern "jazz" performance venues became distanced from Kansas City–styled jam sessions. In typical Kansas City sessions, mistakes could often be made and corrected without being preserved in a fixed document where performers and listeners could always find indelible historical reminders of their every musical move. Innovators gradually adapted to the demands imposed and knew they did not need large orchestras, fancy costumes, and stage layouts, or any other expensive tools and equipment to produce meaningful music. Coltrane and Parker needed only a quartet. Yet, as author Valerie Wilmer asserts, the music continued to evolve rapidly.

> Black music has never stood still. One theory to explain the need for this constant change is that it occurs from necessity, that the protagonists are forced to invent new techniques and systems in order to stay one step ahead of white imitators and codifiers. Possibly the musicians of the past were not blessed with an acute political consciousness (hardly surprising in view of their position in society—

"entertainers" playing in brothels and bar-rooms); perhaps it is true to say that until Charlie Parker came along none of them referred to their music as art, but in the "sixties" and "seventies" the "different drummer" that Black musicians heard was as often motivated by nationalist considerations as by the aesthetic desire to play something new.[3]

Randy Weston, Betty Carter, Charles Mingus, Horace Silver, Dizzy Gillespie, Sun Ra, and other African-American "jazz" artists attempted to establish their own record labels for several decades, only to find that the real problem lay in breaking into the mainstream distribution networks. Their early record labels paved the way for later artist-owned independent publishing and record companies such as Charles Tolliver's Strata East, Andrew White's Andrew's Music, Wendell Harrison's Wenha, and many others. In an interview conducted by drummer and author Art Taylor, composer-pianist Randy Weston responds inexorably unequivocally to Taylor's question, "Do you think musicians should produce their concerts and records?"

I believe the musician of today and of the future has to own everything. He should own his own nightclub, even if it's no bigger than a small room. He should either have his own record company or be able to record his own material and lease it to record companies. I am convinced that it's the only step for us to take now.

Considering our experience and how artists are exploited, particularly black artists, we must forget about working for other people.[4]

Weston's roster of the musicians working with him on the Roulette label was quite impressive. It included

Clark Terry, Richard Williams, Freddie Hubbard, Benny Bailey. We had only two trombones: Jimmy Cleveland and Quinton Jackson. Julius Watkins was on French horn. Cecil Payne, Yusef Lateef, Budd Johnson, Gigi Gryce, and Jerome Richardson were in the reed section. Les Spann was on guitar. Max Roach, G. T. Hogan, Charlie Persip, Armando Peraza, Candido Camaro, and Olatunji were the drummers. Ron Carter and George Duvivier played the bass.

Melba Liston conducted her own arrangements on this session and used the Swahili language to demonstrate the beauty of African language and to show "how the African language is also part of the African rhythms." The album was recorded in early 1960. Weston continues:

It came out during a time when we could see things going down. It was not as bad as it is now, but we could feel it happening. We wanted this to be a symbolic gesture by Afro-Americans, to show our pride that some of the

countries in Africa were getting their
freedom. So the album was called
Uhuru Africa. *Uhuru* means "freedom" in
Swahili.

This particular album was packaged
and put together in 1961. At the time it
was a bit unpopular, especially with
white people—even white people who
were friendly to me. They would hear it
once and they wouldn't hear it
anymore. Especially the first part,
where you have the poem. The other
problem was with Roulette Records.
They wanted to make some sort of a
deal where I would be giving them
power over my music. They promised to
do a big promotion on me, but I have
learned one lesson: Never sell a song.
Never give the rights of a song. I don't
care how sad you think it is. Never sell
a tune! I refused, and therefore the
album got buried. There was no
publicity put behind it. So because of
that and because of the message on the
record, it was hard to find.[5]

Weston discussed the gradual erosion of
economic power and stability among African-
American musicians from the beginning of the "jazz"
era:

In the twenties and the thirties, black
artists had a lot of power. They had a
lot of strength. They had a hotel in the
neighborhood of Sixth Avenue around

Fiftieth or Fifty-first Street. It was called the Clef Club. The Clef Club was worth a million dollars. It was a place for black entertainers. Black entertainers and musicians were organized. If you were hungry, if you were a musician or an artist and you came to New York and you didn't have a place to go and didn't have anything to eat, you could go there.

Our ancestors in this business used to give their own vaudeville shows, because segregation was so rough in those days that they had to do a lot of things on their own. And that's how powerful an organization they had. But when they started to build the Sixth Avenue subway, they tore it down. Harlem started to happen, and everybody got split up. So what happened is this: The old timers let us down, and the reason is because they didn't keep records. It's very hard to find. I've got a book on the history of our people in show business in this country. It's just unbelievable what was happening in the twenties and thirties. But the old people let us down by not having enough written data on this material. A lot of us grew up playing the music not knowing its history, not knowing how the old people used to work together, support one another and feature each other. And we got away from it more and more. The white man

took over more and more, and now he's
also pushing his artists. See, in those
days we didn't have to worry about that
too much."[6]

Horace Silver formed his own Silveto label for
a number of personal reasons. He suspected that
Blue Note was phasing out "jazz" and also wanted to
be free to release his spiritual records. Silver said:

> I was playing the Keystone Korner in
> San Francisco, and got the newspaper
> to read a review on our performance.
> On the other side of the page there was
> a review on this book *How to Make and
> Sell Your Own Records.* I sent for the
> book and that's what turned me on to
> saying maybe I should put my money
> where my mouth is.
>
> I had a couple of offers from labels. I
> said to myself, "If I'm gonna do
> straight-ahead, it's okay, but if I want
> to do this metaphysical thing, they're
> gonna fight me on it, knock me down, I
> won't be able to do it. So why don't I
> just go ahead and start my own label,
> so I can do my spiritual thing?"
>
> That's why I started the Silveto label.
> About eight years ago. [mid-1980s] I
> wasn't thinking about another label. I
> was just thinking about doing what I
> wanted to do without fighting anybody.
> After I had made at least three albums
> for the Silveto label, I thought, "Why

not start another label, the Emerald
label, for straight-ahead?" Instead of
losing fans who didn't want to go this
way. With what I'm doing they can have
both.[7]

By the 1960s musicians and other artists
were ready to move away from European American
business constraints and regain control of their
social, political, and expressive domains. For many
musicians this meant a move back to their African
heritage.

Restructuring Musical Approaches

Saxophonist Archie Shepp stresses the
importance of the oral tradition and its cultural
transformation in the twentieth century in his
forward to Ben Sidran's book *Black Talk.*[8] Shepp
makes clear that the process through which "jazz"
(or most African-American music) is passed on
through generations differs from educational
methods traditionally employed with other forms of
music. What is taught orally and aurally isn't
necessarily notes or technique exclusively, but
includes more esoteric information involving the
inherent spirit and other affective aspects of music.
The emotional feelings that inspire or overcome
musicians or listeners are intangible.

As experimental musicians began to define
themselves stylistically during the 1960s, they
rejected labels previously forced upon their music. It
was clear that terms like "jazz" and "classical" were
political labels in America.

During the 1960s, modern "jazz" music began a poignant expansion beyond the traditional set of musical elements particularly associated with instrumental "jazz" styles. This movement involved modifications to conventional approaches to syncopation, stylized "swing" feel, and others that previously served as technical elements and parameters used by mainstream musical society to describe "jazz." Titles of compositions such as Coltrane's "Meditation" and "A Love Supreme" provide conceptual clues to the basis of some new approaches modern innovators explored. "Jazz" musicians traveled worldwide and absorbed from all the cultures with which they came in contact. Musicians from abroad were also making their new homes in America, bringing rich cultural information with them. (Mongo Santamaria, Ali Akbar Khan, Ravi Shankar, Babatunde Olatunji, Mariam Makeba, and Hugh Masakela are a few examples.)

Through a new cross-fertilization musical, philosophical and conceptual seeds were planted in fertile artistic soil. A greater number of "jazz" musicians emerged with conservatory and other institutional training during the modern "jazz" era (Miles at the Juilliard School of Music in New York City, Coltrane at the Ornstein School of Music in Philadelphia, Cecil Taylor at the New England Conservatory in Boston, and Ornette Coleman and Don Cherry at the Lenox School of Jazz in western Massachusetts—where John Lewis was director). The integrated multicultural aesthetic and spiritual base that resulted enabled artists to separate, recombine, classify, assimilate, and apply a vast amount of knowledge to their artistic approaches in fissionable manners. New idiosyncratic laws and principles merged with an ecumenical understanding of music, which each artist adapted to their individual goals and aspirations.

The integration of spiritual concerns with artistic thinking provided a level of insulation for themselves and their art that the consumption of drugs had not provided during earlier periods. The synergy of these new conceptions now limited the systematic destructive potential of certain malicious influences (typically associated with the "jazz" environment).

As African-Americans adopted the slogan "black is beautiful" during the 1960s, their music was relabeled *black classical music, great black music* (the Art Ensemble of Chicago's slogan), *black jazz,* and the like.[9] The new terms of identification were a proactive movement toward reclaiming all aspects of their art form, as African Americans expressed their dissatisfaction with centuries of discrimination and exploitation at the hands of the dominant society. The Pan-African nationalism that reemerged during the 1960s permeated African-American culture generally; music was not an exception.

As young Americans explored alternative lifestyles in defiance of the conservative values promoted in the 1950s, many African-American innovators liberated themselves from musical limitations that impeded creative expression. As new languages evolved, it appears that some European-American critics embarked on a mission involving sustained condescending assaults aimed at the "demystification," systematization, and denial of "jazz's" spirituality through labeling the music of some innovators of the era "angry," "anti-jazz," "nihilistic," etc.

The 1960s liberation movement produced music that was not packaged for conventional radio formats (three- to five-minute songs, etc.). Recording artists produced LPs with expansive and continuous compositions (filling one or more sides of an album) in both rock and "jazz" genres. Listeners took time to give these recordings a thorough listening. Music that evolved during this period contained a broader range of individualized approaches than any other music in twentieth-century America. Many genres of music in America engaged this era of experimentation. Since most experiments were absorbed by a significant portion of the younger Americans' subculture (who were beginning to obtain a sense of communal participation), the lack of a mature sociocultural foundation led to instability. Consequently, principles learned were quickly abandoned once youths within the majority culture cut their hair and headed off in the direction of yuppie individualism during the 1970s.

The easily identifiable styles of artists who reached maturity during the 1960s, such as John Coltrane, Jimi Hendrix, Cecil Taylor, Aretha Franklin, Albert Ayler, Carlos Santana, Janis Joplin, and Sun Ra, set the standards for many of the experimental approaches used today. Much of the postmodern and poststructural music that caught on in the 1980s (the lower east side of New York City artistic crowd is an example) have clear prototypes in music of the sixties and early seventies.

The 1960s innovator often created musical manifestations that involved a method of communication that transcended the limitations of words. Raahsan Roland Kirk's composition "Inflated Tear" tells the story of a southern physician who caused his blindness by prescribing the wrong eye drops when his mother took him in for treatment of an eye infection when he was very young.[10] Coltrane's "Alabama" was written in response to the bombing of a Sunday school class at an African-American church by European-American supremacists, which resulted in the death of three young girls. Jimi Hendrix's version of the "Star Spangled Banner" performed live at the Woodstock Festival (among other places) during the sixties conveyed more than the original words could have ever transmitted. Miles Davis' album "Nefertiti" was an affirmation of his pride in the African tradition and beauty. It was recognition of the importance of African-American music that helped Davis decide to leave Juilliard at the beginning of his career:

> I was learning more from hanging out, so I just got bored with school after a while. Plus, they were so fucking white-oriented and so racist. Shit, I could learn more in one session at Minton's than it would take me two years to learn at Juilliard. At Juilliard, after it was all over, all I was going to know was a bunch of white styles; nothing new. And I was just getting mad and embarrassed with their prejudice and shit.

> I remember one day being in a music history class and a white woman was the teacher. She was up in front of the class saying that the reason black folk played the blues was because they were poor and had to pick cotton. So they were sad and that's where the blues

comes from, their sadness. My hand
went up in a flash and I stood up and
said, "I'm from East St. Louis and my
father is rich, he's a dentist, and I play
the blues. My father didn't never pick
no cotton and I didn't wake up this
morning sad and start playing the
blues. There's more to it than that."
Well, the bitch turned green and didn't
say nothing after that. Man, she was
teaching that shit from out of a book
written by someone who didn't know
what the fuck he was talking about.
That's the kind of shit that was
happening at Juilliard and after a while
I got tired of it.[11]

As audiences absorbed a wider cross-section
of the world around them through engaging a wider
range of styles and artistic ideas (including the
music of non-Western cultures), vocabularies began
to make the crossover. This melding of styles
resulted in the creation of new "fusionary" and
"fissionary" approaches. In the former, the individual
musical components involved remain fairly distinct.
In the latter, elements are first broken down
deductively to expose their fundamental constituents
and then recombined into new formations that
produce unique qualities and conceptual
approaches.

John Coltrane, for instance, studied a wide
assortment of musical styles but did not merely
imitate or fuse together musical ideas in his
compositions. His understanding of the basic
principles of blues, twelve-tone composition,
microtones, harmonics, quasi-modal composition,

and principles from certain non-Western musical traditions launched an evolution toward a personal language. Coltrane evolved through more distinct styles than most other "jazz" masters (Ellington and Miles, of course, did likewise), embracing rhythm and blues, bebop, hard bop, quasi-modal, avant-garde, and other musical forms that are difficult to label (such as those involved in the compositions *Giant Steps, A Love Supreme, Ascension, Interstellar Space,* etc.). Joe Goldberg mentions that Coltrane had expressed an interest in twelve-tone music; but when asked about the seeming impossibility of improvising serially he replied, "Damn the rules, it's the feeling that counts; You play all twelve notes in your solo anyway."[12]

Artistic Expression or Entertainment?

Bebop introduced an immutable dilemma for many artists. Do performing musicians focus solely within themselves (individually or with the ensemble onstage), or should the primary concern be satisfying the audience? In the African-American community the answer had been clear; a musician plays for both. Once the music moved into a more unfamiliar (and often hostile) European-American community, some African-American musicians directed a significant proportion of their attention to fellow musicians and their individual musical goals rather than to their new audiences (which may have appeared hostile or indifferent to their musical presence). Focusing musical attention on the circle of musicians became a subtle feature of a significant portion of the innovative musical experiments of the 1960s.

Music and art of the sixties often caused audiences, who expected to be entertained in a particular or prescribed fashion, to reconsider their positions. The new musical presentation did not always blend well with stylized descriptions to which some critics had grown accustomed. Words like "swing" and "jazz" would have to be reevaluated, replaced, or redefined. The act of reducing music to descriptive terms poses metalinguistic problems impossible to surmount. The relationship between words and other sociocultural phenomena can often be direct, but the indirect nature of instrumental music often conveys abstract yet more intimate meanings.

Titles and descriptive programs sometimes offer narrow sets of possible musical meanings in order to make listeners more comfortable with their subjective interpretations. Without such aids, however, critics may freely project their own ignorance, fears, fantasies, etc. onto the void formed when they feel alienated from unfamiliar music.

Author James Lincoln Collier, for instance, foolishly wonders whether Coltrane had an "oral fixation" that caused him to devote so much time to practicing his saxophone.[13] Readers are less likely to read such insulting comments about European-American composers, whether virtuosos or journeymen. Few have accused writers like Collier of having anal fixations for spending so much time sitting at a typewriter, for instance. Everyone celebrated as artistic geniuses throughout Western history accomplished mastery over their discipline through spending exorbitant amounts of time enraptured and intrigued by their chosen course of study. Judging by some of Coltrane's expressed comments regarding his passion for music, it is more reasonable to conclude that he may have been spiritually and artistically inspired to express himself so incessantly.[14]

We have not yet perfected a metalanguage that allows us to discuss sounds and their spectrums of organization effectively. This limitation becomes increasingly more complex with unfamiliar music. Some spectators tend to blame the art for not conforming to their personal expectations, limitations, aesthetic preferences, and individual temperaments, whether or not they are familiar with the sociocultural traditions, stylistic contexts or particular artistic idioms. Descriptions such as too loud, too fast, too abstract, too many things going on at once, too intense, etc. are obviously all subjective observations.

African-American music that began to receive a series of stigmata during the 1960s (Free "Jazz," New Thing, Avant-Garde, etc.) was a combination of at least several fundamental convergences: it initiated a new movement toward trans-African musical values; it included a liberated and ecumenical approach to all elements of music making; and it sought new forms of expression. African-American musical styles now embraced more aleatory forms of music (where the composer introduces an element of chance or unpredictability, expressing possibility rather than necessity) and relied less on the tendency of functional harmony to assume that all chord combinations of a key area are variants of the tonic, dominant, or subdominant chords. This new music not only involved changing and abandoning key centers but also expanded timbral notions to include a variety of untempered forms of pitch collections. The musical "cry," the growled "bent" tone, and other expressive factors of traditional African music became increasingly pronounced.

In the exploration of quasi-modality,[15] introduced by Miles Davis and others during the 1950s and expanded during the 1960s, the range of musical possibilities extended further horizontally. Modes were in fashions more akin to usage in traditional African styles, such as that of the Hausa-speaking Muslims in Nigeria. The scale specifications for various praise songs involve flexible approaches to modes such as the ascending configuration E-G-A-B-C-D-E-[F]-G-A.

Ornette Coleman, Eric Dolphy, Albert Ayler, Cecil Taylor, Sun Ra, and other innovators were among those involved in the expansion beyond quasi-modality. With freer approaches to "jazz," traditional forms and patterns were replaced by still more liberated criteria. There are at least four common musical elements that can be discerned in free "jazz": (1) tone color often functions as a structural element, (2) a greater emphasis is (once again) placed on collective improvisation, (3) liberation from traditional roles involves not only the solo functions but applies equally to traditional roles of accompaniment, and (4) all traditional musical rules and elements are open to question, redefinition, and revision.

Free "jazz" covered a large number of musical approaches and sounds. Ornette Coleman (often depicted with his white plastic saxophone) was one of the leading contributors to early free "jazz." In an interview for *Down Beat* magazine, Coleman talks about some of the ways he attempted to expand musical horizons between the 1960s and the 1980s:

When I had my place on Prince Street, I wanted to not worry about categories, and have people playing all kinds of music, regardless of instrument—it could be a kazoo, or a violin, anything. In the Western world, there's only a few instruments that people adopt to a lead, like the saxophone or guitar. You can't have a person with a Jew's harp be the leader of a band. But why not? It's just another sound.

When you see an African person taking a little handmade instrument and blowing your mind, you know the bassoon is not the only instrument that can have new properties to it.

Basically, all the music in the Western world that's tempered is played on the same notes; the solfeggio system is still used today to get people to say, "Well, you're too flat or you're too sharp, you can sing or you can't." Imagine what it was before they had that. . . . Everyone was concerned about how they felt . . . . To me, lots of intellectual things have eliminated the naturalness in human beings. And it has really castrated lots of the pureness of people's hearts.

What I want to do is to make the *coloring* the melodies. Not to *color* the melody, but make the melody the actual statement itself. We do that in Prime Time. That's what it is.

> In Prime Time the melody can be the
> bass line, the modulation line, the
> melody, or the second or third part. In
> fact that's how I see harmolodics.[16]

During the early and mid-1960s, as Cecil Taylor, John Coltrane, and Albert Ayler began to assert their influence upon the development of "jazz" in New York City, Coltrane's music seemed to generate the greatest degree of controversy. Coltrane mastered blues, rhythm and blues, quasi-modal, and hard bop styles, and his influence was becoming widespread. Coltrane's music transcended ideological boundaries to a greater degree than the music of Taylor, Coleman, and Charles Mingus managed before him.

Of course, not all music in the 1960s was experimental. Musical styles from the past continued to stay alive and sometimes thrive (blues, ragtime, Dixieland, boogie woogie, rhythm and blues, swing, bebop, hard bop, cool, etc.). After the swing era, two distinct concepts of music making clearly emerged and diverged. Duke Ellington, Mary Lou Williams, Art Tatum, and others who emerged from the swing era created forms of music that were not necessarily dance based. The jump bands led by Louis Jordan and others retained a particular connection with the African-American dancing community that later inspired Cannonball Adderley, Horace Silver, and other artists to create a "funky" brand of "jazz." Their intent was to perform African-American music that would be easily accessible for those seeking groove-oriented styles that retained an ethnically identifiable rhythmic pulsation. Adderley and others were not swayed by those accusing them of engaging musical forms that were geared to entertain rather than crafted to appeal more to the intellect.

A stylistic tendency toward African themes also emerged during the swing era (Ellington's "Caravan" and other "jungle music," for instance). This direction gained momentum during the forties (Dizzy Gillespie's "Night in Tunisia," for example) and then found highly fertile soil during the fifties and sixties (Yusef Lateef's "Mahaba'" Coltrane's "African Brass," Miles' "Nefertiti," etc.).

Betty Carter

Betty Carter (1929-1998) masterfully fused artistry, showmanship, exuberance, and surprise into each of her performances. Willard Jenkins describes her this way:

> A fan's remembrance of Betty Carter begins onstage. For although she made numerous successful and eminently swinging recordings, Betty Carter was most assuredly a creature of the living stage. Her presence, colorfully gowned and tastefully coifed, was not of the regal, untouchable variety, but more an earthy forbearance – a hip African-American earth mother of the first magnitude. She kept all eyes riveted on her every move; twisting, turning, pivoting, she moved her body to the rhythm in a sort of calisthenic of swing that was peerless.[17]

Born Lillie Mae Jones, Carter studied piano before beginning her professional career as a singer in

1946. She sat in with Dizzy Gillespie's big band and with Charlie Parker's quintet before touring with Lionel Hampton from 1948 until 1951. Billie Holiday and Sarah Vaughan inspired her unique stylistic approach. She moved between scat singing and lyrics with remarkable clarity with her own exciting and highly varied arrangements. She formed her own record company, Bet-Car Records, when she came out of a self-imposed retirement to raise her children (until 1969). She introduced many young pianists, bassists and drummers to the international "jazz" community as members of her trios. Pianist Cyrus Chestnut worked with Carter between 1991-93. He felt that, "Betty was one of the major mentors in my development. She really encouraged me to try to find something new; she refused to let me just go on automatic pilot. She always wanted the musicians to be sensitive and get all the love the music had."[18]

Carter was an innovative composer and vocalist whose musical insurrections stand out as prominently as those of Charlie Parker, Thelonious Monk, John Coltrane, and Miles Davis. Her consistent ability to find young and gifted musicians made the Betty Carter School perhaps as significant as that of Art Blakey, from which many of today's young masters graduated. Carter's audiences enjoyed the high level of showmanship as riveting as any of the greatest artists of the twentieth century.

Inspired by Billie Holiday and Sarah Vaughan, Carter began as a singer in Detroit in 1946 and sat in with Charlie Parker, Dizzy Gillespie, and other bebop musicians. She toured with Lionel Hampton as Lorraine Carter between 1948 and 1951. During the early 1960s Carter toured, after recording with Ray Charles, Japan (1963) and Europe (1964). She then retired to raise her children before resuming her performance career in 1969. During the 1970s many considered her music too radical, but audiences soon caught up to Carter's experimental nature.

Her powerful compositions and arrangements underscored Carter's vocal agility, much akin to that of Sarah Vaughan and Ella Fitzgerald. Her songs, filled with unpredictable shifts in moods and dynamics, transported listeners on amazing voyages to exciting musical regions. She was one of the select few artists who pressed impressive albums on her own label (Bet-Car Records).

Alice Coltrane (b. 1937)

Alice Coltrane, nee Alice Farrow, was born in Detroit, Michigan, on August 27, 1937. She came from a musical family that included her bassist brother, Ernie Farrow. After formal studies in Detroit, she formed her own trio. Bud Powell heavily influenced her after her journey to Europe in 1960. Soon she became the successor to Terry Pollard as vibraphonist with The Terry Gibbs Quartet.

Alice met John Coltrane in 1963. They were soon married and had three children. She replaced McCoy Tyner in Coltrane's quartet in 1966 and continued to perform and promote her husband's music after his death. Alice Coltrane played piano and vibraphone early in her career, but following the death of her husband she extended her talent to include the organ, harp, tamboura, and percussion in live and recorded sessions. In his autobiography on John Coltrane, "jazz" scholar Bill Cole remarked: "If for no other reason, bringing Alice into the band would have been appropriate at this time, if only because of the need to promote more women players."

Unquestionably, there has been tremendous male chauvinism in jazz and too often women have been treated as mere sex objects or exploited as Billy Holiday was by members of the orchestra. But there is certainly more to Alice Coltrane than just her symbolic value in the band."[19]

During the final years of her husband's life musical spiritualism and mysticism became the nucleus of both Alice's and John's philosophical thinking. Alice credited her husband with having taught her "to explore . . . to play thoroughly and completely," and said, "I would like to play music according to ideals set forth by John and continue to let a cosmic principle, or the aspect of spirituality, be the underlying reality behind the music as he did."[20]

Eric Dolphy and the "Jazz" Critics

John Coltrane's first recording for the Impulse record label (*Africa/Brass*)[21] featured arrangements by Eric Dolphy, based upon compositional ideas on which Coltrane and Tyner collaborated. The session utilized an unusual instrumentation: trumpet, four French horns, alto saxophone, baritone saxophone, two euphoniums, two basses, piano, drums, tuba, and Coltrane on soprano and tenor saxophones. Dolphy said, "John thought of this sound, he wanted brass, he wanted baritone horns, he wanted that mellow sound and power."[22] Coltrane listened to many African records for rhythmic inspiration and for a general musical direction. He seemed pleased with the results that were obtained and commented, "I had a sound that I wanted to hear . . . And what resulted was about it."[23]

Alto saxophonist, bass clarinetist, and flutist Eric Dolphy, like Coltrane, continued to maintain ties between his (hard bop) roots and the more radical degrees of musical experimentation he engaged. The contribution Dolphy made to the polyrhythmic fabric while a member of Coltrane's ensemble is particularly robust, piquant, and diametrical in approach. His solo on *My Favorite Things* in the Burrill Crohn film *John Coltrane: The Coltrane Legacy* provides a clear example of his musical contribution. In that performance, Dolphy breaks away from the overwhelming predominance of triplets to create a contrasting new and independent layer of melodic and polyrhythmic tension. Similarly, the melodic lines Coltrane improvised added unusually elongated phrase dimensions. The longer rhythmic cycle provided yet another level of polyrhythmic tension to the manifold musical mosaic extant on that performance.

While Coltrane's stylistic development evolved gradually from traditional hard bop to a freer musical approach in a highly systematic and methodical fashion, Dolphy continued to oscillate between opposing stylistic poles. He participated as co-leader in the 1960 *Free Jazz* recording with Ornette Coleman. The next year Dolphy recorded with Oliver Nelson and Booker Little in sessions that were decisively hard-bop oriented. Dolphy's influence on Coltrane served as a catalyst that yielded far-reaching consequences in directing the tenor saxophonist's music toward "free jazz."[24]

Coltrane and Dolphy were friends for many years. During Dolphy's numerous visits to Coltrane's home they often practiced together, eventually realizing their mutual ideas about music. They agreed that there should be a somewhat divaricated quality to their music in order to move away from limitations of conventional constructs and closer to the abstract perfection of nature.[25] Coltrane felt that Dolphy's presence in the band opened up new possibilities along such lines. "Eric and I have been talking music for quite a few years, since about 1954. We've been close for quite a while. We watched music . . . discussed what was being done down through the years, because we love music. . . . Since he's been in the band, he's been a broadening effect on us. There are a lot of things we try that we never tried before."[26]

To Dolphy, exemplifying an attitude related to that of Ornette Coleman's, tempered intonation in "jazz" was of secondary interest. While Coltrane expanded the humanlike quality of his sound with harmonics and multiphonics, Dolphy augmented the timbre of his individual voice with an extraordinarily natural and limpid sound that often avoided restricting musical fixation upon precisely definable pitches. Just as Coltrane's spontaneous compositional vocabulary assimilated the various aspects of the entire range of his career into a unified vocabulary, Dolphy too integrated the variegated musical elements involved in his highly unusual sonic language, creating a style that reflected the natural qualities of the human voice. The strikingly human quality of Dolphy's sound exceeded attempts by other artists to accomplish a similar effect.

Dolphy's disdain for traditional approaches to sound production brought about the same degree of skepticism that critics had attached earlier to Lester Young's music. Young broke with the standard conventions established by Ben Webster and Coleman Hawkins by altering pitches with substitute fingerings. Young also took a linear rather than arpeggiated approach in his melodic conception. To the astonishment of critics, Dolphy admitted that bird songs inspired the conceptual basis for his flute playing.[27]

The longest trip the Coltrane group made was its European tour in 1961. While in Germany, bassist Reggie Workman recalls, Coltrane remarked that he had dreamed (back in 1957) of the band he now led, so he felt that this group had been coming into fruition for quite a while.[28] Shortly after this tour, Eric Dolphy joined the ensemble, and then, Workman says, "we began to deal with another dimension in the music."[29] In live performances Coltrane's solos became longer when Dolphy was in the ensemble. Both men liked to play extended solos and had the techniques, stamina, and the powerful imagination needed to do so convincingly. The fact that they were inspired by each other's musical contributions was the catalyst.

Once connected to the labels conjured up by journalists, such as the "New Thing," Dolphy and Coltrane were at once praised and damned by the press. In a November 23, 1961, *Down Beat* article, associate editor John Tynan became the first critic to take a strong position against these two musicians.

> At Hollywood's Renaissance club, I listened to a horrifying demonstration of what appears to be a growing anti-jazz trend exemplified by these foremost proponents of what is termed avant garde music. I heard a good rhythm section . . . . go to waste behind nihilistic exercises of the two horns . . . . Coltrane and Dolphy seem intent on

deliberately destroying [swing]. . . .
They seem bent on pursuing an
anarchistic course in their music that
can but be termed anti-jazz.[30]

Although such opinions have damaged the
careers and economic status of many innovative
"jazz" musicians throughout the century, the claims
are generally amateurish, nebulous, perfidious, and
clearly devoid of real musical substance. The content
of this brand of writing rests upon unsubstantiated
and highly subjective lay opinions. This led Cecil
Taylor to express a sentiment shared by many of his
musical colleagues when he disclosed his general
contempt for critics in a 1963 *Village Voice* interview.
"Critics are sustained by our vitality. From afar, the
uninformed egos ever growing arbitrarily attempt to
give absolutes."[31]
Critics rarely assume more meaningful and
appropriate positions, restricting their comments to
technical, sociocultural or historical aspects of
music they are qualified to evaluate. Furthermore, as
Frank Kofsky points out, not only are these writers
usually lacking in musical, sociological, or historical
credentials, but most do not derive the major portion
of their income from criticism. Often they are
dependent for their livelihoods on other unrelated
employment sources. Even the more fortunate few
end up writing liner notes for record jacket or
preparing advertising copy for the record industry.
Consequently, the most basic prerequisite of artistic
criticism, that which demands that the critic be free
to arrive at his or her verdicts without being subtly
or overtly coerced by the conflicting interests of
political lobbies or influences, is often preempted by
self-serving media politics. Despite such

inadequacies, many critics wield influential pens that alter the thinking of a sector of the public at large. One manifestation of this influence is the annual *Down Beat* International Jazz Critics Poll each year.[32] An equally unqualified and improper body of people (controlling a significant economic factor in the business of "jazz" production) rarely brandishes similar influence in any other American or European art forms outside "jazz" (movie critics may be an exception). Critics and readers polls for symphonic organizations do not exist.

Admittedly, all art experiences some level of political control, but the added onerous burden of residual "slave owner" or "plantation" mentality exasperates the problem with African-American music. The effects of powerful artistic innovation have gradually transformed this situation over time, nonetheless.

> Audiences haven't changed much. They say Dizzy and Bird had to face a lot of hostility; but they had their good audiences too. Eventually, the listeners move right along with the musicians.

> Jazz is so much a music of individuality that every new artist with any originality effects a change in the overall scene. Lester Young represented as great a change, in his time, as some of the things that are happening now. So did Bird.[33]

Paradoxically, "jazz" writers, who have demonstrated an affinity for experimental music, are often labeled "the radical critic-polemicist."[34] Those

who apparently fail to acknowledge or understand
the unfortunate interchange that occurs between
African-American "jazz" and European-American
racism misjudge such writers. Kofsky writes:

> I believe that the editorial staff of *Down
> Beat* is thoroughly ingrained with the
> precepts of white supremacy—so much
> so, indeed, that they are an integral
> part of the magazine's frame of
> reference which can be taken for
> granted without conditional reiteration.
> That is why black nationalism, as well
> as other forms of radicalism, which
> threatens to disrupt the status quo, are
> anathema to its editors, why they are at
> such pains to discredit all radical
> ideologies.[35]

The social and journalistic condition to which
Kofsky refers is apparently still in evidence today.
Radano feels that "at times the polemic of the white
radical critic equaled or surpassed that of (Leroy)
Jones . . . unquestionably the most hostile was
Frank Kofsky." It is painfully revealing when the rare
situation occurs where a European-American "jazz"
critic shares an "unpopular" perspective with
African-American artists regarding revolutionary
African-American music. Taking such a position
remains threatening, socially unacceptable, and
newsworthy in the world of American "jazz" literature
even at the close of the twentieth century.
Unfortunately, interracial agreement rarely occurs in
America, so Kofsky's several-decades-old position
still stands as a severely polemic notion.

Pointless cavil certainly affected the careers of Dolphy, Coltrane, and many other artists. Coltrane was delighted with Dolphy's playing and admired the fact that "Eric's into everything."

> He just came in and sat in with us for about three nights and everybody enjoyed it, because his presence added some fire to the band. He and I have known each other a long time, and I guess you'd say we were students of the jazz scene. . . . We'd exchange ideas and so we just decided to go ahead and see if we could do something within this group. Eric is really gifted and I feel he's going to produce something inspired, but although we've been talking about music for years, I don't know where he's going, and I don't know where *I'm* going. He's interested in trying to progress, however, and so am I, so we have quite a bit in common.[36]

Heavy critical protests led Coltrane's record company advisors to eventually convince him to ask Dolphy to leave his ensemble.[37] Although these advisors have not been identified by name in any of the sources I have found, it is certain that the decision made was heavily influenced by responses to Coltrane's and Dolphy's music in the press.[38] Here we come upon a poignant example of the negative influence of opprobrious press on the music of two African-American innovators. Some people felt that if Coltrane had been able to keep his ensemble with

Dolphy intact, it could have turned out to be "one of the most interesting in jazz."[39]

In March 1962, Dolphy left Coltrane's ensemble as a regular member and formed his own group. Although he had worked and recorded regularly with Coltrane, surprisingly few of the recording sessions in which Dolphy participated were ever released; and of those commercially issued recordings on which Dolphy performed, his solos were often edited out.[40]

In an effort to clarify issues and hyperbole surrounding their musical conceptions at the time, Coltrane and Dolphy agreed to an interview with critic Don DeMichael in an article that was printed in *Down Beat* on April 21, 1962.[41] The musicians merely stated the obvious in that interview: basically each said they just wanted to make beautiful innovative music.

Eric Dolphy was one of the motivating forces behind the musical idea for the construction of Coltrane's composition "India." This composition frequently employs bass ostinato and pedal note patterns to provide underpinning for free-flowing improvisation on winds and drums. It also directs emphasis toward the lead melody (played in similar motion by Coltrane and Dolphy at the interval of a fourth apart) or soloist. Ekwueme examined the use of pedal notes in Ibo music and found that they added emphases to the words of choral music. "Pedal notes are used usually, but not always, when more than two parts are involved. The two upper parts follow the shape of the tune (and the intonation of the words) in parallel or similar motion. The lowest part can, therefore, afford to dispense with the limitations of speech inflection in its melodic line, and simply repeat a basic drone while other parts indicate the meaning of the words in their own melodic movement."[42]

These Afrocentric ostinato and pedal note patterns, as well as other related musical devices, provide both tonal and rhythmic orientation despite the unpredictability of the soloists and percussion. It was similarly applied in traditional African instrumental ensembles, where the ostinato provided temporal orientation within polyrhythmic frameworks. With African music, for instance, Ekwueme finds ostinati useful organizers. "Accompaniment patterns are useful delimiters. When an instrument (or hand clapping) repeats the same pattern over and over in a piece of music, the duration of one such pattern is probably the best 'bar line' delimiter that one may use, especially in measuring temporal durations, in the form of the music. These patterns common in African music, have been called by different names, such as *clap patterns, bell pattern,* or simply, *standard pattern.*"[43]

Coltrane created the thematic materials, but Dolphy investigated Indian music long before settling in New York. He introduced Coltrane to certain aspects of Indian music and the nucleus of Coltrane's composition, "India", emanated from Coltrane's association with Dolphy. Eric explored a range of references to exotic scalar configurations over the quasi-modal framework. At the end of his association with Coltrane, Dolphy's performances on this and other recordings show his focused and matured compositional awareness and his control over the technical devices with which he continued to experiment. Earlier in his career, some musical devices sounded more tentative. Dolphy's understanding of formal structure within an improvisational context was also advanced through this synergistic association. Dolphy, Coltrane, Cecil Taylor, Ornette Coleman, and other innovators relied upon symmetrical patterns to provide musical coherence to their work when other tonal devices were abandoned. Call-and-response patterns and the use of refrains in Afrocentric music are related expressions of symmetry. The use of symmetry was also of paramount importance in African music. Ekwueme observed that Africans felt a need to express the duality they found so frequently in nature.

> Many Ibos will not accept gifts that do not come in pairs, and will reject such offers with the statement that they have not been nursed with milk from only one breast. Where there is lack of proportion, balance, or equality, therefore, there is an error in concept or an accident in the execution of the form.
>
> . . . The idea of symmetry in nature has probably been overworked, especially as there are many asymmetrical things in nature. Yet it must be borne in mind that the Ibo, like his fellow African, is much closer to nature than his counterpart in the western world. He accepts nature and natural forces without attempting to discover empirical justification for their existence. He subsists in and by nature. His ethics and philosophies are dependent on the forces of nature, and his art comes from it. Symmetry is

> therefore sought after in all artistic
> endeavors—music, dance, drama,
> literature, sculpture, painting, textiles,
> etc. In choral music . . . symmetry is
> not limited to the form of the songs; it
> is present in the scales from which the
> tunes are themselves constructed.[44]

Dolphy enjoyed the reception he received in Copenhagen and other places in Europe, so he eventually settled there. He was able to secure recorded broadcasts and concerts of his music as a leader in Europe. The *Berlin Concerts* and *Stockholm Sessions* are albums issued posthumously (on the Enja label) that document Dolphy's stellar performances on some of these occasions (despite the inferior rhythm sections on the dates comprised of freelance musicians picked up in Europe).

Dolphy's cadenza-like (unaccompanied) approach to Billie Holiday's composition "God Bless the Child" demonstrates the unchallenged level of virtuosity he obtained on bass clarinet. His ability to make any composition his own through personal interpretations of standards is also revealed in his performances of Holiday's composition. Other compositions such as "Spiritual" represent a big leap forward in his development, leading toward the definitive Dolphy seminal *Out To Lunch*. Dolphy's music, and the music of other 1960s innovators, reflect an important connection between the African-American "jazz" movement of the time and the creative expression of various other revolutionary artists (such as author James Baldwin). Many artists were seeking truth and meaning through their work during this salubrious period of artistic development.

Artists often found powerful expression through liberated art forms as they attempted to create new identities for themselves and for their musical traditions. These sincere and uninhibited individuals left interesting records of the period.

Albert Ayler

Albert Ayler (1936–70) was one of the younger musicians who influenced John Coltrane during his late periods of development. Ayler was fascinated with the sound of the saxophone and felt that "you really have to play your instrument to escape from notes to sound."[45] Essentially a melodist with a distinctive vibrato and instantly recognizable tone, Ayler created an approach to "jazz" that was unprecedented.

The works of Charlie Parker significantly affected Ayler. His haunts, shouts, and whines on his instrument created an emotional and vibrant music that used melody as both a motivating force and continuity factor at the root of his free improvisations. This musical freedom was contained within clearly organized structures, episodes of contrapuntal interaction, and was often sustained through motivic developments. His emotional intensity was counterbalanced by the gentleness that could be found in "Saints" and in certain other compositions. He explored the dirge like genres of music akin to that Ornette Coleman often engaged. Ayler used this particular conceptual approach to explore variations in expressive timbres. This basic principle was applied to his composition "Witches and Devils" and others. Ayler felt that

When there is chaos, which is now [December 18, 1966], only a relatively few people can listen to the music that tells of what will be. You see, everyone is screaming "Freedom" now, but mentally, most are under a great strain. But now the truth is marching in, as it once marched back in New Orleans. And that truth is that there must be peace and joy on Earth. I believe music can help bring that truth into being because music *is* the universal language. That's why it can be such a force.[46]

Coltrane was a musician that Ayler admired, and Ayler wrote his composition "For Coltrane" after the summer when Coltrane died (1967). Ayler said, "John was like a visitor to this planet. He came in peace and he left in peace; but during his time here, he kept trying to reach new levels of awareness, of peace, of spirituality. That's why I regard the music he played as sacred music—John was getting closer and closer to the Creator."[47]

Ayler's compositions insisted that the listener adopt new attitudes for the absorption of music. When Nat Hentoff asked his brother Don Ayler (who played trumpet with Albert) how one should listen to his music, Don told him one way *not* to listen was "to focus on the notes and stuff like that. Instead try to move your imagination toward the sound. It's a matter of following the sound." Albert added, "You have to relate sound to sound inside it. You have to try to listen to everything together." Don concluded, "The pitches, the colors, you have to watch them move."[48] Albert Ayler called the overwhelming vitality of his music spiritual energy that was "purely music of love. While it comes from meditation, it has nothing to do with mysticism. It tries to help bring about new approaches to living for everyone."

Ayler says his composition "Our Prayer" "has its own very distinctive thing to say. It's a prayer to the Creator, a song about the spiritual principles of the universe." Albert Ayler's career was cut short when he was murdered and his body thrown into a river in New York City in 1970. Donald Ayler went into seclusion. They both came in peace and left in peace.

Ayler's intense musical message contained swirling figures with voicelike timbre. He stretched the upper register of the tenor saxophone and based his melodies on European classical and folk rhythms that lacked the conventional swing feeling. His compositions loosely allude to preset harmonic structures and rhythmic motives. He was among the earliest innovators to improvise without conventional preset chord progressions.

The Association for the Advancement of Creative Musicians

In 1961 Muhal Richard Abrams (b. 1930) formed the Experimental Band (which would later evolve into the Association for the Advancement of Creative Musicians). He then became the AACM's president. Abrams explored new ideas with bassist and multi-instrumentalist Donald Garrett and other musicians for an extended period of time. By 1963 the Experimental Band eventually expanded to include Joseph Jarman (b. 1937), alto saxophone;

Fred Berry, trumpet; Henry Threadgill (b. 1944), woodwinds; Gene Dinwiddie, Kalaparusha, and Maurice McIntyre (b. 1936), tenor saxophones; Lester Lashley, trombone; Charles Clark and Donald Garrett, basses; Jack DeJohnette (b. 1942) and Steve McCall (1933–89), drums; and numerous other musicians. Abrams wrote in what he classified as a chromatic style, while Mitchell's compositional area was polytonal and Jarman's approach involved serialized musical experiments.[49]

Pianists Abrams and Jodie Christian, drummer Steve McCall, and trumpeter Phil Cohran formed the AACM in May 1965. Its original members were from several groups that appeared around Chicago. Their goals involved (1) creating a situation where a brand of music of their own choice could be produced, and (2) maintaining self-reliance and control over their music. John Johnson handled most of the administrative responsibilities. Minimal dues were collected from members to cover operational expenses and concerts were presented around town. Members from other parts of the country became interested in the organization and, if nominated by a member, they joined after being told what was expected of them. Lester Bowie (1941-1999), who had been a member of the Black Artist Group (BAG), came to Chicago with drummers Phillip Wilson and Leonard Smith from St. Louis. Trumpeter Leo Smith came from Mississippi.

Leo Smith later worked with Anthony Braxton (b. 1945—woodwinds) and Leroy Jenkins (b. 1932—violin) during a period when the trumpeter evolved closer to the idea of "total creativity." Braxton felt that the creative impulse had become so suppressed that the distance between the innovative artist and audiences continued to grow wider every year. He began spending more of his time in Europe with musicians like guitarist Derek Bailey (1930), who he felt were immersed in developing their own musical worlds.

The seriousness and gravity of the music eventually attracted more innovative musicians (who heard the concerts and rehearsals) into its broadening ranks. As Roscoe Mitchell (b. 1940—woodwinds) explains, "I was cool; I took dope; I smoked pot; etc. I did not *care* for the life I had been given. In having the chance to work with the Experimental Band with Richard and the other musicians there, I found the first something with meaning/reason for doing. That band and people there was the *most* important thing that ever happened to me."[50]

Many others soon to be prominent innovators studied and digested Muhal Richard Abrams's concepts, including Anthony Braxton and Leo Smith. Smith said, "I only play when there is an opportunity for you to explore yourself, when each occasion would bring to those people and myself a complete challenge. And when I say 'challenge,' I don't mean some reference in the back past, but like challenge *right now*, where we are right now—because it is the future."

The Emergence of the Art Ensemble of Chicago

The Art Ensemble of Chicago was one of the most unusual groups to emerge in "jazz". The Art Ensemble of Chicago left Chicago for France in June 1969 and performed at festivals and clubs and gave concerts all over the European continent. Don Moye

(b. 1946—drums), joined the Art Ensemble of Chicago in Paris. The ensemble recorded a wide range of albums during that period and demonstrated their ability to move between blues and other traditional African-American musical norms en route to a highly personal free style. Jerome Cooper (b. 1946) also played with the Art Ensemble of Chicago. He and Leroy Jenkins were also members of the Revolutionary Ensemble.

Lester Bowie, the son of a music teacher and trumpeter, was born in Frederick, Maryland. He began to play the trumpet at age five and developed an eclectic performance style that incorporates the St. Louis half-valve trademark, gut bucket and heraldic trumpet playing. He also experimented with a wide variety of other techniques that span the history of twentieth-century trumpet. He worked as a traveling musician with Jackie Wilson, Joe Tex, Little Milton, and other rhythm-and-blues-oriented bands, while occasionally sitting in with musicians such as James Clay and David "Fathead" Newman (b. 1933). His long association with Julius Hemphill (1940–95), Oliver Lake (b. 1944), Phillip Wilson, and other innovative musicians date back to bebop sessions in St. Louis. Eventually, he became music director for singer and pianist Fontella Bass, who later became his wife. Bowie felt that "if you get a job playing rock-and-roll, you can maybe be a little hip on it, but you're still basically dealing with the idiom. With bebop and free jazz, the boundaries are defined. But with Mitchell there was no limitation about what you could deal from."[51]

Born in 1937, double bassist Malachi Favors was the oldest member of the original quartet that became known as the Art Ensemble of Chicago. He was the son of a preacher in Lexington, Mississippi, who was drawn toward the bass as a teen. In addition to being a unifying musical force in the ensemble, he also branches out from the bass to balafon, banjo, zither, voice, and an assortment of small percussion instruments.

Joseph Jarman (b. 1937), as poet and philosopher, became the spokesperson for the Art Ensemble of Chicago. He had joined forces with Phillip Wilson in 1961 while attending Wilson Junior College, where Jarman wrote stream-of-consciousness-style compositions for words and music that rejected the established musical norms.

The distance between any two opposing poles of phenomena is actually a force that contributes to the definition of the instances at either end of a central void or nucleus. Silence too is such a force. Some musicians realize that this seemingly empty space contributes as much to a musical statement as the notes that surround it. The relationship between space and silence can be methodically controlled to yield profound results. Monk and Randy Weston (b. 1926) are spontaneous composers who bring high degrees of meaning to the silences between their sonic events. Along with an understanding of the use of flexible rhythmic placement over a metronomic pulse, both Monk and Weston derive dramatic effects through unpredictable rhythmic augmentation, diminution, and hypermetrical time maneuvers that transform would-be musical simplicity into rich and surprising artistic occurrences.

The inherent strength and beauty of a melody or motive allows it to undergo various transformations and to enjoy a long life within musical situations that demand that continuity be maintained over extraordinary lengths of time. Once established during a musical exposition, working with familiar elements of these types enable the creative composer to transmute an incomplete or abstracted version of the central ideas into an unlimited set of metaphorical possibilities. The constant references to, or embellishments of, the original melodies or motives provides powerful composers like Monk flexible structures for the creation of well balanced musical abstractions.

Whether musical variations and permutations be subtle or profound, various degrees of tension and release are provided as the music finds new ways to breathe that are no longer determined by simple cadences, phrase structures, and binary or ternary formal devices. The music becomes fresh and personal, not only because an individual harmonic and melodic vocabulary has been formulated, but also because musical choices have been enhanced by spontaneously evolving sets of spatial relationships. As a creative artist expands the voids that form the silent centers between sonic events, new territory is excavated that demands exploration. Seemingly empty space can begin to take on personal dimensions and features of its own that form influential mental constructs. The silences can create moods, rhythms, and attitudes that make us apprehensive, curious, pensive, or excited while anticipating approaching sonic events.

The Art Ensemble of Chicago was one of the first groups to place an extremely heavy degree of emphasis on silence in "jazz." When we realize that silence can become penetratingly animated, it eventually becomes apparent that music contains more than length, width, and depth. It contains immeasurable subconscious elements that register strongly upon our senses but remain difficult to define empirically. These elements, both on our initial and subsequent contacts with certain music, fill our imaginations with images and messages that confirm the presence of countless subtle dimensions, the presence of which our minds, bodies, and emotions cannot deny.

Dewey Redman, Art Davis, and the New York Scene

Dewey Redman, a multi-reed specialist, was born in Fort Worth, Texas in 1931. He began studying music as a clarinetist. After attending Prairie View A&M College he studied the nuances of swing band playing, and admired the work of Johnny Hodges, Earl Bostic, and Charlie Parker. Redman joined the army for a while, then taught full-time in Bastrop, Texas, while occasionally sitting in on alto saxophone with local bands. When he switched to tenor saxophone, Dexter Gordon, Gene Ammons, and Stan Getz became his main influences. He discusses his musical past in a 1992 interview for *Down Beat* magazine.[52] Eventually, "at age 29 I decided to go to New York. And I told myself if I didn't make it in five years, I'd go back to Texas. It didn't work out like that. I've been trying ever since." Dewey Redman later found a stable situation in Ornette Coleman's band. Redman said,

> I've always been into Ornette's music—I knew him when he first started playing. When I got to New York he was in a hiatus, but he had a loft on Prince Street and he'd say, "Well, you're here, so . . ." He'd write out a tune, and I'd go

over it; then he'd write out another
tune, and I'd go over that. . . . When
Ornette came out of his hiatus, the first
gig I had was with him and Denardo
[Coleman's son, then a twelve-year-old
drummer] and [bassist] David Izenzon.
Later [Ed] Blackwell came into the band
and Charlie [Haden].

. . . Ornette is a genius, and I consider
myself having gone to the University of
Ornette because I learned so much—
about space, phrasing; how not to be
caught up in conventional things, but
to appreciate them too. . . . Like
changes: changes are *okay*, but I'm not
to be limited by them. And not to be
limited in my scope.

My technique isn't always what I want
it to be, and my sidemen might
sometimes play too loud. But it's a
strange thing, man: sometimes when
you think you've played your ass off,
people look at you like you're crazy.
And then sometimes when you played
the worst solo ever, people say, "Wow!
What a great solo that was!"

To play a little avant-garde—or avant-
bop—then a little bebop, and a little
blues, musette, this here, that there; to
make it all come out clean, that's very
difficult to do. Some musicians dabble
in it, say their multi-directional; but I

try to make each one distinct and clear.[53]

Like Ornette Coleman, Redman passed on his musical knowledge to his son Joshua. Joshua Redman (b. 1969) graduated summa cum laude from Harvard and was accepted into Yale (and contemplated a law degree) before turning to music as a profession.

Musical life in New York is not predictable. For those who are ready for the challenge musically, there can be endless opportunities to perform, record, and tour with the best musicians in the world. There are also spells of inactivity that can prove to be financially difficult and discouraging. With African-American music, there are no musical institutions designated to provide stability for professional artists. During the 1960s, virtually all studio jobs, teaching positions, positions with symphony orchestras, or any other stable jobs for professional musicians went to European or European-American men.

By 1969, the year that Arthur Davis (b. 1934) and Earl Madison brought suit against Leonard Bernstein and the New York Philharmonic Orchestra, there had been a dramatic 200 percent leap in the number of professional African-American musicians engaged in the major symphony orchestras. Generally speaking, this usually meant that orchestras now hired two African-American musicians instead of one. With the New York Philharmonic this represented approximately 0.3 percent of the total (525) men and women employed. Since 1965 significant numbers of federal tax dollars, of which African-American citizens often pay a disproportionate share, have been allocated for American symphony orchestras.

In 1969, $20 million were allocated to the National Endowment for the Arts and Humanities by the federal government. By 1972 allocations increased to an appropriation of $60 million devoted to these causes. A sizable proportion of these funds continue to be targeted for American symphony orchestras. Other private foundations, whose tax-exempt status is made possible by philanthropic grants to nonprofit organizations such as symphonic organizations, provide sizable contributions toward the maintenance of musical institutions that were almost exclusively "European only" cultural establishments.[54] Author Ortiz M. Walton discusses the Davis/Madison case:

> For Arthur Davis, who had auditioned for the New York Philharmonic on four occasions, and Earl Madison, who had three times auditioned, the outcome could hardly be termed just. The ruling by the New York Commission on Human Rights, after fifteen months of hearings, found the Philharmonic both guilty and not guilty. [After consultation with attorneys representing Mr. Madison and Mr. Bernstein, the latter's name was dropped from Mr. Madison's complaint.] The Philharmonic was found not guilty of the main charge of discrimination against the two black players in terms of permanent hiring. A guilty-of-discrimination verdict was handed down regarding the hiring of

substitute and extra players, a procedure which, unlike permanent hiring, did not require auditions.[55]

Art Davis had been featured two or three times a week on the Merv Griffin television show before the hearings began on his case with the New York Philharmonic. After the legal proceedings began he lost his job. Walton continues:

> In the music business, things such as reprisals have a curious way of happening to people who dare to speak the truth. We have seen what happened to Scott Joplin when he demanded royalties instead of outright, once-only payment for his masterpieces. He never sold any more music, and was unable to successfully stage a production of this opera, *Treemonisha*. This procedure is aptly enough called blacklisting. Of course, like other forms of discrimination, particularly those which affect the individual performer, the charge is difficult to prove, inasmuch as these actions are covertly accomplished. Erroll Garner, who had contractual disputes with Columbia Records in the early sixties, has rarely been heard of since. Charles Mingus, who dared to vilify in his music such figures as the former governor of Arkansas, Orville Faubus, suffered a similar fate. Word somehow gets around to those non-Blacks who are in

charge of the music industry, and shortly a personal boycott results.

The New York Philharmonic is composed, like other major symphonies, of wealthy and powerful interest groups. Their concern with the arts may be most often viewed as supportive to other roles they play in society, politely masking racism under the facade of culture. This veneer, in addition to a fanatical devotion to the tenets of Western European ideas and civilization, assists in the determination and maintenance of the status quo. When an uppity "nigger" comes along to test these notions, and to assist in the redetermination of culture and values, he will then be pushed, forced out of the business.

The most striking statistic to emerge from the evidence presented was that during the 1960's the respondent [personnel manager Joseph De Angelis] hired at least 277 substitutes or extras who played a total of 1773 weeks during that period. Of these musicians, *one* was black and he played for one week. Interestingly enough, the concerts performed during the week this black musician played included a musical work dedicated to the memories of Dr. Martin Luther King, Jr., and Robert Kennedy. Despite general agreement that this black flutist acquitted himself well, he has not been invited by the respondent to return, although white flutists have since been engaged as substitutes.[56]

The *New York Times* reported on November 18, 1970, that cellist Earl Madison and bassist Arthur Davis offered to play against each member of the New York Philharmonic orchestra cello and bass sections if screens were provided to preserve anonymity. Madison said, "We have nothing to lose. They have nothing. They say they are the greatest, so let them prove it." The New York Philharmonic remained intransigent on the issue of screening players during auditions.[57]

Amina Claudine Myers (b. 1942)

Composer Amina Claudine Myers is also a pianist, organist, and vocalist. She was born in Blackwell, Arkansas, on March 21, 1942. Myers began playing and singing as early as age four and began formal lessons at age seven. She served as pianist and organist for both school and church choirs throughout high school. While enrolled at Philander Smith College she was concert choir pianist and, for two years, student director.

In the mid-1960s Myers played organ with The Gerald Donavan Trio and became one of the few female composers affiliated with the Association for the Advancement of Creative Musicians (AACM). She established meaningful contacts during that phase of her development and began touring the country with saxophonist Sonny Stitt in 1970.

Myers soon began a two-year musical association with tenor saxophonist Gene Ammon's Quartet, worked with the AACM Big Band, played with the Vanguard Ensemble led by drummer Ajaramu (Gerald Donovan), performed in Muhal Richard Abrams's piano trio, and played duets with Joseph Jarman. After moving to New York she went on a tour of Europe with Lester Bowie.

In 1977 Myers premiered her musical *I Dream* in Chicago, which received a repeat performance in 1978 in New York City. She has performed solo concerts at numerous universities throughout America and took part in the "Big Apple" Jazz Women band of New York City that gave a highly acclaimed performance at the Kansas City Women's Jazz Festival, in 1979 ("Salute to Women in Jazz"). In addition to recordings made with various gospel groups, Myers has worked and recorded with Little Milton, Lester Bowie, Fontella Bass, Kalaparusha, Henry Threadgill, and her own groups.

Pharaoh Sanders

Pharaoh Sanders was born in 1940 in Little Rock, Arkansas. Sanders was always interested in art and initially wanted to be a painter or commercial artist. He later became fascinated with the music of Coltrane, Dolphy, Ornette Coleman, Rollins, and other African-American innovators. Allowing musicians to recount aspects of their careers can be insightful. An examination of Sanders's career (from his own perspective) provides a glimpse of the West Coast music scene, the musical camaraderie that existed at the time, and the struggle involved in coming east during the

1960s. In an article in *Jazz Change* Sanders recalled:

> My grandfather was a school teacher; he taught music and mathematics. My mother and her sisters used to sing in clubs and teach piano. For myself, I started playing drums in the high school band. Then I played tuba and baritone horn, clarinet and flute. In 1959, I started playing tenor saxophone, still in the school band. At the same time I was listening to Jimmy Cannon, my band teacher, who played jazz. Richard Boone, the Count Basie trombone player—he's from Little Rock too. He would sometimes sit in with the concert band.
>
> In my own playing I was more or less into rhythm and blues. I liked Earl Bostic a lot. When I finished high school in 1959, I was supposed to take either a music or an art scholarship. I didn't want to stay in Little Rock so I left for the West Coast. I went to Oakland Junior College for a couple of years, and then moved over to San Francisco. I majored in art. But I was getting some rock 'n' roll gigs playing tenor. I also played alto, flute, clarinet, and baritone whenever possible, but I had fallen in love with the tenor.
>
> On those blues jobs, I played mostly by ear, but I had some private lessons in

Oakland which taught me about harmonics. By this time I was listening to Sonny Rollins, who was a big influence at first; John Coltrane, who was a later big influence; and Ornette Coleman, Eric Dolphy, Booker Ervin, Hank Mobley and Horace Silver's group. I loved Benny Golson on *Moanin'* with Art Blakey.

When I heard Coltrane's *Blue Train* LP, I really didn't know what he was doing. I had never heard anybody play tenor like that before, with that range. Most of the guys played just in the middle register. When I first heard Ornette's music I liked it—*really*, it was something! It seemed so natural, as if he weren't limiting himself, as if he wanted to let himself just go to the music. I remember talking to Ornette in 'Frisco. I don't know whether he remembers me from then.

By that time I had begun to try to play that way myself. Sonny Simmons, and a lot of people I was playing with in Oakland at the time, were playing a lot freer. They had been playing that way before I came to California. They heard me and invited me to come down and play sometime. I was kind of skeptical about it because up to that point all I had been playing was rhythm and blues. What they played had a good feeling, but I was wondering, what are they doing? Were they crazy? But it felt good. So, I just fell in with it too. Later, I started playing jazz more conventionally and studying the basics—getting my chords and my scales.

Actually I have never had a jazz gig of my own long enough to see what I can really do on conventional tunes. I would like to get one for at least six nights a week so I could try to express myself fully "inside" and see both sides of it. I still take different kinds of jobs. I play rock 'n' roll for dances, usually in Brooklyn. It's a big help financially, and my profession is music, so it's my business to be able to play any kind of music.

Once when John Coltrane came out to San Francisco, he was asking around about mouthpieces. So I told him that I had a bunch of mouthpieces, and that he could try them. I also said I would take him around to the different places in town if he wanted to try some more. I never thought he'd take me up on it, of course—he was a giant to me then. But he showed up one morning, saying, "Are you ready, man?" I was really shook up! At the time, my own horn was in the repair shop and he offered to pay the bill so I could get it out. All day long we went around to pawn shops and more pawn shops, trying out different mouthpieces.

Sanders drove across the country with a couple of musician friends in 1962. It took awhile to get established in New York once he arrived.

> I slept in the subway—the police didn't bother me—or in tenement halls under the stairs. And I pawned my instrument.

> I think my first gig in New York was one in a coffee house in the Village called the Speakeasy, with C Sharp and Billy Higgins. . . . We made $8 a night. The job lasted almost a year. I used to live on wheat germ, peanut butter and bread—I still carry a jar of wheat germ in my instrument case. It's good food. I began seeing a lot of Billy Higgins. We would play together, talk, eat; might be together all day long. If he wasn't playing on his drums he would play on the table, or glasses with spoons or whatever else he found.

> I took some other jobs. Once I was a combination cook, waiter and counter-man, and all I got was what I ate. Then I caught on that I should be paid, and I split. I was trying to survive, and it is harder to survive in New York than in Oakland or San Francisco. If I wasn't thinking about trying to survive, I was thinking about music. I didn't think

much about commercial art by this
time.

A friend of mine who lived in Brooklyn,
someone I had known in San
Francisco, invited me to stay at his
place. That's where I met Don Cherry,
and we began rehearsing and playing
together. We got one job at Pratt
Institute in Brooklyn. There was an
exhibition of student art work and they
wanted some of our kind of music along
with it. I had to get my horn out of hock
for that one, and the other guys in the
group helped me by putting up the
money.

When I play, I try to adjust myself to
the group, and I don't think much
about whether the music is
conventional or not. If the others go
"outside," play "free," I go out there too.
If I tried to play too differently from the
rest of the group, it seems to me I
would be taking the other musicians'
energy away from them. I still want to
play my own way. But I wouldn't want
to play with anybody that I couldn't be
pleased with the way I play. Anyway,
Don Cherry seemed to like what I was
doing. I was getting different sounds
out of the horn then. For my part, I was
just trying to express myself. Whatever
came out of the instrument just came
out, as if I had no choice.

Naturally, you have elements of music and musical skills to work with, but once you've got those down, I think you should go after feelings. If you try to be too intellectual about it, the music becomes too mechanical. It seems that for me, the more I play "inside," inside the chords and the tune, the more I want to play "outside," and free. But also the more I play "outside" the more I want to play "inside" too. I'm trying to get a balance in my music. A lot of cats play "out" to start with. But if I, myself, start off playing "inside" and then let the spirit take over, wherever it goes, it seems better to me. I'm not trying to do anything that is over somebody's head. My aim is to *give* people something. When I give them something they can give me something, the energy to continue.

(Sanders had the good fortune to sit in with Coltrane's quartet at the Half Note in New York.)

We had become pretty close and had been talking a lot. He would call me and we would talk about religion and about life. He was also concerned about what he wanted to do next in his music, about where he was headed. We got pretty close and sometimes he would say, "Come on down and play something with me tonight," almost as though we were continuing the

conversation. So I would just come
down and start playing.

By that time, I thought of him not just
as a great musician but also as a wise
man. But I was still a little self-
conscious and wasn't sure what to do
with him musically. I thought maybe I
was playing too long, and on some
numbers, I wouldn't play at all. And
sometimes I would start to pack up my
horn. But he would tell me not to.
Anyway, I'd never play as long as he did
because, you know, he might play for
an hour on one tune.

Sanders was never asked officially to become
a member of Coltrane's group but played with
Coltrane whenever he was asked to.

He (Coltrane) might say, "I have a job
down in Washington for a week. How
about coming on down with me?" Or,
he'd say he had a record date coming
up and would I like to play on it too.

Always, it was like a communication
through music, like he knew some
things that I wanted to know that he
could express musically, and that I
maybe had some things to contribute
too. It's hard to talk about it, except in
spiritual or religious terms, actually.
Still, he had a lot of things on his mind
musically. He wanted to decide what he
should turn to next, and he needed

time to find out. He was a perfectionist,
and he wanted to grow, always.
Whatever he did, he wanted it to come
from inside himself, and he did not
want to hold anything back, or hide
anything he found there. Good or bad,
it had to be expressed. Once he asked
me what I thought he should do next,
what he should work on—how could he
create something different. I told him
maybe he should try to better some of
the things he had already done, go
back and try again on older tunes. I
don't really know if that was any help
to him; I don't know whether that was
what he was looking for or not.

In regards to Pharaoh's own playing he says,
"In a group, I like to play with anyone who really
wants to play, who really wants to put out the
energy. If the players don't put out the energy it
takes away my own."[58]

Archie Shepp

Archie Shepp, a saxophonist influenced by
Ornette Coleman born in 1937 in Fort Lauderdale,
Florida, completed his B.A. in dramatic literature at
Goddard College in 1959. He intended to become a
playwright when he moved to New York. He joined
forces with Cecil Taylor instead, and, after playing
alto saxophone in local dance bands around the city,
met John Coltrane, who greatly influenced Shepp's
approach to music. Shepp eventually formed a
quartet with trumpeter Bill Dixon (b. 1925), which

later became the New York Contemporary Five
(including Don Cherry and John Tchicai). With the
aid of John Coltrane's recommendation, he recorded
the album "Four For Trane" for Impulse Records in
1964. Shepp became an influential figure within the
avant-garde music scene in the late 1960s. He
collaborated with Bobby Hutcherson (b. 1941),
Roswell Rudd (b. 1935), Grachan Moncur III (b.
1937), Beaver Harris (1936–91), and other
experimental artists. Shepp is also an educator. After
gains made through the efforts of the Civil Rights
movement were beginning to take effect, the
American university was gradually becoming a
potential system of patronage for a few African-
American artists.

Shepp began to lead his own groups
beginning in the mid-sixties. Roswell Rudd, Beaver
Harris, Bobby Hutcherson, and Grachan Moncur III
were featured in his ensembles. From 1969 to 1974
he served on the faculty of the black studies program
at the State University of New York (SUNY) and in
1974 accepted a faculty position at the University of
Massachusetts. He was eventually promoted to
associate professor. Shepp credits Duke Ellington,
Max Roach, and Charlie Mingus as his chief musical
influences because they fused music with
sociopolitical opinions. His political views were also
shaped by Langston Hughes, Richard Wright, Ralph
Ellison, and other writers.[59]

Shepp articulately voiced anger and
resentment toward the oppressive tendencies of the
dominant society. His messages permeated all levels
of his artistic utterances throughout the 1960s,
chiding racial policies that discriminated against
African-American musicians. He characterizes the
economic situation for African-American innovators:

"Music for a nigger *is* a hobby! White folks make a lot of money playing black music. A nigger will never make a dime; if he makes a dime, he's lucky. But that's good, because this country is giving up less and less. I'm opposed to what I see, and I'll go on record as being opposed to what I see being done to my people!"[60]

Author David Such argues, "Shepp also posits causal relationships between jazz and certain political and social attitudes."[61] Shepp states clearly that he feels African-American "jazz" is, "self-expression. . . And a certain quality of human dignity despite all obstacles. Despite the enslavement of the black man and then his oppression. And each of the great players has had so distinctive, so individual a voice. There is only one Bird, one Ben Webster, one Cootie Williams."[62]

Many European Americans, including David Such, consider Shepp's views racist. When commenting on the oppression they encounter and witness in America, African-American musicians have always been criticized flippantly by the majority society.

It was two centuries after the first institutions of higher education were opened in America (in 1636) that an African-American obtained a diploma from a college or university in the United States.[63] As "Black" studies departments began springing up throughout America, a small number of African-American musicians gradually found positions on university faculties. Some, like Bill Dixon, who had taught art history at the university level, found academic life suitable. Dixon found an academic home at Bennington, Vermont.[64]

In 1970 Cecil Taylor joined the University of Madison, Wisconsin. He moved to Antioch College in

Yellow Springs, Ohio, when the atmosphere became less accommodating in Madison after a considerable number of his students there failed his course. He was able to establish the members of his performing ensemble as artists-in-residence for a fruitful two-year period at Antioch. Both Jimmy Lyons and Andrew Cyrille benefited from the temporary economic stability and artistic growth the college position provided. Taylor had always experienced difficulty in getting musicians to play his music. Within a university he could develop his compositional ideas and have them played by ensembles that rehearsed regularly.

Of all the universities in the United States that have offered "jazz" courses and performance programs, relatively few have hired educators from the enormous pool of established African-American "jazz" masters. Charlie Parker, John Coltrane, and Miles Davis were never offered tenured positions on university music faculties. Many members of symphony orchestras (who often lack advanced degrees) are frequently employed on university faculties as professors. Since the early 1970s, nonetheless, Donald Byrd, Jackie Byard, John Handy, Yusef Lateef, Art Davis, David Baker, George Russell, Art Davis, Ron Carter, Andrew Hill, Max Roach, Milford Graves, Buddy Collette, Nathan Davis, Jackie McLean, Ken McIntyre, Charles Tolliver, and Clifford Thornton are among the African-American artists who have taught for various periods of times at American universities.

In the 1970s Shepp became a tenured professor in the African-American Music Department in Amherst. He realizes that African-American music has remained a reflector of changing times. In an interview with Charles Gans in the *Jazz Forum*

(February 1985), Shepp offered an explanation as to why there are fewer African-American innovators extant at the end of the twentieth century.

> Today people pay money to see a show much like in the '20s and '30s. The music that surfaced in the '40s after the war—so-called bebop music with the small quartets, the virtuosic combinations culminating in John Coltrane—has become perhaps out of step with the times. Young people don't seek to emulate that kind of music anymore. They may try to play like a particular virtuoso. Many saxophone players today try to emulate John's (Coltrane's) music almost note for note regardless of what idiom they play in. But that style of music—so-called "jazz" music—is rapidly disappearing.
>
> When a music loses its history and its connection to its tradition, it is very hard pressed to stay alive. . . . I mean you don't find many young black people playing that kind of music or the blues—a few but not many. And with so-called "jazz" music, I think relatively few black youngsters are coming into the tradition, so eventually it will lose its innovative aspect . . .
>
> This is perhaps the only music created in the Western world that kept pace with technological innovation. When you hear reggae and those types of

music, they are very influenced by
African-American blues from the United
States. It's the beat that really gives the
samba and those kinds of music their
specific identities. Many of those
rhythms can be found in Africa. They
haven't been changed that much.

When we talk about Baby Dodds and
Cozy (Cole), Roy (Haynes) and Max
(Roach), you are talking about different
drummers. But when we talk about the
drum set, I think it is an ingenious
invention. The American Negro player
exchanged the African chorus for the
trap set, where one man does what
three men used to do in Africa. In
Africa the ilya ilyu, kere kere and gudu
gudu form a drum choir. But Max
Roach with the tom tom, snare and
high hat does that same thing . . .

The interesting thing is that people
don't play it anymore, at least black
people don't. I think that's a sad
commentary on the ultimate meaning
of that music, because it was made by
black people and now it is being
neglected and relinquished by black
people. That's why it no longer has life.

. . . I would suspect that most people
don't think of black people in the
United States as having created any
culture at all. But that's quite an error,
and I think our music is an example of

that. It's so distinct and different—and
not only so-called "jazz" music . . .
Negro music is quite easily identified.

Shepp was well aware of the economic
realities that engulf even the most stalwart
musicians. He feels that some of the most prominent
innovators in "jazz" began to allow economic
concerns too strongly affect their artistic judgment.

What perhaps is more negative is that a
very strong figure like Miles Davis is
trying to play like Michael Jackson too.
. . . All of Miles' group—Herbie
(Hancock), Wayne (Shorter) and all the
cats—are playing something else. I
think we should make some kind of
statement about this music—that it is
worth something and is valid—because
even the people who created it are no
longer playing it. In fact, they speak
rather despairingly of it.

The thing about it is that it's less of a
commentary on him than on America.
Somehow he was discouraged from
being the genius that he's always been,
and money was the root of it. According
to this book by Clive Davis, the former
head of Arista, there was a big shakeup
at Columbia when Miles decided that
he would not be a jazz musician
anymore. He hadn't played for a long
time and was supposed to have come
and asked for a raise. They told him,
"But, gee, Miles, we can't give you a

raise, in fact we were thinking of giving you a cut in salary, because jazz doesn't sell the way other kinds of music sell." And Miles reportedly said, "Well, fuck it, I don't play no more jazz then. If it don't sell why play it."

. . . But Blacks who created it are too caught up in the day to day efforts of survival to continue to innovate in this music and therefore it will not last, because this music grows out of a whole cultural matrix, and particularly the Afro-Christian church.[65]

Alcohol and heroin took their toll on many great artists during the 1950s[66]. Money and peace of mind may have become the new lures from the 1970s onward. "Cross-over" musicians from the latter era have included Sony Criss, Yusef Lateef, Don Pullen, Don Cherry, and Sonny Rollins. Usually artists see such ventures as temporary ones allowing them to access a wider audience and to gain capital to finance more creative projects in the future. Whether this process ever in fact reaches the suggested goals still remains to be seen.

EVIL

Looks like what drives me crazy
Don't have no effect on you—
But I'm gonna keep on at it
Till it drives you crazy, too.

—Langston Hughes

Joanne Brackeen

Pianist-composer Joanne Brackeen, born in California in 1938, was largely self-taught as a child. By the time she was a teenager she won a scholarship to the Los Angeles Conservatory of Music, but left the school after just three days, explaining that she "wasn't interested in the classical training it offered." She instead began sitting in at local clubs, where she was able "to learn from such top jazzmen as saxophonists Dexter Gordon and Harold Land." She continued to study and copy the solos of Charlie Parker, Bud Powell, and John Coltrane. Linda Dahl considers Brackeen's playing "informed by a passionate, relentlessly exploratory harmonic approach and ceaseless rhythmic complexity, and her high level of technical expertise is matched by her intense concentration."[67]

Joanne married saxophonist Charles Brackeen in 1960 and left the professional scene for a while (they have since separated). "When I got married, making sure my children had a mother during their younger years was what mattered most to me. [She has four children born close together in time.] I still played and wrote music, and that was enough. It wasn't until we moved to New York in 1965 that I began to appear in public again."[68] By 1969 Joanne secured a job with Art Blakey and the Jazz Messengers and remained as pianist with the band until 1972. She remained the only woman to play with the Messengers for a significant period of time. "I heard Blakey's group in a club. The piano player was just sitting there, but he wasn't playing. He didn't know where they were in the tune. So I went up on the bandstand and started playing. After

I finished I thought it was pretty strange for me to do this, but that must have been how I got the job."[69]

Brackeen played with saxophonist Joe Henderson's group from 1972 to 1975 and then joined saxophonist Stan Getz until 1977. She left at that point to begin a career as a solo performer committed to playing her own unique compositions. She moved from California to New York. Since arriving on the East Coast, Joanne has recorded frequently as a leader and has received numerous awards. Her manager Helen Kean observes, "It's hard to believe those delicate arms and hands can get that strength out of the piano, and she has the kind of courage to do *her* material. The real heavyweights in the music compliment her for this. They say, 'Yes, that's what you *must* do. We need something new, we need variety, we need to be excited by something.'"[70]

Her views on the position of women in "jazz" are close to the attitude expressed earlier by Mary Lou Williams, who also insisted that she had to work with musicians best suited for the job. "If I want a bass player, I want a player at Eddie Gomez's level. What woman can I call?" Brackeen asks.

> If a woman wants to be fine and bother to develop the music . . . it has to be at the same level that men have taken it to. She can't come fifty years later and be fifty years behind—and let me tell you that they *are*—most of them are. You'll hear them playing the notes but you will not hear the feeling, the flow, the maturity, the spirituality, the thing that you hear from the man. It's not because they're women, it's because

they haven't developed . . . . They may
think that because they have a little of
it, they can see further than they can
and they actually think they're great,
and they are *good*, some of them are
very good, but there's no Charlie Parker
on the saxophone, there's no Art Blakey
on the drums, there's no Stan Getz on
the saxophone.[71]

Charles Tolliver

Down Beat Magazine voted Charles Tolliver
(trumpetist, flugelhornist, and composer) Critics'
Choice for the trumpet in 1968. After beginning his
professional career with Jackie McLean (making his
Blue Note debut with the saxophonist in 1964), he
performed with such renowned artists as Roy Hayes,
Horace Silver, McCoy Tyner, Sonny Rollins, Booker
Ervin, The Gerald Wilson Orchestra, Oliver Nelson,
Roy Ayers, Art Blakey and the Jazz Messengers, Max
Roach, and many others.

Tolliver formed the quartet Music Inc. in
1969, which gained international recognition for its
innovative approach. His tour with this ensemble
has taken him to festivals, concerts, radio and
television stations throughout the world.

Toshiko Akiyoshi

Toshiko Akiyoshi was born in Manchuria in
1929. She and her three sisters studied ballet,
Japanese traditional dancing, and piano when they

were young. Toshiko said, "I dropped the dancing and the ballet right away, but I loved the piano. But it was all classical music. I didn't know a thing about jazz, and in fact, didn't like it at all."[72] Akiyoshi was eventually exposed to "jazz" as a teenager when it and other Western music flooded her native Japan during with the American Occupation after World War II. Manchuria became a battleground for contending Japanese, Soviet, and Chinese forces during the thirties and throughout World War II. The Akiyoshi family returned to Japan in 1947 as the Chinese Communists were consolidating their control over Manchuria.[73]

Postwar Japan was a good place for studying "jazz" through recordings, and pianist Teddy Wilson and other musicians influenced Toshiko. She worked in Tokyo as a dance-band accompanist, and she recalls these early experiences: "I didn't know the chord names or anything." Nevertheless, by 1952 she was leading her own band and working steadily. Akiyoshi recorded an album for Norman Granz in Tokyo (1953) and eventually won a full scholarship to study at the Berklee College of Music in Boston with the aid of recommendations from Oscar Peterson and other artists. After moving to America in 1956, Toshiko remembers she "dealt with both racial and sexual prejudice. I played clubs and TV wearing a kimono, because people were amazed to see an Oriental woman playing jazz."[74]

Toshiko married saxophonist Charlie Mariano in 1959. She worked in New York and Japan in a small group context, often with bassist Charles Mingus. Akiyoshi's compositional style is firmly rooted in her Asian identity. This quality gave her music a distinctive rhythmic and melodic style. "I came to think that being Japanese was not a negative aspect [in the "jazz" world]. Rather it was a positive aspect in that I could draw something from my own culture and perhaps return to the jazz tradition something that might make it a little bit richer than before."[75] Akiyoshi has always avoided performing pop charts of any kind and has always maintained a big-band book of almost exclusively her own compositions. She was the first Asian and the first woman to win numerous *Down Beat* polls. Most of her fame and notoriety would come in subsequent decades.

Akiyoshi debuted as composer and leader at Town Hall in New York in a concert that included original solo, trio and big-band compositions in· 1967. She then began to set the foundation for her future orchestra, which would begin to mature during the following decade. In 1969 she married saxophonist-flutist Lew Tabackin and formed a quartet with him (having divorced saxophonist Charlie Mariano, with whom she had a daughter). When Tabackin was called to Los Angeles to work in the *Tonight Show* band, the couple began organizing a "jazz" ensemble.

There was "a tremendous amount of skepticism about a Japanese woman writing for a jazz band in Los Angeles."[76] Akiyoshi discussed the difficulty she encountered in several interviews:

> Being female I think you have a little difficulty because you're taking a man's job. Maybe now it's much better than before. . . . when we formed the band it was a new experience for the musicians to rehearse under a woman. I had to think that aspect through very carefully. I think that emotionally a

man still has a hard time taking orders from a woman.[77]

. . . Competition wasn't as tough [in Japan] as in the United States, so I could rise to the top quicker. . . . There was less female competition in Japan. Whenever women competed in a man's world in the United States, they didn't succeed. Those that did, became separated from the mainstream and wound up as piano players in the more sophisticated, high class clubs, such as the East Side Club or the Hickory House in New York. A few, such as Marian McPartland, did succeed.[78]

"Traditional Jazz" Continues

Throughout the sixties, the big bands of Stan Kenton (1912–79), Woody Herman (1913–87), Maynard Ferguson (b. 1928), and other musicians continued to advance the stylistic forms initiated by swing during the thirties. The big bands of this era focused on inflexible "tight" arrangements and powerful dynamics rather than on individual soloists and innovative approaches to improvisation. Herman, who was never an exceptional clarinetist, recruited young men into his "Thundering Herd" who were good section players. Kenton, who started out as a cocktail pianist, had been forced to disband his organization during the 1940s. The 1960s witnessed the Kenton organization embarking upon a new era with a brass dominated band, subtitled the Mellophonium Band because he added four mellophones to the five trumpets and four trombones that rounded off his brass section. Maynard Ferguson continued to base his approach upon his ability to play in the extreme upper register of the trumpet for extended periods of time. In terms of instrumentation, trumpeter Don Ellis (1934–78) had the most unusual big band of the period. He experimented with complex meters and later incorporated electrified string quartets, synthesizers, and made other exotic augmentations to achieve his unique ensemble sound.

1960s Music outside African-American Culture

Related evolution had taken place elsewhere in the African Diaspora. The roots of reggae music are also fixed in slavery. A rich mixture of African peoples and variegated cultures survived after the abolition of slavery in Jamaica (1838), and can be heard today in rural Jamaica. Elements of the musical traditions and cultures of the Ibos, Yoruba, Noko, Sabo, Nago, as well those of African people from the Gold Coast (Mandingos, Coromantee, Hausa, etc.) are among the influences still present in the songs, dances, and rhythms of the region. Jamaican music such as Kumina (a ritual involving neo-African song, dance, worship, and animal sacrifice), etu, pocomania, gumbe, buru, and tambu retain many traditional African characteristics. Mento, a music related to calypso music of Trinidad, became the most common music in Jamaica until the early 1950s.

Reggae was an outgrowth of the influence of American rhythm and blues by way of several regional musical forms. Local itinerant deejays ("sound system men") played Jamaican r & b music and eventually the term "ska" was coined for the new dance created for the music. Thus reggae was born during the national insecurity that took place in Jamaica following its independence from Great Britain in 1962. "Ska" was replaced by a dance music involving a smaller instrumentation called "rock steady." Reggae emerged from "rock steady" around 1968.

Artists involved in twentieth-century European-American art music were also busy redefining musical traditions during the sixties. Composer John Cage documented some ideas he developed and expanded during the era of the 1960s in his book *Silence*.[79] Some of his perspectives on modern music are voiced in his commentaries and rhetorical questions found within this document:

> If words are sounds, are they musical or are they just noises?
> If sounds are noises but not words, are they meaningful?
>
> We know, don't we, everybody else's religion, mythology, and philosophy and metaphysics backwards and forwards, so what need would we have for one of our own if we had one, but we don't, do we?
> But music, do we have any music?
> Would it be better to just drop music too?
> Then what would we have?

Jazz?
What's left?

Debussy said quite some time ago, "Any sounds in any combination and in any succession are henceforth free to be used in a musical continuity."
Why, if everything is possible, do we concern ourselves with history (in other words with a sense of what is necessary to be done at a particular time? . . . In order to thicken the plot?

What is the nature of an experimental action? It is simply an action the outcome of which is not foreseen. It is therefore very useful if one has decided that sounds are to come into their own, rather than being exploited to express sentiments or ideas of order.

. . . one is no longer concerned with tonality or atonality, Schoenberg or Stravinsky (the twelve tones or the twelve expressed as seven plus five), nor with consonance and dissonance, but rather with Edgar Varese who fathered forth noise into twentieth-century music.[80]

Summary: The American Society That 1960s Music Reflected

The music created during this decade reflected a colorful and influential American transition that left an indelible mark on world society. Much of the music of the 1960s concerned itself with eliminating barriers standing in the way of free expression. There was a tendency toward viewing creative evolution as a natural state of being that did not necessarily depend upon conspicuous music knowledge, conventions, and obligatory displays of technical efficiency. For the liberated artist, the world of conceptions expanded without the approval of those who traditionally took it upon themselves to measure (and dictate the value of) artistic expression according to preconceived Western standards.

The seeds of the unprecedented social and political changes of the 1960s era in the United States were sewn during the 1950s. The *Brown vs. the Topeka Board of Education* case made the separate but equal doctrine invalid in American education in 1954. A year later, Rosa Parks was arrested for refusing to give up her seat to a "white" man on a bus in Montgomery, Alabama. In 1957, Dr. Martin Luther King organized the Southern Christian Leadership Conference. In 1958 "A Raisin in the Sun" became the first play by an African-American woman produced on Broadway.

During the 1960s, as African-Americans struggled to organize politically and gain equality in America, undercover government agencies made plans to infiltrate and disrupt "black" organizations. Their efforts were directed at fostering chaos among political groups and preventing individual leaders from emerging within the "black militant" community. In 1960 the first student protests involved sit-ins at "whites only" lunch counters at North Carolina A&T University (Greensboro, North Carolina). Wilma Rudolph won gold medals at the

Rome Olympics in the 100-meter run, the 200-meter run, and in the 400-meter relay that year. It was also the time John F. Kennedy was elected President of the United States. Two African-American musicians, Ella Fitzgerald and Count Basie, were awarded Grammy Awards for the first time.

America broke off diplomatic ties with Cuba in 1961. That year African-American and European-American "liberals" from the Freedom Riders (a loosely organized group whose mission was to test and demand integration in the South) had men and women members of their organization attacked and beaten by "White" citizens in Anniston and Birmingham, Alabama.

In 1962 three thousand federal troops were ordered to protect James Meredith and suppress riots as he struggled to enter the University of Mississippi. The following year European-American citizens and police attacked and beat civil rights demonstrators and leaders in Birmingham, Alabama, culminating in the arrest of Dr. Martin Luther King, Jr. More than 250,000 people marched on Washington and heard King's "I Have a Dream" speech. The same year (1963), Medgar Evers was assassinated. President John F. Kennedy was also assassinated in Dallas, Texas, that year, and W. E. B. DuBois died in Ghana.

The Civil Rights Act of 1964 was passed during the year Dr. King received the Nobel Prize for Peace. Violence soon struck again in 1965 when Malcolm X (b. 1925) was assassinated in Harlem. Violence erupted in the form of uprisings in Watts (a section of in Los Angeles). Thirty-five people died as a consequence of the riots and four thousand citizens were arrested. The Ku Klux Klan shootings continued in Selma, Alabama, after Dr. King led four thousand marchers there to present a "Negro" petition.

In 1966, Huey Newton and Bobby Seale established the Black Panther Party in Oakland, California, and the Student Nonviolent Coordinating Committee elected Stokely Carmichael its leader. Also that year, a Massachusetts Republican, Edward Brooke, became the first African-American elected to the Senate since the Reconstruction era, and Mrs. Indira Gandhi (Nehru's daughter) became prime minister of India. Maulana Karenga founded an American organization on the basis of Kawaida principles in 1966 as well; it was the first human rights organization to recognize the need for cultural reconstruction of the African-American people.[81]

The National Organization for Women (NOW) was also formed in 1966. Their focus would soon turn toward legislative and judicial reforms to check discrimination against women in education and employment. NOW also became involved with issues such as women in the media, child care, discrimination in consumer finance, and, after hesitation and debate, eventually affirmed that abortion was a women's rights issue.

In 1967 Thurgood Marshall became the first African-American appointed to the Supreme Court in the United States, and Shirley Chisholm became the first African-American female member of the House of Representatives.

The year 1968 was the unfortunate time of the assassination of Dr. Martin Luther King in a Memphis, Tennessee, hotel. James Earl Ray was arrested in London and extradited to the United States to stand trial for King's murder. The Chicago police rioted against citizens in the city's park during the 1968 Democratic National Convention. While on their uncontrollable rampage, police clubbed innocent bystanders to the ground, tear-gassed women and children at point blank range, and systematically assaulted the varied mixture of peace activists, clergy, academics, long-haired hippies, and other victims while they chanted, "The whole world is watching." Student rioting also broke out in Paris that year.

In 1969 James Earl Ray was sentenced to ninety-nine years in prison for murder. The final year of this proactive decade, students at Cornell University seized the Willard Straight Hall student center. The purpose of their actions was to protest the harassment of African-American females at Cornell and the burning of a cross by European-American students on campus.

Communal living during the 1960s meant that individuals within a group could break with standard social regiments. Many people graduating from high school chose to travel, to put a band together, to "just hang out," or to adopt some other unconventional lifestyle. The extra time these alternative lifestyles provided enabled people to read longer books for pleasure, engage in longer casual conversations (often about philosophical concerns, social conditions, war, and politics), indulge in more "mind expanding" drugs (marijuana, LSD, hashish, psilocybin, and other psychedelics), and listen to longer musical compositions. Although history has often focused upon the drug culture that was highly conspicuous during the 1960s, it was also a decade involving the awakening of a new sense of social responsibility.

By the end of this revolutionary decade it was clear that a capitalist society could not afford to tolerate loss of control to such a degree. When students protesting against the Vietnam War at Kent State University in Ohio were fired upon in 1970 by the American National Guard (killing four people), this culminating display of destructive force initiated a new age of intolerance and a durable, hyperconservative attitude in American politics and culture. Finally, most European American hippies reconsidered their "liberal" political philosophies, activist postures, and moral awakenings, virtually terminating the 1960s social revolution for the mainstream American youth culture.

Lynching of African-American sociopolitical prisoners continues in America under the high-tech guise of legal action. Out of a total of 3,817 executions between 1930 and 1969, more than fifty percent (2066) involved African-American citizens. Angela Davis described how Marie Hill got on death row in a North Carolina prison.

> Sister Hill was arrested in October, 1968 in South Carolina, and at the age of 15 charged with the murder of a white grocery store proprietor in Rocky Mount, North Carolina. The unfolding of events in the aftermath of the arrest is a classic study in the transformation of the law-enforcement-judicial network into a tool of terror against Blacks.
>
> She was coerced into signing a confession, without having received the advice of an attorney, a confession she later repudiated, saying, "I had no choice." Ill-informed of her right to resist extradition, she was speedily transported to North Carolina.

Intensive in-custody interrogation—inherently coercive—with no accompanying attempt to apprise her of her right to remain silent led her to break down once again. This throng of white policemen even tricked her into waiving a preliminary hearing.

A week had already passed before she was permitted to speak to her parents or even confer with her attorney.

On December 17, 1968, she was brought to trial. The prosecution had no evidence of her guilt save her own confession which she vigorously repudiated on the witness stand. The state could not even offer proof that she had been present at the scene of the killing, and although the prosecution referred to objects touched by the perpetrator of the crime, no fingerprints were produced.

After two days, Marie Hill, then 15 years of age, was found guilty of first-degree murder and was sentenced to die.

In their appeal to the U.S. Supreme Court, her lawyers have stated: "Such a penalty—not law, but Terror—is the instrument of totalitarian government. It is a cruel and unusual punishment, forbidden by the Eighth Amendment.

Emmett Till was lynched outside the law, Marie Hill (was) being lynched under the color of law.[82]

---

[1] Listen to the album by Randy Weston/Melba Liston, *The Spirit of Our Ancestors* (1991).

[2] Recorded in 1950--JWS-500; reissued as OJC 041.

[3] Valerie Wilmer, *As Serious as Your Life: The Story of the New Jazz* (New York: Serpent Tail, 1992), p. 30.

[4] Arthur Taylor, *Notes and Tones: Musician-to-Musician Interviews* (New York: Da Capo, 1993), p. 20.

[5] Ibid., pp. 22–23.

[6] Ibid., pp. 24–25.

[7] Gene Lees, *Cats of Any Color: Jazz Black and White* (New York: Oxford University Press, 1994), p. 30.

[8] New York: Da Capo, 1981.

[9] Listen to the album *Reese and the Smooth Ones: Reese Part 1* by the Art Ensemble of Chicago, recorded August 12, 1969, and explore the expressed perspective on "Is jazz . . . as we know it . . . dead?"

[10] The physicain purposely caused Kirk's blindness, according to trumpeter Lester Bowie who tells the story on the video "The Leaders In Paris."

[11] *Miles: The Autobiography*, p. 59.

[12] Joe Goldberg, *Jazz Masters of the Fifties* (New York: Da Capo, 1965), p. 210.

[13] James Lincoln Collier, *The Making of Jazz: A Comprehensive History* (New York: Dell Publishing Co., 1979), p. 490.

[14] See the liner notes to Coltrane's album *A Love Supreme*, for instance.

[15] Use of harmonic and melodic formations based on the church modes, a medieval system of eight scales each using the white keys of a C-major scale; a reaction against classical harmony.

[16] Ornette Coleman, "The Color of Music," *Down Beat* 61, no. 2 (February 1994); originally issued December 1982. Harmolodics is the term coined by Coleman to describe his approach.

[17] Willard Jenkins, *Down Beat*, December 1998, p. 67.

[18] Ibid. p. 68.

[19] Bill Cole, *John Coltrane*, p. 192.

[20] "Alice Coltrane Interviewed by Pauline Rivelli," in *Black Genius*, p. 122.

[21] Recorded June 7, 1961.

[22] From the liner notes to the album *Africa/Brass*.

[23] Ibid.

[24] Ekkehard Jost, *Free Jazz*, p. 27.

[25] Bill Cole, *John Coltrane*, p. 134.

[26] Don DeMicheal, "John Coltrane and Eric Dolphy Answer the Critics," in *Down Beat*, April 12, 1962, pp. 20–23.

[27] Ibid., p. 28.

[28] From the liner notes of the album *Coltrane Legacy*, comments by Coltrane.

[29] Ibid., Workman's remarks.

[30] Bill Cole, *John Coltrane*, p. 148.

[31] A. B. Spellman, *Four Lives in the Bebop Business*, (New York, Limelight Editions, 1985), p. 30.

[32] Frank Kofsky, *Black Nationalism*, pp. 71-76.

[33] Leonard Feather, "Coltrane Shaping Musical Revolt," *New York Post (Jazz Beat)*, October 18, 1964.

[34] Ronald Radano in the *Annual Review of Jazz Studies*, 1985.

[35] Quoted in "*Jazz Avant-Garde (with Eric Dolphy)*" (Tunbridge Wells, England: Costello, 1989) pp. 76–77.

[36] "Conversation with Coltrane," p. 7.

[37] Goldberg, *Jazz Masters of the Fifties*, p. 205.

[38] Ibid. Goldberg's observation is echoed by Vladimir Simosko and Barry Tepperman in their biography, *Eric Dolphy: A Musical Biography and Discography* (New York: Da Capo, 1971), pp. 62–63.

[39] Simosko and Tepperman, *Eric Dolphy*, p. 62.

[40] Ibid., pp. 63–67.

[41] Karlton Hester, "The Melodic and Polyrhythmic Developments of John Coltrane's Spontaneous Composition in a Racist Society," (Lewiston, NY: Mellon Press, 1997).

[42] Lazarus Edward Nnanyelu Ekweume, "Ibo Music--Its Theory and Practice." (New Haven, CT: Yale University Press, 1972) p. 225.

[43] Ibid., pp. 69–70.

[44] Ibid., pp. 112–13.

[45] Liner notes to his album *Witches and Devils*, Arista Records (1975).

[46] Liner notes to *Albert Ayler in Greenwich Village*, Impulse A-9155.

[47] Ibid.

[48] Ibid.

[49] Wilmer, *As Serious as Your Life*, p. 117.

[50] Ibid., p. 116.

[51] Ibid., p. 121

[52] Howard Mandel, "Cringe of the Lone Wolf: Dewey Redman," *Down Beat*, February 1992.

[53] Ibid., pp. 22–24.

[54] Ortiz M. Walton, *Music: Black, White and Blue*, pp. 129-137.

[55] Ibid.

[56] Nat Hentoff, "Un-chic Racism at the Philharmonic," *The Village Voice*, December 17, 1970, p. 30.

[57] Providing a screen so judges are forced to be impartial to the musician's auditioning.

[58] As quoted in Martin T. Williams, *Jazz Changes*, (New York: Oxford University Press, 1992), pp. 121–26.

[59] David Such, *Avant-Garde Jazz Musicians* (Iowa City: University of Iowa Press, 1992) pp. 25–26.

[60] Baker, Belt, and Hudson, *The Black Composer Speaks*, p. 300.

[61] *Avant-Garde Jazz Musicians*, pp. 25–26.

[62] Rivelli and Levin, *Giants*, p. 119.

[63] Robert Bruce Slater, "The Blacks Who First Entered the World of White Higher Education," *Journal of Blacks in Higher Education* 4 (Summer 1994): 47.

[64] Wilmer, *As Serious as Your Life*, p. 241.

[65] Charles J. Gans, "Archie Shepp: In the Tradition," *Jazz Forum: The Magazine of the International Jazz Federation* 93 (February 1985): 37.

[66] According to the *San Francisco Sunday Examiner and Chronicle*, July 24, 1977, p. 41.

[67] Linda Dahl, *Stormy Weather*, pp. 70–72.

[68] Quoted in George Nelson, "Joanne Brackeen, Pianist for a New Era," *Down Beat*, July 1980.

[69] Quoted by Amy Duncan, *Baltimore Sun*, May 25, 1980.

[70] Interview by Linda Dahl, June 1981.

[71] Quoted by Don Nelson, *Jazz Times*, April-May 1981.

[72] Quoted in Takashi Oka, "Japanese Jazz Artist Perfects Skills in U.S.," *Christian Science Monitor*, October 12, 1956.

[73] *Stormy Weather*, pp.165–67.

[74] Quoted in Leonard Feather, "Toshiko Akiyoshi: The Leader of the Band," *Ms.*, November 1978.

[75] Quoted in Charles Gans, "T.A.L.T. Conference: A Conversation with Toshiko Akiyoshi and Lew Tabackin," *Jazz Forum*, February 1980.

[76] Peter Rothbart, "Toshiko Akiyoshi," *Down Beat*, August 1980.

[77] Quoted in Gans, "T.A.L.T. Conference."

[78] Quoted in Rothbart, "Toshiko Akiyoshi."

[79] Cambridge: M.I.T. Press, 1971.

[80] John Cage, *Silence* (Cambridge: M.I.T. Press, 1971).

[81] *Historical and Cultural Atlas of African Americans*, p. 188.

[82] Angela Davis et. al., *If They Come in the Morning: Voices of Resistance* (New York: New American Library, 1971), pp. 104–5.

Figure 24: Eric Dolphy

Figure 25: Joe Henderson

Figure 26

Figure 27: John Coltrane

Figure 28: Toshiko Akiyoshi

Figure 29: Cecil Taylor

Figure 30: Donald Byrd

Figure 31: Adela Dalto

Figure 32: Akua Dixon

Figure 33: Billy Taylor

Figure 34: Contemporary Jazz Art Movement

Figure 35: Pamela Wise

Figure 36: Wendell Harrison

XI
Innovators Emerging
between 1970 and 1980

The life of man is a self-evolving circle,
which, from a ring imperceptibly small,
rushes on all sides outwards to new
and larger circles, and that without
end. The extent to which this
generation of circles, wheel without
wheel, will go, depends on the force and
truth of the individual soul. For it is the
inert effort of each thought, having
formed itself into a circular wave of
circumstance, as, for instance, an
empire, rules of an art, a local usage, a
religious rite, to heap itself upon that
ridge, and to solidify and hem in the
life. But if the soul is quick and strong,
it bursts over that boundary on all
sides, and expands another orbit on the
great deep, which also runs up into a
high wave, with attempt again to stop
and to bind. But the heart refuses to be
imprisoned; in its first and narrowest
pulses, it already tends outward with a

vast   force,   and   to   immense   and
innumerable expansions.
                    —Ralph Waldo Emerson, "Circles"

Changes Around the World

During   the   1970s   America   once   again
declared the death of "jazz." According to earlier self-
proclaimed pundits of "jazz" history, the music had
died before at the end of the swing era when bebop
was in its nascence.

In 1971 George Jackson, author of *Soledad
Brother*, was killed at San Quentin Prison in San
Francisco and Angela Davis was acquitted of all
murder and conspiracy charges. In her book, *If They
Come in the Morning: Voices of Resistance* (written
while still a political prisoner in America), Davis
says, "As a consequence of the racism securely
interwoven in the capitalist fabric of this society,
Black   people   have   become   more   thoroughly
acquainted with America's jails and prisons than any
other group of people in this country. Few of us,
indeed, have been able to escape some form of
contact—direct or indirect—with these institutions at
some point in our lives."[1]

In 1974 the cost of food, fuel, and other goods
soared as worldwide inflation (heightened by boosts
in oil prices) slowed economic growth to near zero in
most   industrialized   countries.   ABC   television
adapted Alex Haley's book *Roots* in 1977 . The series
drew the largest television audience of any program
in history.

In 1978 a military junta seized power in
Afghanistan   as   violence   swept   Nicaragua.
Muhammad Ali lost the "crown," only to regain his

world heavyweight title from Leon Spinks, becoming the first person to win the heavyweight championship three times. In 1979 Franklin Thomas became the first African American to head a major foundation when he was named president of the Ford Foundation, and the Nobel Prize for Economics went to Arthur Lewis, an African American.

Spiritual "Jazz" and New Musical Settings

Duke Ellington, Mary Lou Williams, and other early twentieth-century innovators established a connection between religion and music through their compositions. During the sixties Coltrane, Albert Ayler, Pharaoh Sanders, Mingus, and others were among the expanding communities of African-American musicians who labeled many of their compositions with sacred music titles. "Jazz" always maintained a connection with spiritual music on both technical and emotional levels. For those pianists and vocalists who began their musical careers in the church, this connection was particularly difficult to avoid. Since the majority of African-American children attended churches during the first half of the century (where music making was a communal experience), most musicians who lived in those communities shared a common knowledge base of African-American spirituals and sacred music. Michael J. Budds outlines the long tradition of religious connections with African-American music in his book *Jazz in the Sixties: The Expansion of Musical Resources and Techniques.*

Although there has always been a close
family relationship among spirituals,
gospel music, the blues, and jazz in
musical terms, the latter two have
evolved and prospered in the realm of
secular life. The blues and jazz sprang
from the rituals of Friday and Saturday
nights; spirituals and gospel soared
from the ceremonies of Sunday
morning. During the sixties such
arbitrary restrictions between sacred
and secular were disregarded as
leading jazz musicians reevaluated the
role of music in their own lives. Many
discovered a vital connection between
their spiritual beliefs and their musical
activities and deliberately set out to
bring these two important aspects of
their lives into closer harmony. It is not
too far-fetched to propose that some
jazz musicians began to perform as
preachers, with the music taking the
place of sermons. Others were content
to bear witness to their faith by the
nature of their lifestyles and the
attitudes reflected in their music. The
more noticeable, perhaps, were those
who embarked on a spiritual journey
into non-Western religious thought and
came to perceive their own
performances as a form of meditation.
In effect, by employing their music to
express personal religious convictions,
these individuals expanded the jazz
tradition in purpose and content.[2]

Many instrumentalists and vocalists began broadening and transforming established musical norms and conventions as the "loft jazz" era of the 1970s created new performance possibilities. The levels of experimentation generated by the AACM and BAG, and other organizations that promoted the development of innovative art forms in the late 1960s, were advanced by a new experimental venue that enabled independent musicians to maintain greater control over their artistic directions.

While most club owners preferred hiring established musicians who played styles of music that their clientele theoretically preferred, the "loft jazz" scene generally provided open formats in which a variety of stylistic or conceptual approaches could be tested. A direct line to audiences bolstered the confidence and productivity of experimental musicians, dancers, poets, and visual artists who presented works in "loft jazz" settings during this era during the early 1970s.

Some of the most important and striking stylistic changes in "jazz" took place in alternative performance spaces that eventually drew fairly large and responsive audiences who preferred hearing challenging new music in unpretentious and relaxed settings. Unlike music presented in typical concert halls and commercially oriented clubs, many alternative venues seemed the quintessential contemporary environment. The alternative music scene inherited the task of educating, cultivating, and enriching their audiences, many of whom may have experienced experimental or abstract art forms for the first time. A sampling of the diverse spectrum of musical styles presented during this brief era was preserved on the limited issue five-record set *Wildflowers (1–5): The New York Loft Jazz Sessions.*

Recorded live in 1977, *Wildflower* was produced by Alan Douglas and Michael Cuscuna in association with Sam Rivers. Over sixty musicians performed on the twenty-two performances that were released. Sam Rivers is an innovative saxophonist (and flutist) who played with Miles Davis briefly and continued to develop a highly personal and unique spontaneous compositional approach during the 1970s.

Changing Attitudes in Europe

A serious exodus of African-American musicians to Europe began in 1969 when the BYG record label initiated the Actuel Festival of Jazz, Rock and New Music. Rock groups such as Pink Floyd and Frank Zappa were headliners originally signed, but the festival invited "jazz" musicians if they paid their own way overseas. Upon arrival in Europe, there were often possibilities for "jazz" musicians to record. BYG released a series of albums immediately after the festival. Only a small proportion of the money collected from the sale of those recordings went to the performing artists, however.[3]

While some "jazz" innovators gained a nominal degree of exposure and recognition at home and abroad, their music was not always well received. Performances of Afrocentric experimental music rarely made huge profits for the artists involved.

Andrew Cyrille (b. 1939) was touring Europe with Cecil Taylor during that time and recorded a solo percussion album *(What About?)* that displayed an original approach to drumming. He had little success with this particular recording in America.

John Hammond at Columbia records said, "The computer is not interested in creative drumming, it's interested in making money." He also assured Cyrille that no other company would be interested in his material either.[4]

The original European festival planned to host a similar festival in Paris at Les Halles. Trouble with earlier festivals there in 1968 made local business establishments reluctant to allow another such episode so soon afterward, so the plan was denied. The festival took place in Amougies, Belgium, nevertheless, inside a huge tent. Over 75,000 people witnessed the concerts. Joseph Jarman, Sirone, Archie Shepp, Steve Lacy, Sunny Murray, Don Cherry, Leroy Jenkins, Grachan Moncur III, Frank Wright (tenor saxophone), Noah Howard (saxophone), Ray Draper, Earl Freeman, and others participated. Veteran drummer Philly Joe Jones (1923–85) performed with Shepp, Moncur, Freeman, South African musicians Johnny Dyani (bassist), and Louis Moholo (drummer). Frank Zappa sat in with this ensemble as well.

Experimental music proved completely accessible to the new breed of young European audiences. At the Ann Arbor Jazz and Blues Festival two years later, promoters avoided the term "jazz," and the experimental music avoided making their presentations esoteric form of mysterious art. As a consequence, audiences drawn to the familiar names of rock and blues artists adapted favorably to the new musical approaches presented by the innovators of the day.

In time, European audiences grew less receptive to African-American "jazz" musicians, as Britain and Germany became nationalistic in their "jazz" preferences, favoring local (European) adaptations of African-American styles to the music of the originators. For a slightly longer period, France preferred to hear African-Americans perform Afrocentric music.

French presenters generally provided appropriate performance conditions and fairly good earnings, while French fans remained enthusiastic. Many musicians adopted Paris as a home base and were able to gain enough business leverage to negotiate favorable contracts, enhance their performance resumes, and were granted a temporary break from the bleak New York scene. The Art Ensemble of Chicago had the means and foresight to buy property in the Paris suburbs where they could work and live. Nevertheless, only on rare occasions was an African-American group able to sustain a comfortable life as musicians in Europe after 1975. The Frank Wright Quartet was a notable exception. Wright's group included Bobby Few and Alan Silva, and Muhammad Ali (Rashied Ali's brother) was the drummer.[5]

For a while, Europeans considered African-American musician an exotic and artistic revolutionary, on display for reasons that often had little to do with music. Although most African-American innovators did not perceive of themselves as merely entertainers, much of the audience, apparently attending purely for the novelty of the occasion, wanted entertainment much as that imported during the era of the early black-faced minstrels.

Connecting Fusion, Miles Davis, and Jimi Hendrix

Miles Davis was at the forefront of another musical movement when he began his experiments with electronics during the late 1960s. His 1969 album titled *Bitches Brew* maintained a shift of focus toward the rhythm section and continued to incorporate fewer chord structures. Woodwind specialist Benny Maupin (b. 1946) recalls:

> Miles was in top form, and the condition of his life was so high that we each responded to his non-verbal communication. He never really stated what he really wanted with words. Through his actions it was clear to me that everything he wanted from each of us should be based on trusting our intuition and the courage to move from one note to the next with total confidence in each other and the music.[6]

Miles based a large portion of his musical unfoldings upon bass ostinati and other short rhythmic bass patterns. The form of the album relies upon medleys, presenting musical "environments" rather than standard improvisational formats. In the 21st century *Bitches Brew,* the album that shocked a significant segment of the musical world, remains in vogue and remains one the most unorthodox departures from the "jazz" mainstream. Drummer

Jack DeJohnette (b. 1942) sums up the recording date:

> Miles assembled an experiment with musicians he liked. He wrote a few sketches, but the idea was to get the spontaneity down. It wasn't a stop-and-start recording. It was Miles conducting an orchestra in real time. He was like a painter changing the canvas by conducting his group.[7]

A variety of electronic instruments provided environmental textures and colorful arrays of evocative timbres, while keyboardists take surprisingly few solos on *Bitches Brew*. Davis continued to incorporate electronics on both the *Live Evil* (1970) and *On the Corner* (1972) albums, while also beginning to experiment with multiple drummers.

Miles incorporated electronics into various styles throughout the seventies. This drew sharp criticism. Larry Birnbaum asserts in his article "Metal Steps To Heaven" that "back in the days of platform shoes, blow-out Afros, and blaxploitation flicks, Miles Davis—to the disgust of jazz critics, former colleagues, and lifetime fans alike—plunged headlong into funk."[8] Despite claims that Miles sold out, the albums from this period actually sold few copies and missed the young African-American audience for which they were allegedly targeted.

Recordings from two live sets at Osaka Festival Hall in Japan (February 1, 1975) were released by Japanese CBS/Sony on double LPs. Aghartha, the matinee performance, was the only recording of the performances issued in the United

States, however. The recording produced some of Miles's most unconventional and least accessible music of his career. His compositions, laced with thick polyphonic textures, involved ametrical percussion coloration that typical 1970s American audiences found difficult to digest. Some critics attacked it with vacuous terms (such as those associated with certain of Ellington's works such as the bigoted label "jungle music," for instance). Miles simply felt his new approach was "a deep African-American groove."[9] Guitarist Reggie Lucas, an AACM member, provided a Hendrix-inspired ambiance, while veteran Al Foster established a strong rhythm foundation. Michael Henderson·was the bassist, and James "Mtume" Foreman (Jimmy Heath's son), supplied additional percussion. Sonny Fortune, on temporary leave from McCoy Tyner's ensemble, was the woodwind specialist in this electrifying performance. Typically, Miles directed the ensemble through the spontaneous moods of each movement with his trumpet statements.

Davis was attracted to the electronic music produced by African-American musicians who generated huge popular followings during the 1960s and early 1970s. Miles talked about his musical and personal association with Jimi Hendrix in his autobiography:

> The music I was really listening to in 1968 was James Brown, the great guitar player Jimi Hendrix, and a new group who had just come out with the hit record, *Dance to the Music*, Sly and the Family Stone, led by Sly Stewart, from San Francisco. The shit he was doing was badder than a motherfucker,

had all kinds of funky shit up in it. But it was Jimi Hendrix that I first got onto when Betty Mabry [Miles' wife at the time] turned me on to him.

I first met Jimi when his manager called up and wanted me to introduce him to the way I was playing and putting my music together. Jimi liked what I had done on *Kind of Blue* and some other stuff and wanted to add more jazz elements to what he was doing. He liked the way Coltrane played with all those sheets of sound, and he played the guitar in a similar way. Plus, he said he had heard the guitar voicing that I used in the way I played the trumpet. So we started getting together. Betty really liked this music—and later, I found out, she liked him physically too—and so he started to come around.

He was a real nice guy, quiet but intense, and was nothing like people thought he was. He was just the opposite of the wild and crazy image he presented on the stage. When we started getting together and talking about music, I found out that he couldn't read music. Betty had a party for him sometime in 1969 at my house on West 77th. I couldn't be there because I had to be in the studio that night recording, so I left some music for him to read and then we'd talk about it later. (Some people wrote some shit

that I didn't come to the party for him
because I didn't like having a party for
a man in my house. That's a lot of
bullshit.)

When I called back home from the
studio to speak to Jimi about the music
I had left him, I found out he didn't
read music. There are a lot of great
musicians who don't read music—black
and white—that I have known and
respected and played with. So I didn't
think less of Jimi because of that. Jimi
was just a great, natural musician—
self-taught. He would pick up things
from whatever he was around, and he
picked up things quick. Once he heard
it he really had it down. We would be
talking, and I would be telling him
technical shit like, "Jimi, you know,
when you play the diminished chord . .
." I would see this lost look come into
his face and I would say, "Okay, okay, I
forgot." I would just play it for him on
the piano or on the horn, and he would
get it faster than a motherfucker. He
had a natural ear for hearing music. So
I'd play different shit for him, show him
that way. Or I'd play him a record of
mine or Trane's and explain to him
what we were doing. Then he started
incorporating things I told him into his
albums. It was great. He influenced me,
and I influenced him, and that's the
way great music is always made.
Everybody showing everybody else

something and then moving on from there.

But Jimi was also close to hillbilly, country music played by them mountain white people. That's why he had those two English guys in his band, because a lot of white English musicians liked that American hillbilly music. The best he sounded to me was when he had Buddy Miles on drums and Billy Cox on bass. Jimi was playing that Indian kind of shit, or he'd play those funny little melodies he doubles up on his guitar. I love it when he doubled up shit like that. He used to play 6/8 all the time when he was with them white English guys and that's what made him sound like a hillbilly to me. Just that concept he was doing with that. But when he started playing with Buddy and Billy in the Band of Gypsies, I think he brought what he was doing all the way out. But the record companies and white people liked him better when he had the white guys in his band. Just like a lot of white people like to talk about me when I was doing the nonet thing—the *Birth of the Cool* thing, or when I did those other albums with Gil Evans or Bill Evans because they always like to see white people up in black shit, so that they can say they had something to do with it. But Jimi came from the blues, like me. We understood each other

right away because of that. Both him
and Sly were great natural musicians;
they played what they heard.[10]

Hendrix, while appreciated by many African
musicians, did not gain the wide acceptance in the
African-American community that Sly Stone enjoyed.
In *The Death of Rhythm and Blues*, author Nelson
George   discusses   possible   reasons   for   this
phenomenon:

> Hendrix used blues and R&B as his
> building blocks, and Sly Stone worked
> from gospel and soul. Hendrix was
> rejected, while Sly was viewed, before
> the drug days, as a hero.
>
> The difference was that Hendrix drew
> from   a   style   blacks   had   already
> disposed of; Sly shrewdly stayed just a
> few steps ahead of the crowd. Both
> were   children   of   the   R&B   world.
> Hendrix   had   been   sideman   for
> numerous R&B bands after leaving
> Seattle in his teens, including the Isley
> Brothers. Sly, baptized as Sylvester
> Stewart, was reared in a roof-raising,
> sanctified church and worked as a
> popular deejay on several Bay Area
> stations. And both Sly and Jimi
> rebelled   against   the   narrow-
> mindedness in which they grew up. It is
> not coincidental that they blossomed in
> environments   removed   from   the
> traditions of black America, Hendrix in
> London and Sly in "free-love" San

Francisco, where they each plunged into the hippie life-styles of those two countercultural centers, emerging in black-based sound drenched in flower-powered rhetoric that had little in common with the soul consciousness of James Brown or Aretha.

After a prolonged sabbatical following this period, Miles made a successful comeback in 1981. Other experimental material was introduced fifteen years later during the emergence of a 1990 funk-metal movement.

Jazz-Funk Fusion

Virtuoso pianist and composer Herbie Hancock (b. 1940) thoroughly absorbed the new experimental formulas he encountered while performing with Miles Davis, and he displayed this influence on his album *Crossings* in 1972. This direction continued as Hancock evolved toward a heavily funk influenced style on subsequent albums: *Headhunters* (1973), *Sextant* (1973), and *Thrust* (1974).

The electronic hues Hancock produced on Arp Synthesizers, Fender Rhodes electronic piano, Echoplex, Hohner D-6 Clavinet, and other new instruments were exciting and impressive. His jazz-funk albums set new standards for the genre in the early 1970s. The electric bass was now an established instrument in the jazz-fusion idiom. Bassist Paul Jackson, who played on several of Hancock's early fusion albums, helped to codify the new virtuoso bass vocabulary. Scott La Faro used the two-finger plucking style that allowed the modern electric bassist greater intricacy and speed on the instrument, creating melodic flexibility, grace, and rhythmic fluidity in the low register of new electric ensembles. Jackson too used multiple fingers to gain speed, but grounded his style in an understanding of complex funky rhythms.

Stanley Clark (1951) is another electric bass guitarist to emerge during the 1970s. Clark worked with Pharoah Sanders, Getz, Gordon, Blakey, Gil Evans, Horace Silver (b. 1928), Joe Henderson (b. 1937) and Chick Corea (b. 1941). He was a founding member of Corea's group Return to Forever. His early influences include Charles Mingus, Paul Chambers, Ron Carter, Jimi Hendrix, and James Brown. His approach to the electric bass involves precisely executed rapid bass lines, slap bass technique, and a powerfully articulated attack to his melodic and syncopated phrasing.

Pianist Ramsey Lewis, traditionally a hard-bop-style pianist, collaborated with the popular ensemble Earth, Wind & Fire in 1974 to produce a "cross-over" album titled *Sun Goddess.* Another interesting "cross-over" album from the early part of the seventies was vocalist Flora Purim's Brazilian-influenced *Butterfly Dreams* (1973).

Jazz-Rock Fusion

The Don Ellis jazz-rock fusion big band recording *Electric Bath* (Columbia--CS 9585) employs multiple and complex time signatures in its compositions. Ellis' augmented big band (with strings, sitar, woodwind doubles, etc.) also explored systematic experiments with pitch musical elements that produced interesting results. (Ellis played a quarter-tone trumpet.)

Chick Corea's first influence was Horace Silver. His father, a trumpet player, led his own groups, and started Chick on piano at age four. After transcribing Silver's solos, Corea studied the music of Bud Powell and Bill Evans. His introduction to Latin music arrived before Chick graduated from high school in 1959. He attended the Juilliard School of Music before realizing two months later that the training he wanted was best obtained playing with New York's Latin-jazz groups. He performed with Mongo Santamaria, Willie Bobo, Herbie Mann, Blue Mitchell, and Stan Getz before recording his first solo album, *Tones for Joan's Bones* (later retitled *Inner Space*). The Latin rhythms and melodies recorded during the seventies on albums like *Light as a Feather* (Polydor PD 5525) and the jazz-rock oriented *Musicmagic* won him a popular following.

Saxophonist Wayne Shorter (b. 1933), pianist Joe Zawinul (b. 1932), and bassist Miroslav Vitous (b. 1947) formed the nucleus of the jazz-rock group Weather Report, which began to evolve in 1971. Shorter and Zawinul incorporated many of the musical lessons introduced by Miles Davis while they were associated with the trumpeter's band into their new ensemble. Weather Report explored novel approaches to collective improvisation through fusing rock-and-roll elements with emancipated rhythmic and metrical approaches. Weather Report placed emphasis upon electroacoustic timbres, a mixture of interesting textures, and on the employment of simple structural and formal conceptions.

As one of jazz-rock's longest lasting groups, Weather Report produced *Sweetnighter* (1973), *Mysterious Traveler* (1974), *Black Market* (1976), and a number of experimental albums during the 1970s. The distinction between soloist and accompaniment was blurred intentionally as conventional instrumentation mixed with electronic ambiance. Both bassists with the group, Miroslav Vitous and Jaco Pastorius (1951–87), continued to advance the virtuosic techniques introduced and developed by Paul Jackson, Scott Lafaro (1936–61), and other bassists operating earlier in the 1970s. Electric bass virtuosity began to flourish as the requirements of the new fusion music demanded expanded flexibility, speed, and diversity of styles.

Donald Byrd (b. 1932)

Donald Byrd, a "jazz" pioneer, innovator and scholar, came through the hard bop school of the 1950s before establishing another type of fusion in the seventies with his highly successful group, the Blackbyrds. He grew up in Detroit and was educated at Wayne University, the Manhattan School of Music, and Columbia University. He also studied composition with Nadia Boulanger in France. Byrd, one of the first teenage trumpet wizards, is hailed historically as one of the most creative and influential musicians of all time. In the 1950's, his career flourished in the realm of bebop and hardbop. At the age of 23, his collaboration with Art Blakey and The Jazz Messengers was only the beginning, as he later went on to work with jazz giants including Max Roach, Sonny Rollins, Charlie Parker, Thelonious Monk, Coleman Hawkins, Lionel Hampton, John Coltrane and Herbie Hancock, among others. In the late fifties, he began recording on the legendary Blue Note label. His artistry on that label is exemplified by the classic album *Black Byrd,* which became the largest selling album in the history of Blue Note.

Then, through phenomenal hits like "Rock Creek Park", "Happy Music", "Blackbyrds Theme", "Places and Spaces", and "Do It Fluid", Dr. Byrd became a living legend. The jazz fusion movement of the early 70's, which enjoyed success in both mainstream as well as purist circles, thus established Dr. Byrd as a pioneer of a new sound. With over 60 albums to his credit, his range in style and his ever-expanding spiritual strength continue to reach far beyond the traditional jazz scene.

In addition to being a major force as an artist, Dr. Byrd has also been a seminal figure at the forefront of jazz education. He has helped bring to fruition jazz programs at institutions such as Rutgers University, Howard University, North Carolina Central University, Oberlin College and Queens College. His ability to thus embrace jazz on all levels has captured the hearts and minds of whole generations since he started his career. Recently, his work with Guru's *Jazzmatazz* project introduced him to a younger audience whose jazz inheritance was gained through hip hop's breaks and samples. Not only did the *Jazzmatazz* project fuse two musical genres, it is in essence generations coming together. Dr. Byrd is a creative force in many different disciplines. He has started his own line of Bb cornet and trumpet, The Blackbyrd. For 1991 alone, he toured in Japan and around the world for Phillip Morris; appeared on The McCreary Report and BET's Noon Day Live; participated in the Louis Armstrong House Committee, the Louis Armstrong Archive Committee, the Dizzy Gillespie Committee and the music panel at the Black Congressional Caucus; lectured at the Brooklyn Academy of Music and the All Faith Church in Berkeley, CA; and raised $50,000 for the Girls and Boys Club of Central Newark, NJ. Currently, he is archiving original African American art with a collection of over 100 pieces.

Byrd remains a frequently recorded artist,[11] with more than fifty albums to his credit, and he has often been criticized for embracing popular formulas to gain that success. In a 1990 interview with Leonard Feather,[12] Dr. Byrd explains his perspective on the music business.

Byrd begins by responding to Brazilian musician Mayuto's argument that the profit motive was severely affecting the quality of music and that producers (and not great composers) have become a powerful force in shaping the listening public's tastes. Byrd's reaction was simply to state that times have changed. Musicians who have adapted with the times are themselves producers and know the ways of business.

> It's just a lack of understanding and education on the part of the artist. When I was in law school, I learned the rules of the game. . . . Mayuto should stay within the scope of his understanding, and that's music.

> He [Mayuto] worked with me , but we never really sat down and really talked the way I've talked with men like Freddie Hubbard. I spent one whole day talking strictly business with Hubbard. Mayuto only knew me as a musician. Similarly, during the last conversation I had with John Coltrane

before he died, he never got into any of
those mystical, ethereal things he was
identified with; we dealt with whether
or not he could get back certain
copyrights.

It would be like denying the existence
of people like James Brown. . . . I've
never in my life been as impressed by a
musician as I have been by James
Brown. . . . People like James Brown
and Berry Gordy are much more
meaningful to me, in my life, than a lot
of so called historical jazz figures. They
have done more for black people.

This is not a racial issue. The same
thing is happening to white musicians
who are being put in the position where
they have to compromise. . . . If they
are, it's because they've been emulating
the black musicians.

. . . I think that which sells the best *is*
best.[13]

Beyond the knee jerk reaction that Byrd's
comments may invoke from some readers, there is
an important perspective being delivered. Byrd
apparently feels that eschewing the "starving artist"
image is important for musicians' advancement in a
capitalist society. He also realizes that most people,
given the opportunity to think for themselves, are
intelligent enough to appreciate beautiful music. The
music of Bach, Mozart, Beethoven, and other
European innovators remains popular among many

people today, although the artists themselves had more than their share of struggles with the audiences of their times. Innovators do not choose to be unappreciated "starving artists." Therefore, if we calculate ticket or record sales by centuries instead of months, then Byrd's points become crystal clear.

Today, after initiating "jazz" programs at Howard University, Oberlin, and elsewhere, Byrd is active as a teacher, art collector, historian, music theorist, and remains an influential innovator. Other current projects involve developing compositional and pedagogical approaches combining music, art and math in new ways.

African-American music managed to evolve consistently throughout the twentieth century. This may result from sociocultural adaptations cultivated as a survival technique in a hostile and bigoted American environment. Author and photo-journalist Valerie Wilmer feels:

> Black music has never stood still. One theory to explain the need for this constant change is that it occurs from necessity, that the protagonists are forced to invent new techniques and systems in order to stay one step ahead of white imitators and codifiers. Possibly the musicians of the past were not blessed with an acute political consciousness (hardly surprising in view of their position in society— "entertainers" playing in brothels and bar-rooms); perhaps it is true to say that until Charlie Parker came along none of them referred to their music as art, but in the "sixties" and "seventies,"

the "different drummer" that Black
musicians heard was as often
motivated by nationalist considerations
as by the aesthetic desire to play
something new.[14]

The Crossroads of Stylistic Evolution

Historians generally divide the evolution of
"jazz" into distinct periods by isolating distinctive
elements of style and tracing origins and innovations
through the most dominant musicians of each era.
There was little attempt to evaluate "jazz" seriously,
objectively, or in a scholarly manner before World
War II. The bias against African-American music
maintained by many writers was obvious from the
scarcity and inferior quality of "jazz" documentation.
A general lack of knowledge and diminished respect
for a sociocultural subject has always produced
inaccurate reporting (take the history of women in
the Western world before 1950, for instance), and
this was often the case with African-American music.
After the Second World War, a greater effort was
made to examine African-American music more
empirically. Unfortunately, references often used to
substantiate research still failed to involve primary
subjects, the African-American musicians who
produce the music, and rarely involved total
transposition of the music examined.

Total transcription places all notes performed
on a musical occasion on a fixed score. Such a
process enables theorists to make meaningful
studies of the interactive nature of "jazz." Thorough
study requires an advanced knowledge of Afrocentric
music theory and requires a significant investment

of time. Most transcriptions of "jazz," unfortunately, include only curt efforts involving the examination of small portions of an improvised melody isolated from its musical context. Chord symbols are traditionally written above the melody on the lead sheets. The chord symbols alone have limited meaning since serious practitioners never play chords as reflected by written symbols. Limiting the investigation to superficial dimensions allowed almost anyone an opportunity to become an instant "jazz" analyst. Like the "emperor's new clothes," these methods usually stand unchallenged, resulting in an unfortunate perpetuation of the status quo.

Where a person studied, how many performances they have attended, or the size of the record collection they own has less validity to non-Western cultures than an individual's knowledge of the given culture. Many cultures (including African-American "jazz" culture) measure knowledge according to an individual's performance proficiency or other tangible criteria. Ward states: "A collective 'us,' whether a reference to Westerners, white males, or ethnomusicologists, is no more valid than a collective 'them,' which lumps people with different abilities and levels of knowledge about tradition and culture."[15] This fact was a poignant one in the early "black" and "white" minstrel tradition in the United States, where grossly distorted perspectives about "us" and "them" were held by minstrels of all colors. Distance between "us" and "them" must first be reduced if meaningful analysis of African-American music is to emerge from within the majority culture.

Although musicians still perform all substyles of "jazz," historians tend to present an individual era as though its rise, peak, and decline follow predictably before the subsequent cycle begins. The careers of Ellington, Miles, Coltrane, and others tell us otherwise. The evolutionary development of "jazz," from early New Orleans styles to bebop cannot be restricted to stylistic differences that serve to simplify historical reporting.

Not only do bebop and hard bop share many common elemental features, but seemingly diametrically opposed styles such as "free jazz," swing, and New Orleans "jazz" also maintain essential similarities. All of these styles involve blues-based foundations that share sustained intensity, syncopation, complex rhythms, improvisation, and other characteristics rooted in an African-American dialect. Innovators of each new era generally acknowledge a connection to Afrocentric tradition, and often perform and record tributes to past eras. Many "jazz" styles borrow from a repertoire of standard compositions and share a common approach to fundamental harmonic orientation and melodic phrasing. There is much to be learned through the examination of differences; but there is an equal amount to be learned from considering similarities and retentions.

More Conceptual Expansion

Charles Mingus Reemerges during the 1970s

Mingus was a recluse from 1966 to 1970, falling into temporary obscurity, playing no music publicly, and producing no recordings. He emerged early in the 1970s, formed a new band, and released several memorable large-ensemble and small-group records. His big band performances in New York City on September 23 and November 28, 1971, included compositions (some of which were arranged by Sy Oliver) that were eventually released on an album entitled *Charles Mingus: Let My Children Hear Music*.[16] A concert billed as "Charles Mingus and Friends" in 1972 was another project involving a large ensemble on which Mingus collaborated with Sy Oliver.

The 1977 release of the album *Three or Four Shades of Blues,*[17] Mingus's best-selling record ever, fully revived his career. Mingus uses three electric guitarists on the album, which sold over fifty thousand copies. Shortly after his remarkable comeback, Mingus was diagnosed as having amyotrophic lateral sclerosis (Lou Gehrig's disease). By 1978 he was unable to play the bass, but he continued to compose for large ensembles. On several dates, his new works were recorded while Mingus led the musicians from his wheelchair (including the session that produced the album *Me, Myself an Eye*). Some of these recordings were released posthumously, and other extensive compositions were also performed after his death.

His wife, Sue Mingus, selected Gunther Schuller to edit and prepare the manuscript for a concert of Mingus's *Epitaph,* written for an assembly of thirty musicians and never performed during the composer's lifetime. That Mingus was not able to gain support for a performance of this piece—which Schuller accomplished—is conspicuous evidence of the American racism he encountered while trying to produce his own music after being "blacklisted" following his recording of his composition "Fables of Faubus." Mingus was not known for either a lack of motivation or inadequate business competence. It is perhaps due to frustrating sociocultural obstacles that account for the resignation reflected in Mingus's notes for *Epitaph*, where he simply said that he "wrote it for [his] tombstone." He apparently realized that his composition would never be performed during his lifetime. Mingus' multimovement *magnum opus* (composed intermittently between 1940 and 1962) was recorded at Avery Fischer Hall in 1989.

Mingus attempted to produce his own large-scale works once before in 1962 for an ill-fated concert at Town Hall in New York City. The date for the concert was originally set for November 15, 1962, then United Artists advanced the date forward five weeks earlier to October 12. The inconsiderate rescheduling placed Mingus in a position where outside arrangers had to be hired to try to rush to complete his music by the new deadline. This was the first of a series of inconsiderate circumstances and unfortunate events. Gunther Schuller discusses other experiences that occurred at the performance of the work:

> The first series of tragedies occurred when Mingus, out of strain and frustration, swung-out at his long-time friend, trombonist Jimmy Knepper, who had been assisting with the preparation of the score. With scant rehearsal time Mingus assembled his musicians at Town Hall where two copyists were seated with the orchestra on stage, preparing instrumental parts from the newly finished score while the musicians played! The recording engineers were unable to provide playback monitors on stage or even to see the musicians, and thus

communication was almost non-existent. Furthermore, when Mingus discovered the promoters had advertised the event as a concert and not as an open recording session with its stops and starts, he encouraged customers to demand their money back.

The full realization of his music was thwarted not only by a lack of rehearsal but by the fact that he had to act as composer, contractor, conductor, bassist/soloist, consultant, advisor, and virtually, director and producer. Mingus persevered until midnight when the unionized stagehands began to close down the hall. One musician, Clark Terry, broke into Ellington's "In A Mellow Tone," and as the weary artists sought release through a jam session on a familiar theme, the stagehands brought down the curtain. What came out of the Town Hall recording issued by United Artists is fragmentary and disparate. Titles were mislabeled, splicing and editing was done without Mingus' knowledge, and little of the two hours of recorded music appeared on the album. And if this wasn't enough, Mingus found himself in court on two counts: one to bring suit against United Artists for more than $18,000 in copying costs and, later, to answer assault charges made by Knepper.

Although trouble frequently plagued
Mingus, the fiasco at Town Hall and the
drama of his eviction in 1966 [captured
on film by Tom Reichman] illuminated
in a dark way the strength and
sensitivity of one of America's greatest
composers.[18]

Experimental music-making with the
controversial bassist/composer was dubbed by his
sidemen "the University of Mingus." His workshops
(which took place either in closed rehearsals or live
performances) involved long rehearsals where sloppy
playing and attitudes were forced to confront the
composer's wrath. If Mingus felt the playing lacked
musicality and sincerity at any point during the
"workshop," he had no qualms about stopping a
composition midstream to chastise an individual
musician or the entire ensemble, reminding them
that they should always treat music (melody in
particular) with "respect."

Anthony Braxton

Woodwind multi-instrumentalist and
composer Anthony Braxton (b. 1945) has remained a
major figure in contemporary instrumental music
since the mid-seventies. He contributed to the body
of experimental music produced by members of the
Association for the Advancement of Creative
Musicians (AACM), and still continues to resist
categorization. His unique contributions as a
composer distinguish him in the evolution of
African-American music, particularly of the 1970s.
Braxton's interest in exploring unconventional
approaches to timbre, formal construction, and other

compositional elements is expansive. His technical proficiency on woodwinds extends to a variety of rarely seen horns including such instruments as the sopranino and contrabass saxophones.

Braxton's recognition as a composer, whose works form a bridge between contemporary African-American "jazz" and European "classical" avant-garde idioms, is becoming increasingly more widespread. He has received a Guggenheim Fellowship and a National Endowment for the Arts grant for composition. The range of his work extends from solo performances to scores for multiple orchestras. Between those poles Braxton creates music for an array of small and large "jazz" ensembles, as well as unusual compositions for various other settings. He has also written film soundtracks, pieces for dance companies (including Merce Cunningham's) and has received chamber orchestra commissions.

Braxton studied harmony and composition at the Chicago School of Music and pursued graduate work in philosophy at Roosevelt University. His first love was European "classical" music, but the influence of cool-style saxophonists Paul Desmond, Lee Konitz, and Warne Marsh inspired his interest in "jazz." Upon receiving a discharge from the army in 1966, following a two-year tour of duty in Korea, Braxton joined the AACM. The experimental AACM workshop offered a conducive environment for Braxton's conceptual explorations of new synergetic musical resources related to the vanguard styles of both "free-jazz" players like Ornette Coleman, and the music of musicians such as John Cage, Karlheinz Stockhausen, and other European and European-American vanguard composers.

In 1967 Braxton, trumpeter Leo Smith, and violinist Leroy Jenkins formed the Creative Construction Company and recorded Braxton's debut album with those fellow AACM musicians later that year: *Three Compositions of New Jazz* (Delmark Records, 1967). During the following year, Braxton began to document his groundbreaking solo performances with his recording *Anthony Braxton, For Alto* (Delmark Records, 1968), which featured Braxton on unaccompanied alto sax. The critical acclaim for both releases created little financial profit for Braxton, a typical economic situation in the "free jazz" subculture. During this period Braxton often earned his living through engaging in hustling chess games on the street.[19]

Braxton became associated with the European electronic music scene shortly after he and many of his AACM peers moved to Europe (in 1969). He performed with the Italian improvising ensemble Musica Elettronica Viva in 1970. Avant-garde musicians during the 1970s expected to find a more sympathetic audience for their music abroad. It was during that period that Braxton joined pianist Chick Corea, bassist Dave Holland, and drummer Barry Altschul to form the short-lived group Circle. The musical empathy and improvisational inventiveness of Circle was documented on a recording of a live performance in Paris.[20] After Circle disbanded in 1971, a recording date the following year with the Dave Holland Quartet involved the multi-instrumentalist on an album entitled *Conference of the Birds* (that featured Braxton on reeds and flute).[21]

Braxton found that the delayed impact of his album *For Alto* eventually increased the demand for him as a solo performer in Europe. Braxton's burgeoning reputation at the time was reflected in the estimation of him as "the greatest living alto saxophonist," according to Coda, Canada's premier "jazz" magazine.[22] His African-American peers, who certainly knew better than to make such deluded claims, did not share this inflated enthusiasm for his playing. Braxton music included more elements of European musical approaches to the saxophone than did most African-American altoists. His command of the instrument, and his inventiveness as a spontaneous and premeditative composer, certainly did not surpass contributions of Coleman Hawkins, Lester Young, Charlie Parker, John Coltrane, Cannonball Adderley, Ornette Coleman, or countless other innovative African-American saxophonists.

Braxton moved to New York in 1974 and recorded with his former AACM and Circle colleagues. He also found work with other musicians in small-combo settings (duets, trios, and quartets). These efforts produced several unusual albums including *Anthony Braxton, New York, Fall 1974* (for quartet on Arista Records, 1975); *Anthony Braxton, Five Pieces* (for quartet on Arista Records, 1975); *Anthony Braxton, Duets with Richard Abrams* (Arista Records, 1976); *Anthony Braxton, for Trio* (Arista Records, 1978). Braxton began to compose records for large ensembles during this phase of his career, and he created an early masterwork, *Anthony Braxton, Creative Orchestra Music* (Arista Records, 1976). His compositional imagination became intensified during the next two years. He toured Europe with his own experimental ensemble in 1978 and released a three-record set that documents a huge aggregation of 160 musicians organized into four orchestras performing on-stage at Oberlin

College in Ohio (*Anthony Braxton, For Four Orchestras*, Arista Records, 1978).

Braxton's concern seems directed toward constructing new musical and structural paradigms. His music often involves pulse track structures:

> The term pulse track refers to the horizontal placement of given factors in the forward space of the music, horizontal variables that define how the space is conceived in the same sense as vertical harmony does, except here we're · dealing with conceptual areas that I've generated in my own music, areas that in this context have to do with the nature of event-forming and construction dynamics. And these horizontal variables establish a dialogue, on the first level between the individual and the process, then the individual and the other players; then later the individual and the composite group consciousness.[23]

The World Saxophone Quartet

The World Saxophone Quartet was formed in St. Louis in 1977 by three saxophonists from the Black Artists Group who became prominent during the 1970s and a younger Bay Area born saxophonist. Oliver Lake (b. 1942), Julius Hemphill (1940–95), and Hamiett Bluiett (b. 1940) were the members of BAG who founded the WSQ with saxophonist David Murray (b. 1955). Their complementary styles are demonstrated in numerous recordings of live and studio performances. The range of influence includes elements as diverse as Ornette Coleman, the Art Ensemble of Chicago, and Albert Ayler, on the one hand, with Duke Ellington, Igor Stravinsky, and Charles Mingus on the other. Their music incorporates humor, world music, traditional African-American music, and a diverse spectrum of sources.

The World Saxophone Quartet's longevity (over twenty years) was not permanently interrupted in April, 1995, when Hemphill died. Multi-reedist John Purcell joined the quartet as a performer, producer, and saxophone consultant. Purcell has worked with Tito Puente, Dizzy Gillespie, Stevie Wonder, and others. In an article for *Down Beat* magazine, Bluiett attributed the staying power of the quartet to a strategy against the tendency of the American music industry to divide and conquer African-American artists: "We have managed to stay together by not trying to stay together. This was my formula because I know this industry. If you try to stay together, it will pull you apart. By pursuing our own careers, we somehow kept coming back together, and it was just a matter of making ourselves available for the various concert and recording dates. But we also like playing together. And furthermore, we are not just a group, we are a non-profit business, and no decision is made unless we all agree."[24]

Joe Henderson

Joe Henderson first came into prominence in a group he co-led with trumpeter Kenny Dorham

(1924–72) between 1962 and 1963. He later made classic recordings with Horace Silver (b. 1928) and organized the Jazz Communicators with trumpeter Freddie Hubbard (b. 1938). He played a televised concert with Herbie Hancock, Ron Carter, and Tony Williams in 1985 and recorded his highly acclaimed recordings live at the Village Vanguard around that time.

Favorable things finally began to happen for Henderson during the early 1990s, as the general public finally began to realize what all "jazz" musicians had always known: Joe was one of the most powerful tenor players to emerge from the 1960s. He absorbed from all the great tenor players that came before him but emerged with his own distinctive melodic style. He is one of the contemporary masters.

McCoy Tyner

Pianist McCoy Tyner, perhaps best known in connection with the Coltrane ensembles, was the driving force in front of his own varied groups by the early seventies. He transfers his powerful piano solo style to big band scores on occasion, but, Tyner says, "I do big band dates in Europe from time to time, but only a couple of times here in the States. It's expensive and I don't want to be on the road constantly."[25]

Tyner's mother, a pianist, encouraged and instructed young McCoy. Bud and Richie Powell were his main influences, and Tyner soon led his own teenage "jazz" band in his native Philadelphia. McCoy always followed his devout Muslim religious beliefs closely, and adopted the name Sulaimon

Saud around that time. Tyner always used his original name when he performed, however.

In 1959 Tyner played with the Jazztet, a group co-led by Art Farmer and Benny Golson. He then joined the Coltrane sextet for five years (1960–65). His album with Joe Henderson, Ron Carter, and Elvin Jones that followed the period with Coltrane is one of the important recordings to come out of the late sixties. When asked about the Coltrane influence on his playing McCoy replied:

> We can never recapture anything, because it [the world] is always changing. It's always different. People leave the planet but their styles remain here. They're here in spirit. What I'm saying is that to try and duplicate anything doesn't make sense. That's the reason why when I left John, Jimmy [Garrison] and Elvin [Jones] were ready to leave, and they said, "Let's play as a trio." I said, "No," because it's like a tree, your roots are there but you branch off. What I'm doing is like an extension of what I did with them. It's 1995, and I'm still drawing strength from those roots. . . . John is always present. Like Charlie Parker, he's there, and that's good.[26]

The pianist was also influenced by Monk and Art Tatum. He has, in turn, influenced the younger generations of pianists. McCoy says, "I try to listen to music from many different countries: Africa, India, from the Arabic world, European classical music . . . all kinds of music are interconnected."[27] Tyner made a number of impressive recordings during the 1970s. He participated in an all-star tour in 1978 with Sonny Rollins, Ron Carter, and Al Foster. He later made a film as a solo pianist in 1985 when Blue note relaunched its label. He continues to experiment with modern Afrocentric music at the piano. In 1996 he remarked: "I take a particular interest in African culture because it's in me and it's reflected in a lot of my songs."[28]

Instrumental Style Continues to Evolve

The saxophone continued to remain among the most dominant "jazz" instruments, exerting a wide-ranging influence during the seventies. Yet the trumpet, piano, bass, trombone, flute, and other instruments began to make impressive strides as well. A careful examination of American trumpet history shows we can trace an uninterrupted and powerful line through the styles of King Oliver, Louis Armstrong, Roy Eldridge, Dizzy Gillespie, Miles Davis, and Lester Bowie. Each of these innovators acknowledged the importance of past traditions, but contributed a salubrious personal style that produced a votary of followers.

When a new mainstream style reasserted itself during hard bop, Horace Silver, Randy Weston, Tommy Flanagan, Elmo Hope, Herbie Nichols, Mal Waldron, and other pianists emerged from that movement. Ramsey Lewis, Wynton Kelly, Ray Bryant, Andrew Hill, and others created an eclectic piano style that revitalized an interest in blues, gospel, and other soulful African-American music, while often incorporating elements of European impressionism,

Latin styles, and other elements drawn from around the world. Pianists McCoy Tyner, Herbie Hancock, Milt Buckner, and Bill Evans had popularized the use of quartal harmony making its usage increasingly more common.

The interval of the fourth was a favorite of other musicians (during the 1950s) who introduced quartal dyads and triads as supporting chord structures or as extensions of chromatic harmony. Later, compositions like Hancock's "Maiden Voyage" experimented with combinations of quartal harmony, harmonics, and polytonality. Interestingly, as Kubik notes, the !Kung of Southeastern Angola and other Africans employ a related harmonic approach.

> Tonal systems based on the use of harmonies over two fundamentals [Hancock uses four fundamentals in "Maiden Voyage"] . . . frequently encountered in areas where the musical bow is known, particularly the mouth-bow in its varieties. These fundamentals are yielded either by two segments of the string when it is divided by means of a brace or noose on an unbraced bow when the string may be stopped with a finger or a stick and thus shortened to obtain the higher note. . . .

> The tonal system of the !Kung of Southeastern Angola is tetratonic with frequent pentatonic extensions. My surprise finding, however, while doing research in the area of Kwitu-Kwanavale in 1965, was that the !Kung

> tetratonic system manifests itself in three different phenotypes with different intervals, depending on the width of the basic interval to which the music bow is tuned. . . . Unaccompanied vocal music is totally in line with the bow harmonics, and a song stands in any of the three phenotypes, unless of course, it is pentatonic.

Hard bop musicians and other stylists also became interested in making modern "jazz" more appealing to African-American audiences during the mid-fifties and mid-sixties.

Since the dawn of modern "jazz," saxophonists consistently excelled as the most influential innovators of each eras beginning around 1940. The innovations of Charlie Parker that marked the beginning of the modern "jazz" era were honed into new approaches during the late fifties and early sixties by Ornette Coleman, Eric Dolphy, Sonny Stitt, Cannonball Adderly, and other saxophonists. Coleman restructured small-group "jazz." His "harmolodic" revolution defied most of the tonal and harmonic conventions established by the hard bop and cool styles. Coleman was instrumental in the creation of what became known as "free jazz." With Dolphy's approach, saxophone style was again modified, expanding harmonic, melodic, timbre, and other expressive borderlines while introducing the bass clarinet as a new lead instrument. Dolphy was also instrumental in liberating the role of the flute in "jazz."

The synthesis of styles developed by Sonny Rollins, John Coltrane, Eric Dolphy, and Ornette

Coleman became the new extension of the saxophone legacy established by Ben Webster, Coleman Hawkins, Lester Young, and Charlie Parker. Many saxophonists of the seventies and eighties (such as Julius Hemphill, Dewey Redman, Branford Marsalis, Oliver Lake, Sam Rivers, Yusef Lateef, Joe Henderson, David Murray and Arthur Blythe) can trace their musical approach back to that stylistic "school." The hard bop approach that developed between 1955 and 1965 branched out into two distinct styles: those players who continued to be guided by preset chord changes, and those who moved away from prescribed forms, melodies, and harmonies.

In the seventies an additional type of "jazz" saxophone style emerged. "Jazz" saxophone style was influenced by popular styles of the day and, in turn, influence styles of popular music. The music that resulted was labeled jazz-fusion and jazz-funk, but this line of influence extends back to the rhythm-and-blues style of the late forties and fifties (produced by musicians such as Illinois Jacquet, Flip Phillips, Earl Bostic, and others). Their lineage continued into the sixties, affecting the musical directions of David Fathead Newman, Cannonball Adderley, Hank Crawford, Tina Brooks, King Curtis, Gene Ammons, Grover Washington, Jr., and Stanley Turrentine. Grover Washington Jr. (1943-99) developed an influential lyrical saxophone sound (particularly on soprano) that eventually became the primary prototype for a much more watered-down and popular smooth-jazz saxophone sound.

Other saxophonists developed styles that, while not as influential as the more dominant innovators, were clearly outside the mainstream sound. Among these personal styles are the Texas tenors Booker Ervin and Jimmy Tyler; soprano saxophonist Steve Lacy; saxophonists Joseph Jarman, Albert Ayler, and Roscoe Mitchell; and multi-instrumentalists Anthony Braxton and Rahsaan Roland Kirk. These musicians' distinctive approaches have less clearly defined links to the two adjacent saxophone dynasties mentioned above.

The general temperament of the African-American community was reflected in the styles of many musicians during the sixties. The nature of this movement contributed to redefining African-American sociocultural and personal identity, as well as to reshaping modes of artistic expression. The music of the seventies, on the other hand, began to become more assimilated into mainstream American culture and world musical styles, as the social environment briefly became somewhat neutralized. Perhaps several totalitarian shows of force during the early 1970s caused activists (of all colors) to rush to the barber shops across America to shed their Afros and long straight hair. The show of military force at Kent State and then the militarized police aggression in Los Angeles that mercilessly crushed the Symbionese Liberation Army (on national television) were two such incidents. The systematic infiltration and disruption of the Black Panther Party was a related and effectively orchestrated conspiracy. The youth cultures of the 1960s began grooming themselves for radically more conservative lifestyles in America of the 1970s.

The Evolution of the Flute

When Samuel Mordecai writes about the Richmond, Virginia, of the "bygone days" in 1860, he makes it clear that the flute was already an instrument used at American dances. He mentions a famous "Negro fiddler Sy Gilliat" and a "Negro flautist London Brigs" in connection with performances at state balls where they "dressed in a courtly fashion." Mordecai says, "To the music of Gilliat's fiddle and London Brigs' flute all sorts of capers were cut. . . . Sometimes a 'congo' was danced and when the music grew fast and furious, a jig would wind up the evening."[29]

The low audibility of the flute made it difficult for the instrument to be heard in the noisy environments in which early "jazz" musicians performed. Like the double bass and guitar, the flute would eventually enjoy greater popularity when amplification of musical sounds became more refined. Nevertheless, the flute has always had a place in the "jazz" evolution. There were certainly early flute players who failed to gain historical recognition. A flute and piccolo specialist in Chicago named Flutes Morton (1900–62) performed at the Sunset Cafe in the middle of the Roaring Twenties. Norvel E. Morton lived in Chicago for many years and worked regularly with violinist (and multi-instrumentalist) Erskine Tate (1895–1978) and pianist Dave Peyton (1885–1956). In 1932 Morton was a member of the Eddie King band and was with Reuben Reeves's group between 1933 and 1934. He also performed briefly with Louis Armstrong, Earl Hines, and Noble Sissle.

Although the clarinet was the preferred woodwind double of most swing era saxophonists (because of its greater amplitude), the flute found a place in some big bands. One of the first solo flutists to be featured on a "jazz" recording was Wayman Carver (1905–67). He is the earliest master of "jazz" flute. Carver produced not only a beautiful tone, displayed an impressive technique, and improvised superbly on that traditionally delicate woodwind instrument, but he also demonstrated an equally impressive control and imagination on the clarinet and saxophones. He began to study the flute seriously at age fourteen and was soon performing with Elmer Snowden's band (1931–32). Carver worked with Benny Carter (b. 1907) for a couple of years and was featured on a recording session in New York with bassist Spike Hughes (1908–87) that produced "Sweet Sue Just You."

Carver gained his greatest exposure from 1934 to 1940 while a member of master drummer Chick Webb's band featuring Ella Fitzgerald. He was also proved to be an interesting arranger, contributing renditions of "Down Home Rag," "My Heart Belongs to Daddy," and other arrangements in Webb's book. Chauncey Haughton often performed duets with Carver on Gershwin's "I Got Rhythm," Harry White's "Congo," and other diminutive swing-style arrangements for a quintet (formed on the band-within-band principle) from Webb's big band format.

In the early 1950s Yusef Lateef (b. 1920) began to use flute, oboe, and a wide range of other wind instruments from around the world. William Evans (Lateef's name before he embraced Islam in the late 1940s) moved from Detroit to New York in 1946. He soon found work as a tenor saxophonist with Lucky Millinder, Roy Eldridge, and Hot Lips Page before joining Dizzy Gillespie for a year. The exotic compositions Lateef introduced affected the music of John Coltrane and other musicians during the 1960s.

Almost all of the early flute innovators doubled on the saxophone. James Moody (b. 1925) began on the alto saxophone before taking up the tenor the following year. During the 1940s he worked with Dizzy Gillespie, Miles Davis, Tadd Dameron, and Max Roach. Moody was based in Paris from 1948 to 1952 and began to play the flute when he returned to the United States in the mid-1950s.

Eric Dolphy (1928–64) not only created a new role for the flute in "jazz" but was also one of the first vanguard multi-instrumentalists to master all of his instruments convincingly. Dolphy studied with another brilliant Los Angeles–born multi-instrumentalist, Buddy Collette (b. William Marcel in 1921). Collette was a founding member of the Chico Hamilton quintet. In the late 1950s, Buddy Collette's Swinging Shepherds recorded ground-breaking flute quartets (for piccolo, flute, alto flute, and bass flute) with flutists Bud Shank, Paul Horn, and Harry Klee. Collette continued to work with Monk, Dizzy Gillespie, Benny Carter, and others, but soon focused on freelance studio performance and teaching. His ability to maintain a beautiful tone on flute while switching from one instrument to another with utmost ease places Collette in a special class of multi-instrumentalists. Flutist James Newton (b. 1953) studied with Collette, but his style is firmly grounded in Dolphy's musical approach.

Other tenor players who made important contributions to the development of the flute during the 1950s and early 1960s were Frank Wess (b. 1922), Harold Land (b. 1928), Sam Rivers (b. 1930), and Herbie Mann (b. 1930). Wess and Mann began to popularize the "jazz" flute during the mid-1950s. It was Rahsaan Roland Kirk (1936–77), though, who moved furthest away from the idiomatic "jazz" flute approach that was heavily influenced by the prevailing saxophone styles. Kirk's extended flute technique was broad enough to incorporate virtually all twentieth-century flute techniques.

James Spaulding (b. 1937), Art Webb, Lloyd McNeill, and other flutists would follow in the tradition of the earlier flutists. Hubert Laws (b. 1939) put his tenor saxophone aside after working with Mongo Santamaria (b. 1922) and dedicated full energy to moving the flute and piccolo playing to new levels of technical mastery. Although flutists Bobbi Humphrey and Kent Jordan chose to express their musical ideas in fusion and popular styles, both were heavily influenced by Laws.

Hubert Laws's elevated flute technique to a new level of control and virtuosity. His style involved the exploitation of an expanded array of the inherent qualities of the flute. He also introduced his audiences to the piccolo and the alto and bass flutes during his numerous concerts. He studied at the Juilliard School of Music and used this knowledge to engage the innovative improvisational style of 1970s fusion. He was born in Texas, the birthplace of many other innovative "jazz" flutists (including Leo Wright, James Clay, Prince Lasha, John Carter, and the author).

Laws performs both Afrocentric "jazz" and Eurocentric "classical" influenced works with supreme authority. Laws contributed music to the repertoire of 1970s jazz/classical fusion that would continually gain in popularity throughout the decade. His albums *Afro-Classic* (1970) and *The Rite of Spring* (1971) are the earliest of his albums that display an ability to move between baroque, impressionistic, pop, and early-twentieth-century European styles while maintaining stylistic connection with the African-American music tradition.

Although the role of the "jazz" flute is relatively marginal, few orchestral woodwinds or strings have enjoyed the influential status assigned to the saxophone in "jazz" history. Nonetheless, the more subtle sound of the violin has remained attached to the evolution of "jazz." Ray Nance, Stuff Smith, Stephane Grappelli, Joe Venuti, Billy Bang, Michael White, Noel Pointer, Jean-Luc Ponty, and Regina Carter are just a few of the notable musicians who demonstrated the powerful capabilities of the "jazz" violin. Just as all instruments are potentially virtuoso instruments, so each one is capable of "jazz" expression.

Classical-Jazz Fusion and Other New Approaches

"Classical" is a general term that can be equally applied to the music of any culture, including "jazz." The music called "jazz," on the other hand, has its primary traditional roots in innovation and experimentation, and it generally involves an evolutionary process requiring continual artistic revolution. In the past, innovative "jazz" musicians have been less concerned with the perpetuation of tradition than with each finding their own unique voice. Dorothy Donegan, Hubert Laws, and Wynton Marsalis are only a few of a growing number of African-American musicians who consciously direct their musical attention toward building bridges between "classic" African-American and European music.

Cleo Lane is a remarkable vocal recitalist who was living in London when the influence of "jazz" found her. For Lane, this period of discovery (in the

1970s) led to the creation of a fresh vocal approach. Lane's unusually impressive vocal range supported a stylistic approach capable of winning almost immediate popularity. Her 1973 album *I Am a Song* exemplifies a cross-section of Lane's early style. Lane's music on that recording involved yet another example of fresh ways of fusing European musical aesthetics with African-American musical styles.

The various roles of women musicians during the seventies were not restricted to vocalists. Sharon Freeman was playing concerts and studio sessions in the late 1970s. Sharon Freeman was equally adept on the French horn and piano after graduating from New York City's High School of Music and Art and later the Manhattan School of Music (with a Bachelor of Music in Theory and French Horn). She eventually worked with the Gil Evans Orchestra, Sam Rivers' Harlem Ensemble, Charles Mingus' Big Band, Kenny Dorham Quintet, New York Jazz Repertory Company, Jazz Composers' Orchestra Association, McCoy Tyner's Big Band, the French Horn Ensemble (of which she was organizer/leader), and with Carla Bley.

Composer/pianist Carla Bley (b. 1938) composed and performed her own unique brand of experimental music and founded a record distribution company (New Music Distribution Company). Although women instrumentalists were poorly promoted during this period, they continued to create music in a variety of settings. Paula Hampton emerged as a dynamic New York City drummer during the seventies. She appeared regularly with The Jazz Sisters. Hampton was also a featured drummer at the "Salute to Women in Jazz" (in New York City) in 1978. Hampton performed with the Universal Jazz Coalition's "Big Apple" Jazz

Women Ensemble in New York, and was a guest artist at the Kansas City Women's Jazz Festival in 1979.

During the 1970s, saxophonist Oliver Lake (b. 1942) contributed to the innovative evolution of the fissionary variety of spontaneous composition. He and other innovators, unable to find recording companies in America who were eager to embrace their music, began recording abroad for Black Saint records and other European labels. The ideas for compositions on his 1976 album *Holding Together* introduce fresh approaches to musical organization.

As an increasing number of 1970s college music students began to study "jazz" and European music simultaneously, the ivory tower that traditionally elevated European "art music" above all other world music was often forced to justify its lofty claims. Today, examining music strictly in terms of the notes and empirical theories involved makes the justification for Eurocentric musical snobbery an impossible case to prove.

Since the 1970s, African-American musicians began to receive increasingly more institutional support for their innovative work. Ornette Coleman, Cecil Taylor, Charles Mingus, Charlie Haden, James Newton, David Murray, and George Russell have received Guggenheim Foundation Fellowships. Taylor, Coleman, Steve Lacy, and Anthony Braxton are among those who have received MacArthur grants. Billy Harper, Grachan Moncur III, the JCOA, Kenny Durham, and Lee Konitz were among the early recipients of the National Endowment for the Arts (NEA) "jazz" composition grants. Ed Blackwell and other artists received awards from the NEA for producing method books.[30] Despite significant changes in funding policy for the arts in the United

States, the support provided by American corporate agencies and educational institutions for African-American music has remained disproportionately low.

Artistic barriers such as social conditioning, arrogance, and lack of exposure to new music prevent many people from understanding that most world music contains beauty, knowledge, inspiration, and sophistication that can benefit all listeners. Author Alain Danielou offers an interesting perspective on attitudes regarding the eminence of European music:

> Modern Western music was able to develop its polyphonic system only by deliberately sacrificing the greater part of its possibilities and breaking the ties which connected it with other musical systems. Formerly, all the musical systems were near to each other and, in spite of differences, could generally be understood from one country to another; this can clearly be seen in the success that the musicians who came with the Turkish Empress had in China, in that of some Negro musicians in the Mussalman [sic] world during the first centuries of Islam, or that of the Gypsies in Europe. But since the middle ages, there has been, in the West, a tendency to accept those simplifications of the theory which had already been rejected everywhere else as being incompatible with a refined form of Art. Therefore, when, in the words of M. Amédée, 'Guido d'Arezzo

(990–1040), having reduced everything to the diatonic, and given the last blow to the quarter-tones inherited from the Greek melody, directs our scale toward temperament and facilitates the progress of polyphony. D'Arezzo, in reality, only gives a blow to all popular forms of music whose very complex modal and rhythmic forms will place to an official art, heavy and simplified.[31]

There is little difference between solitary or simultaneous occurrences of tones in a planned system and those forming related harmonies spontaneously during improvised music. Sound is sound whether read from a sheet of music or produced spontaneously. There can be elements of predictability and surprise, tension and release, or joy and sadness in any artistic expression. The involvement of inspiration, musical knowledge and technical virtuosity are inherent in music from all over the world.

Race has always mattered in America and the consequences of racism are far reaching. Racism has always affected the way many Americans think and feel about certain music. Bigotry has limited the growth and development of music in America. How much greater contribution could African-American musicians such as Louis Armstrong, Duke Ellington, Art Tatum, Charlie Parker, Charles Mingus, John Coltrane, and countless other innovators have made in their musical quests with institutional support and respect equivalent to that given the composers of European dodecaphonic music? What would the range of possibilities for rap music be if the music and creative arts programs had not been abducted from inner city school programs? Had "jazz" remained a function of the African-American community, how might the music have affected the development of knowledge, self-esteem, and creative imaginations of young people who are now desperately seeking positive African-American role models?

Even as educators across the country seek answers to the problems involved in educating today's morally, economically, and emotionally neglected children, they apparently fail to recognize the importance of artistic creativity in the nurturing and shaping of young minds, bodies, and spirits. If an appreciation of the arts is not a high priority in education, society will eventually devolve toward a point of creative impotence.

Santeria and Musical Freedom

By the 1960s Santeria had made its way to New York City, bringing with its rituals the music of the bata drum. Many of the "free" players were eager to incorporate these new rhythmic sounds into their musical universe, bringing the evolution of African-American music full circle—back (so to speak) to its point of origin (African music).

The origins of Santeria can be traced back to the traditional religion of the Yoruba people of West Africa. Its system of beliefs and rituals emerged in Cuba in the 1940s before making its way to neighborhoods in New York City, where many Cuban, Puerto Rican, and Dominican (Dominican Republican) people resided. John Amira and Steven Cornelius describe interesting aspects of this religion in *The Music of Santeria: Traditional Rhythms of the Bata Drums*.

Traditional Yoruba religion is constructed upon a hierarchical, pantheistic system of thought which stretches from Almighty God in the most rarefied heaven to man on earth. Man can fulfill his destiny by avoiding the wrath of gods, and actually improve his lot through proper veneration and sacrifice to them.

Olorun is The Deity, God Almighty, and is generally considered to be responsible for the creation of the universe. Olorun is an austere and remote God who by representing all things, all possibilities, is beyond human comprehension. Therefore, practitioners direct their entreaties to the orichas, deities who, positioned directly below Olorun, are both relatively fathomable and accessible. Each oricha embodies various aspects from the totality of Olorun. These aspects are personified from natural features (rivers, oceans, mountains) or from elemental forces acting within nature (wind, lightening, disease). Through these associations, each oricha is believed to govern specific aspects of the universe. What evolves from these conceptions are layers of religious belief which reveal multiple notions of, and means to, the sacrifice.

Religious practitioners use music and
various types of prayer to communicate
with and praise the orichas. In turn,
the orichas mediate between man and
God Almighty. Direct contact with the
orichas is sometimes achieved through
spirit possession. This is an important
aspect of worship in some areas of West
Africa and central to New World music
ritual.[32]

In addition to the musical associations "jazz"
musicians had with bata drummers and other people
practicing African-based religions, many African-
American "jazz" musicians were impressed with
other forms of worship. Dizzy Gillespie spoke to Art
Taylor of the difference that his new faith made in
his life. Gillespie was a follower of the Baha'i faith,
which means "follower of Baha'ullah" (Baha'ullah
means "glory of God" in Persian):[33] "Since I became a
Baha'i, which is my religious faith, I've been much
more aware of unity. Because the Baha'is are
destined to bring unity to the world: unity of religion,
of races, of finance, of everything. I'm looking at it
like this: if you have a group, the group is like a
painting, a masterpiece. Each one of the instruments
represents a specific color, and the diversity of colors
makes it beautiful. You've got five pieces, and none
of them sound alike, but they must have unity."[34]

While an audience for the innovative forms of
"jazz" was gradually developing downtown in New
York City as well as in other urban areas, audiences
did not include large proportions of African-
American listeners. Appreciation for an art form is
enhanced through formal and casual education that
is a by-product of direct and continued exposure to

artistic experiences. Young African Americans remained less likely to frequent lofts located in European-American neighborhoods. Just as the proportion of African-American listeners declined when the musicians left the Harlem nightclubs and theaters in New York to perform downtown on 52d Street and other areas (especially during the bebop era), a related trend continued to distance contemporary African-American innovators from young people in African-American neighborhoods. While this trend continued for decades in America, a significant number of young Europeans and European Americans became better exposed to the newer approaches to "jazz" that were emerging than young African-American adults and (especially) children. Thus, as "jazz" became less Afrocentric, socioculturally speaking, it lost its potency and its relevance to young African Americans.

With innovative artists now cordoned off and isolated from their indigenous communities, European Americans began increasing their control over African-American music. In an attempt to build an independent, self-contained, self-defined and viable community infrastructure, pianist Horace Tapscott (1934-99) formed the Pan-Afrikan Peoples Arkestra and organized the associated activist artistic community organization the Union of God's Musicians and Artists (UGMAA) around 1959. It was difficult to sustain such noble efforts. The trend towards Eurocentric controls over Afrocentric music even angered some of the more amiable and broad-minded musicians. Dizzy Gillespie revealed his feelings regarding these developments to Art Taylor. Taylor opens the line of discussion by asking Dizzy, "What do you think about the word jazz?" Gillespie responds:

It's no longer fashionable to say Negro,
which is what the white man named
us. If we want to call it jazz, we'll make
them call it that. It's our music,
whatever we want to call it. I don't
know who made up the word *jazz*. The
blacks might have named it jazz
themselves, but I don't know much
about it. It's a misnomer only when it is
identified with white musicians. On a
television program someone was asked
to say who was known as the king of
jazz. The answer was supposed to be
Paul Whiteman. That's a misnomer,
because he couldn't be the king of our
music.

Take Stan Kenton, for instance: a big
phony, really, because he had a big
band at the same time I did. People
used to walk up to me and think they
were saying something nice, like: "I like
you and Stan Kenton." I'd be looking at
them like this, and I'd question their
taste. History will either off you or
make you valid. History has wiped Stan
Kenton out completely. They thought
he was a master, they thought he was
greater than Duke Ellington, and that
motherfucker couldn't even keep time. I
went on a tour with him as a soloist,
and when I came on, he left and you
didn't see him no more. On the next
show he'd come and do his thing in the
front, then he would announce me and

leave, and the band played my music better than they played his. I found a deeper respect from all his musicians, because all of them came up from my school. Everyone in his band came up under us, not under Stan Kenton. So they recognized the fact, and when I walked on the bandstand, there were twenty smiles. You should see what they looked like when he was playing. It made me feel good.

Anyway, our documentation is so strong now with all our records that they can't get it. I think the idea now is for blacks to write about the history of our music. It's time for that, because whites have been doing it all the time. It's time for us to do it ourselves and tell it like it is. The whites have a whitewash look at our music. Naturally they're going to try to ooze off as much as they can to the whites, but they can't, because we're documented in records, and the truth will stand. History will tell you what it is about.[35]

One thing Gillespie failed to anticipate was that European Americans could take a major portion of the documentation off the market shelves as records in one format (LPs) and reissue this information at will on CDs. Today, only a relatively small sampling of the works of Gillespie, Tatum, Parker, Coltrane, Miles, Donegan, Williams, or any other African-American "jazz" master has been released, although CDs have been widely available

on the market for over a decade. Record companies
are not as concerned about making all the
historically significant documents (formerly released
on vinyl) available to the public as they are
developing market strategies that will insure them a
steady flow of capital. Before the change of format
from LP to CD occurred, a much larger proportion of
artists' works was available in most large "jazz"
record stores as both regular issues or cut-outs. The
types of recordings by "jazz" artists sold in record
stores were altered during the music industry's
transition from analog to digital recordings. This
essentially became a European-American
businessman's editing project that arbitrarily filtered
through the history of African-American music. As a
consequence, yet another revision of African-
American history occurred. In many record stores
across the United States, the recordings of
European-American musicians have replaced many
of the recordings of African-American "jazz"
progenitors.

The intensified and perpetual tendencies of
revisionists to control "jazz" and redesign its history
have haunted African-American musicians
throughout the twentieth century. Thumbing
through any of the numerous current "jazz"
periodicals exposes related revisionist trends in
"jazz." Because the majority of America lacks a basic
education in the history of African-American music,
they are not aware of its many innovators (Herbie
Nichols, Horace Tapscott, Sam Rivers, Ted Curson,
etc.). Therefore, it is difficult for most Americans to
realize what important musical documents are
currently out of print. In a September 1998 *Down
Beat* interview titled "Take Back the Music," the
innovative saxophonist Gary Bartz discusses his

disgust "with the quality of music recorded by top artists who allow major labels to exercise control over the final product."

> Record labels feel like part of their job is to bother the musicians. They think they have a better idea of how to sell the music. I have the best idea: Stay out of the studio and sell the music. Don't tell me to put a young trumpet player on my album when I have a great trumpet player with me already. If I did put a young trumpet player on the album, they still aren't going to sell the record, so what's the deal? They want you to further their cause. They want me to build up a young trumpet player when I'm trying to make music—which is all I'm interested in.[36]

There is an additional sociocultural disposition that complicates this problem. Historically, the majority of European Americans found it difficult to acknowledge the contribution African-American citizens made to American society as inventors, political leaders, inventors, innovators, and spiritual messengers. As a consequence, the European-American "jazz" musician serves as a more "digestible" image for many Americans, thus enabling them to partake in an African-American art form without acknowledging its source. Unfortunately, if African-American musicians finally gain recognition for their greatness (currently Miles, Monk, Mingus, Dolphy, Coltrane, etc.), their physical images are vigorously displayed on posters, T-shirts, calendars, and in other ways that celebrate their exemplary accomplishments only posthumously. African-American artists are often appreciated by the music industry only for the profit they yield, and profit can be made posthumously. When asked why record labels don't sell records, Bartz evaluates the situation this way:

> It's counterproductive for them because they couldn't get a tax write-off in the first year or two after the record comes out. Now, they know when they make the record it's never going to lose money. If it takes 200 years, that record will make its money back. Unfortunately, the musicians don't last quite that long. Musicians have a high mortality rate and die at a very young age, so the record companies have their cake and eat it, too. That's why they don't sell the music. They know if the musician passes away, their recordings become very valuable.[37]

A Historical Summary

From West African musical roots two distinct but related lines of secular music traditions evolved in North America. We will call one a "jazz" tradition and the other a blues tradition. The seeds for the African-American "jazz" evolution originally began to take shape around 1502, when the first slaves arrived in America. The definitive aspects of these traditions culminated in the innovative African-American music of the 1970s.

The blues tradition was an offspring of African-American work songs, field hollers, and protests songs, whereas sacred folk spirituals, which began to appear at the end of the seventeenth century, were influenced by game songs and social songs. The folk spiritual became formalized by the middle of the eighteenth century, when arranged spirituals were heard throughout the country. Traveling musicians like the Luca Family and others sang a brand of spirituals performed around the world a few years later by the Fisk Jubilee Singers.

The influence of spiritual music, songs of both oppression and joy, eventually led to the rural blues around 1880. At about the same time syncopated dance music, which can also be traced back to the 1600s, gradually gave rise to ragtime. The melodies and harmonies of both the spirituals and syncopated dance music were influenced by the European hymns, concert music, and the marches with which it came in contact. African and African-American music, in turn, affected European and European-American music during these early periods of stylistic development.

Around 1890 African-American sacred music produced a folk gospel (gospel hymn) containing elements of rural blues, ragtime, and New Orleans "jazz" (which was a by-product of ragtime). This early "jazz" also contained rural blues elements and, in turn, had an effect on the Vaudeville blues that, along with boogie woogie, was a direct descendant of the early blues and barrelhouse piano. Blues and boogie woogie forms evolved during the birth of the gospel hymn around the turn of the century.

By the 1920s New Orleans "jazz" had made the initial transition into the early big bands, many of which were to emerge as swing bands of the 1930s. Many of the 1930s swing bands retained aspects of stride and boogie woogie styles. By the subsequent decade, however, a new bebop style was born that would mark the birth of modern "jazz." Hard bop and cool styles followed bebop during the 1950s.

The gospel hymn evolved into traditional gospel by 1930, and traces of vaudeville blues exist in the new gospel music. Later, along with soul and rhythm and blues, this sacred style would influence secular civil rights songs during the early 1960s. Traditional gospel not only produced the gospel quartets that became popular around the 1940s but was an important part of the cross-genre pollination that took place between rhythm and blues and urban blues during that period. Other gospel groups emerged later during the 1940s. The new gospel groups' stylistic influence eventually made its way into the work of hard bop musicians like Cannonball Adderley, Horace Silver, and others.

By the 1950s there were African-American gospel choirs of various sizes throughout America. This time it was soul music (born a decade later) that became the secular cross-fertilization partner. By the time Contemporary Gospel entered the picture in the early 1970s, sacred African-American music was enjoying additional influences of both funk and "jazz" fusion.

The urban blues qualities of the 1930s, retained in 1940s rhythm and blues, became the foundation for rock and roll in the early 1950s. Rhythm and blues and urban blues adapted musical elements from the swing bands of the 1930s (by way of the jump bands). Urban blues and r&b eventually merged with certain soul music elements the following decade. Soul, "jazz," funk, disco, and other Afrocentric music inherited these traits. Funk music, with its broad range of power, its popularity, and its ability to sway general audiences, was in this sense the precursor of the "jazz" fusion and rap styles that emerged in subsequent decades. A listener can detect a related influence in other African-American music of the next decade such as techno funk, house music, and go-go.

While cool "jazz" failed to produce an offspring, hard bop figured prominently in the production of both soul "jazz" in the 1960s and "jazz" fusion in the 1970s. A more innovative third by-product of bebop was the experimental music labeled avant-garde that revolutionized the music scene during the 1960s.[38] Many observers have commented on the flexible nature of the "jazz" evolution.

Hard bop and bebop are sometimes considered separately, which illustrates that the differentiation of styles constitutes no more than drawing arbitrary lines at given points along a continuum. The same also applies to labeling performers. It would be a great disservice to Lester Young if one were to label him strictly as a big band saxophonist, since he continually sought to broaden his style of musical performance throughout his career. For example, Young performed in the small group settings of the 1930s; on occasion, he also performed with bebop musicians.

Because the above model for the development of jazz mainly attributes stylistic change to purely musical considerations, it also overlooks certain cognitive components of behavior. For example, the processes of composing and performing music involve a countless number of decisions that performers make on both the conscious and unconscious levels. Leonard Meyer summarizes: "What remains constant from style to style are not scales, modes, harmonies, or manners of performance, but the psychology of human mental processes—the ways in which the mind, operating within the context of culturally established norms, selects and organizes the stimuli that are presented to it."[39]

Such processes operate in situations when jazz musicians assimilate different musical styles. In other words, as jazz musicians come into contact with other styles of musical performance, they may borrow certain features and adapt these to fit their own styles of musical performance. Since the 1940s, jazz musicians increasingly began to look to non-Western music as sources for new ideas. For example, Charlie Parker and Dizzy Gillespie incorporated into their music African-influenced rhythms from Cuba such as the mambo. Furthermore, in the 1950s, Bud Shank and Oscar Peterson recorded tunes using the Brazilian samba rhythm.

The practice of assimilation plays a central role throughout the development of the African-American folk music continuum as well. In the 1700s, for example, African slaves brought to the New World lived amidst the pressures of the dominant European culture. Unable to fully sustain their African musical traditions under these conditions, they began to borrow and adapt features from the music of the dominant culture. In fact, some African slaves became skilled in playing European dance tunes on Western instruments.[40]

David Such also asserts, "aural-oral modes of perception are also important factors of stylistic change in the jazz continuum." It is a set of modes of communication, similar to that which traditional African societies established for the perpetuation and documentation of knowledge, that enabled African Americans to overcome the limitations of oppression and establish sociocultural convergence on multiple levels. It forged a positive force that became "jazz." The transmission of musical information through this system of oral/aural knowledge enabled saxophonist Marion Brown and others to absorb and then modify Ornette Coleman's "free jazz." It is readily apparent in Thelonious Monk's influence on pianist Andrew Hill and others. When Eddie Jefferson performed lyrical versions of "Billie's Bounce" and "Parker's Mood," he was acknowledging the musical sources of those classics while continuing along his personal line of evolutionary "jazz," which requires each artist to contribute something uniquely their own to the tradition. The aural/oral tradition produces unique stylistic qualities and musical expectations that mark Joe Henderson, Stanley Turrentine, and Yusef Lateef as standout tenor saxophonists. Such concludes:

> These, too, are rooted in African culture, in which ideas and knowledge are communicated using mainly non-written forms such as speech. In improvised jazz, the aural-oral mode encourages the direct expression of the performer's inner emotions and creative impulses through musical sound. To ensure the vitality of this process, jazz tends to incorporate highly flexible and relatively noncomplex rules governing performance. This is precisely what enables musicians like Eric Dolphy to extract sounds from the environment and transform them during a musical performance. Saxophonist Ornette Coleman comments, "Regardless of race or nationality, if you are not trying to compare your values with those of other people, but are interested in expressing musically something that you have in your mind and not trying to get anyone's approval—then jazz seems to be the most honest and freest form of taking the opportunity to see if you can express something."[41] Along these lines drummer Elvin Jones adds, "A solo can take any form the artist chooses; he can use any form he wants within the framework of the composition. It goes back to getting

away from the rigidity that jazz had to face when it was primarily dance music."[42] Jones' comments also suggest that when the rules grow too complex or too staid and fresh expression is inhibited, some musicians may seek alternative ways to organize improvisation.[43]

Although Herbie Hancock and other musicians exploring "jazz" fusion during the 1970s relied on traditional African-American dance orientation in their new stylistic approaches, other musicians made metrical, formal, and conceptual modifications that continued to expand the range of elemental possibilities. The music explored by avant-garde experimenters on the forefront of African-American music was on the verge of becoming truly ecumenical.

---

[1] Angela Davis et. al., *If They Come in the Morning: Voices of Resistance* (New York: New American Library, 1971), p. 143.

[2] Michael J. Budds, *Jazz in the Sixties: The Expansion of Musical Resources and Techniques* (Iowa City: University of Iowa Press, 1990), p. 127.

[3] Valerie Wilmer, *As Serious as Your Life: The Story of the New Jazz* (London: Serpent's Tail, 1992), p. 250.

[4] Ibid., p. 229.

[5] Wilmer, *As Serious as Your Life,* p. 252.

[6] Down Beat, December 1999, p. 34.

[7] Ibid.

[8] Larry Birnbaum, "Metal Steps to Heaven" *Village Voice*, August 24, 1990, p. 78.

[9] As he suggested in his autobiography.

[10] *Miles*, pp. 292–93.

[11] Selected Donald Byrd Albums: *Off to the Races* (Blue Note BLP-4007); *Fuego* (Blue Note BST-84026); *Caricatures Blue Note* BN-LA-633-G; *A City Called Heaven* with Joe Henderson and Bobby Hutcherson (Landmark LCD-1530-2); *John Coltrane—Black Pearls* (Prestige-7316); *John Coltrane—The Believer* (Prestige-7292); *John Coltrane—The Last Trane* (Prestige-7378); *Art Blakey Big Band* (Bethlehem-6027); *Red Garland—High Pressure* (Prestige 7130); *Red Garland—Dig It* (Prestige 7229); *Sonny Clark—Sonny's Crib* (Blue Note 1576); *Paul Chambers—Whims of Change* (Blue Note 1534).

[12] As cited in Leonard Feather, *The Passion for Jazz* (Da Capo, New York: 1990).

[13] Feather, *Passion for Jazz*, pp. 100–105.

[14] Wilmer, *As Serious as Your Life*, p. 30.

[15] W. E. F. Ward, "Music in the Gold Coast," *Gold Coast Review* 3 (July-December 1927): pp. 222, 223. As cited in Kofi Agawu, "Representing African Music," *Critical Inquiry* 18 (1992): 260.

[16] Columbia 31039.

[17] Atlantic Records, 1977.

[18] Gunther Schuller, liner notes in *Mingus: Epitaph*, CBS Records (1990).

[19] *Jazz Spoken Here*, pp. 49–50.

[20] ECM Records, 1971.

[21] ECM Records, 1972.

[22] Ibid.

[23] Graham Lock, *Forces in Motion: The Music and Thoughts of Anthony Braxton* (New York: Da Capo, 1988), p 196.

[24] *Down Beat,* September 1996, pp. 23–24.

[25] *Down Beat,* January 1996, p. 20.

[26] Ibid., p.18.

[27] Ian Carr, Digby Fairweather, and Brian Priestley, *Jazz: The Rough Guide* (London: Rough Guide, 1995), p. 654.

[28] *Down Beat,* January 1996, p. 20.

[29] Marshall Stearns and Jean Stearns, *Jazz Dance: The Story of American Vernacular Dance* (New York: Da Capo, 1994), pp. 21–22.

[30] Wilmer, *As Serious as Your Life.*

[31] Alain Danielou, *Introduction to the Study of Musical Scales* (New Delhi: Oriental Books Reprint Corp., 1979).

[32] John Amira and Steven Cornelius, *The Music of Santeria: Traditional Rhythms of the Bata Drums* (Crown Points, Ind.: White Cliffs Media, 1992), pp. 5–6.

[33] Arthur Taylor, *Notes and Tones: Musician-to-Musician Interviews* (New York: Da Capo, 1993), p. 124.

[34] Ibid., p. 123.

[35] Ibid., pp. 126–27.

[36] *Down Beat,* September 1998, p. 24.

[37] Ibid.

[38] Joseph E. Holloway, ed., *Africanisms in American Culture* (Bloomington: Indiana University Press, 1991).

[39] Meyer, *Music,* p. 7, as cited in *Avant-Garde Jazz Musicians,* pp. 31–33.

[40] Such, *Avant-Garde Jazz Musicians,* pp. 31–33.

[41] Morgenstern, "Ornette Coleman," p. 17.

[42] Rivelli and Levin, *Giants,* p. 54.

[43] Such, *Avant-Garde Jazz Musicians,* pp. 31–33.

XII
Innovators Emerging
between 1980 to 2000

Facts do not cease to exist because
they are ignored.

—Aldous Huxley

African-American Music in American Marketplace

African music developed for thousands of
years before the European slave trade. Once
abducted from their indigenous continent and
isolated as a community in America, Africans
developed music, dance, and other art forms over
hundreds of years in an environment that remained
independent of European socioculture. Thus African-
American music can only be as integrated as are
African-American communities. These communities
stand less divided as America approaches the end of

the twentieth century, but a sociocultural hiatus remains a part of American life.

Music throughout time reflects sociopolitical trends. During the 1970s, African-American music moved gradually from fusion forms to the more solid retrospective styles of the following two decades. Whereas African-American innovators were previously members of a progressive vanguard, young musicians now looked to the past for the lion share of their ideas. Due to a decline in music education in America, and a consequent decline in music appreciation and knowledge, the majority of the African-American and European-American communities began championing similar artistic values. The most popular kinds of "jazz" were those that resembled styles created decades earlier. Without an emphasis on invention and musical exploration, African-American "jazz" musicians began playing a conservative style. This was a break for executives in a Eurocentric "jazz" industry, which never wants to take chances on "products" that have not proven themselves. Record companies focused on packaging the types of fashionable youthful images previously exploited in rock and roll.

Rap and other young styles reasserted degrees of innovation and resourcefulness during the 1980s, but because of the unfortunate separation between young people in the African-American communities and senior Afrocentric innovators, these styles reflected a lack of direct connection to elder progenitors of the "jazz" legacy . The lack of instrumental virtuosity, compositional technique, and technical musical depth within the new American musical styles was largely a consequence of deteriorating American music programs, particularly in inner city schools.

The African-American music that enjoyed the widest dissemination from the mid-1970s to the present, therefore, was retrospective, simplified, and easily duplicated. Evolutionary progress equivalent to that which extended through ragtime, swing, bebop, hard bop, quasi-modal, free "jazz," etc. failed to surface. Unlike no other music, "jazz" transformed its musical elements dramatically at least once a decade for the first seventy years of the twentieth century. It is inevitable that a momentary reprieve from such an intense era of experimentation and discovery would occur at some point.

The media increased its control over artistic expression and dissemination during the 1980 and 1990s. In an open letter to Black Music Radio and the music industry published in *Emerge* magazine, Bob Law suggests that the media take a greater sense of responsibility. He suggests that "Black music radio has the ear of [the younger] generation," and he asks that these industries "help us reclaim the minds of our young." During "this critical time, when violence and confusion abound," Law feels,

> What is needed is a rebirth of the cultural arts movement—music, literature, images, and film totally committed to the empowerment of the African-American community. We must return to the level of liberating ideas. Artists and political activists must be on the same mission; they must resist the seductions of a weaker moral self while moving to sustain a stronger spiritual and more perfect self. The true role of the artist and activist must go beyond protest to become shapers of

the future reality. The Black artist must
link his work to the struggle for the
liberation of his people. Unfortunately,
the best efforts of Black artists seem
trapped within a music industry that
has always been willing to sacrifice the
interest of the artist and community in
order to control the profits and flow of
ideas.

Oscar Brown Jr. once told me that we
will have to free the music so that the
awesome power of the music can free
the people. A conscious Black arts
movement is what is needed. I have a
reasonable   request   for   African
American music industry executives:
Just as you have found innovative ways
to serve your bosses, perhaps you can
find some small way to serve your
people.[1]

In general, by the end of the 20th century,
recorded "jazz" became over-produced, nostalgic, and
replete with what Rob Leurentop called "boardroom
concepts" in an effort to popularize the music for
greater profits. When Miles Davis responded to a
question regarding the term "popular" in a
documentary film on Quincy Jones, he said,
"Popular! Doesn't that mean White music?" Miles
implied that genuine African American music is not
popular unless it is packaged with Eurocentric
consumption in mind. Much of the music of the
1980s and 90s was so intended. Younger African
American musicians were led into neo-classic bebop
and hardbop styles because the music's popularity

was already well established. The cultivation of such qualities of "Black" musicians legitimized the general trends of the majority of European and European American musicians to adopt more retrospective and popular approaches to Afrocentric music. As Eurocentric aesthetics began to dominate "jazz", the most conspicuous results were smooth-jazz, various forms of fusion, retrospective trends, and other parodies and diluted forms of Afrocentric music. Inevitably, this trend will remain as long as Afrocentric music remains increasing exploited, marginalized or dominated by Eurocentric culture.

The problems that African-American innovators confronted at the beginning of the twentieth century remain as the century draws to an end. Some Americans remain troubled whenever African-American artists insist upon self-determination. The society that fabricated race records, elected a "White" King of Swing and a "White" King of Jazz, and denied that African Americans were the creators of "jazz" has made some progress. Nonetheless, Law's request comes at a time when *Down Beat* magazine has proclaimed Brian Setzer the "New King of Swing."[2] One disgruntled journalist recently insinuated that those who acknowledge "jazz" as an African-American invention "have falsified the record, indulging in what Plato calls, in the *Republic*, the Noble Lie."[3] Finally, in an article in the *Wall Street Journal* (January 27, 1999), a writer proclaimed that "open admissions . . . has proved as disastrous to education as Coltrane has been to jazz."[4]

The music industry retained a plethora of labels to categorize African Americans. Many African-American innovators and style setters, nevertheless, have preferred the generic term "music" to describe their art. Differences between Eurocentric and Afrocentric sociocultures are reflected in personal aesthetics and musical style. When artists assert that European-American and African-American musicians have distinct sounds that can be recognized, critics often try to trip them up in blindfold tests and such. All such tests prove are that (1) just as a European American can imitate African-American speaking styles (or vice versa), musicians who learn to imitate the style of an innovator may succeed in deceiving some listeners, and (2) people have varying degrees of contact with a continually changing American society, and each person experiences a variety of sociocultural dimensions despite the racial segregation remaining in America. Experiences of individual musicians in America consistently broaden as the distances between social domains shrink. When racism finally wanes and citizens finally desegregate themselves, it will then be possible to create an American music. Some "jazz" masters feel there is a glimmer of hope on the horizon. When asked about the new recordings made during the 1990s, Randy Weston replied:

> I didn't really listen to new records. I still get up every morning and listen to Art Tatum.

> I'm pleased that finally it looks like the world is recognizing how important Africa is and has been. The music and the culture. People are looking back at history, science and art in Western culture, but so much of all that was already happening first in Africa.[5]

Emphasis Moves from Innovations to Youthful Image

Some claim that Paul Whiteman was a popular artist rather than a "jazz" musician because of low levels of improvisation in his music. American audiences considered Whiteman a "personality" more than an innovative artist. Few people remember Whiteman's instrument. The classification "popular" can be tricky, however. Music of the swing era was very popular. Mozart's *Le Nozze di Figarro* (1786) and other comic operas were popular during the European classical era. Labels of this sort do not necessarily give reliable information regarding musical content.

Charlie Christian, Fats Navarro, Charlie Parker, Miles Davis, and others had established their reputations at an early age. Many of these artists did not live much beyond twenty or thirty years. On June 30, 1982, the Kool Jazz Festival presented a concert of new music performed by seventeen exceptional young musicians. The music was released on the Elektra Musician label (cat. no. 60196-1 R) the following year under the title *The Young Lions*. The following musicians were included:

John Blake-violin
Hamiet Bluiett-baritone saxophone
Ronnie Burrage-drums
Anthony Davis-piano
Paquito D' Rivera-alto saxophone
John Purcell-double/single reeds, flute
Avery Sharpe-electric and acoustic bass

Kevin Eubanks-electric & acoustic guitar
Chico   Freeman-tenor   saxophone,   bass
clarinet, flute
Fred Hopkins-double bass
Wynton Marsalis-trumpet
Bobby McFerrin-voice
James Newton-flute
Daniel Ponce-percussion
Craig Harris-trombone
Jay Hoggard- vibraphone
Abdul Wadud-cello

Saxophonist Dave Murray (b. 1955, one of the
founding members of the World Saxophone Quartet),
bassist Stanley Clarke (b. 1951, who played with
Chick Corea and others), pianist Amina Claudine
Myers (b. 1942),[6] and countless other Young Lions
and Lionesses could have been included in this list.
The goals of the project were specific, however. There
were   no   women   or   European-American   "jazz"
musicians on the recording. In the liner notes to the
album Michael Gibbs (a festival organizer) says, "In
the past few years I've been increasingly aware of a
fresh optimism in the jazz world, a new acceptance
of the music as today's young people discover them
for themselves, and a renewed acceptance of it by
the older fans as they recognize their need for it."
The festival and album were aimed at refuting the
notion that "jazz" was dead, as Nesuhi Ertegun
reveals:

> Self-appointed prophets of gloom have
> long played a monotonous chorus: jazz
> is dying, jazz is dead. For decades,
> generation   after   generation   has
> announced the demise of this besieged

art-form. Jazz died with Jelly-Roll [sic] Morton, we were told, then with Bix, then with Pres, then with Bird.

Those great artists created new styles and made enormous contributions, but jazz didn't end with any of them. It even survived Coltrane and Mingus, Ellington and Armstrong.

This album is dedicated to youth and jazz and survival. The Young Lions know and understand their past. They are aware of jazz roots; they know all about fusion and rock and Berg and Cage. They know free and funk, R&B and J.S.B. . . . they have chosen jazz.

Regardless of whether it was the intention of Ertegun and Bruce Lundvall (who together initiated the project) to establish emphasis on Young Lions as a marketing trademark, the youthful image of rock and roll now transferred to "jazz." Other Young Lions entered the scene in the late 1980s and early 1990s. Peter Watrous ran an article on some of the younger performers in the *New York Times* on June 16, 1991. His article, titled "The Youth Movement Puts Jazz Back in JVC," mentions that the younger players had the advantage of having learned jazz in elementary school, attending magnet schools, and an increasing number of high schools for the performing arts.

Roy Hargrove (b. 1969), one of the most heavily promoted trumpet players to follow Wynton Marsalis, is a gifted Texas-born musician who attended an elementary school that taught jazz.

Marsalis discovered the younger trumpeter when Hargrove later attended a special arts school. While at Berklee College of Music, he commuted to New York to perform with Kenny Barron, Harold Mabern, John Hicks, and other master musicians. Record companies competed for his services after his performance at the Mount Fuji Festival in Japan, resulting in the release of several new albums.

Marlon Jordan is a year younger than Hargrove and developed his full-bodied trumpet sound in his hometown, New Orleans. He attended the prestigious New Orleans Center for the Creative Arts, a magnet school in that city. He comes from a musical family: his mother plays piano; his sister, the violin; his father is a saxophonist and teacher; and his brother is a jazz recording artist on flute. He began practicing six or seven hours daily at age six or seven. He decided to stay in New Orleans, rather than moving to New York, because he appreciated the supportive environment there. The faculty at the creative arts school in New Orleans stressed the importance of knowing musical tradition. Jordan said, "I was brought up around serious music, whether it was John Coltrane or Stravinsky." He attended summer music programs such as Symphony School of America and Tanglewood regularly.

As the young players benefited tremendously from formal preparation, they also gained easy access to the music market place because they presented retrospective music that is highly accessible. That they are all attractive young "stars" is no handicap to music promoters in today's youth oriented culture, where "jazz" musicians can receive a style of promotion and treatment formerly reserved for rock and roll musicians. Nevertheless, musicians who serve as models for this new generation of musicians, and the more adventurous and rebellious players from the 1960s and 1970s, are effectively ostracized from the music scene. Jordan is very much aware of this fact: "I feel sorry for the older musicians; we're in the right place at the right time, and between promoters and audience the demand for young musicians has turned into a bit of a freak show. But it makes me feel good, to show America that young black musicians can be serious and not worry only about the financial rewards."[7]

Guitarist James Whitfield is another young musician who anchors his music in the bebop tradition. He also attended Berklee College and performed there regularly with pianist James Williams. Upon George Benson's recommendation, he gained a contract from Warner Brothers, and he joined Jack McDuff's band.

Terence Blanchard attended the New Orleans Center for the Creative Arts and studied "classical" piano at an early age. At Rutgers University, he studied with Kenny Barron and Paul Jeffries before going on the road with Lionel Hampton in 1982. He and Donald Harrison replaced Wynton and Branford Marsalis in the Art Blakey band in the early 1980s. Harrison and Blanchard formed a band in 1986. Harrison has performed on and wrote the music for some of Spike Lee's films (*Mo' Better Blues* and *Jungle Fever*).

Steve Turre is a trombonist and composer. Art Blakey brought Turre from San Francisco to New York in 1973 as a Jazz Messenger. Turre performed and recorded with numerous others and led his own experimental ensembles. He is one of the most imaginative and gifted trombone virtuosos of his generation. Turre expressed his virtuosity as a trombonist in both traditional and avant-garde idioms and has composed music in fresh new ways. He is one of the world's greatest performers on the conch shells, and he has recorded the "jazz" classic "All Blues" and many other compositions on that unusual instrument.

Cellist, composer, and improviser Akua Dixon Turre plays in Quartette Indigo. The ensemble (which includes her sister, Gayle) has recorded on Carmen McRae albums and for Dizzy Gillespie's music for the film, *Winter in Lisbon*. Quartette Indigo also provided music for James Blood Ulmer's album for guitar and string quartet. Dixon arranges or composes most of the quartet's music. She worked with the Neo-Bass Ensemble, performed on the soundtrack for Spike Lee's *School Daze*, and played on Turre's albums *Right There*, *Fire and Ice*, and others. In the late 1980s she received a Rockefeller grant to compose her work the *Opera of Marie Laveau*, presented at the Henry Street Settlement House Playhouse. Dixon also sang on Archie Shepp's album *Attica Blues Big Band* in the late 1970s.

Bassist Christian McBride was another successful "young lion." At the end of the twentieth century he made the following comments:

> The whole "young lions" hype which, unfortunately, I was a part of, peaked in the early 1990s. I say "unfortunately" because the hype was so strong, I don't think any musician from that "movement" will ever be looked upon by certain people as serious musicians. We'll be looked at as puppets for the record companies and managers, or People magazine-type

personalities. Record companies, of course, jumped on the hype to sell some records, and they did ... for a while.

After the young lion hype died down, the focus was put on what's known as "concept" records (i.e. X plays the music of Y; X plays love songs; X plays music for driving to. Fortunately, there have been some concept records that have been wonderful, but I believe that when a record company tries to FORCE a "vibe" on a record, rather than letting the music flow on its own power, we will hear some very untrue CDs. Which, in my opinion, flooded the market in the '90s.[8]

Families of Musicians

Wynton Marsalis (b. 1961), one of the leading trumpeters today, was trained in the European classical tradition and repertoire. Louis Armstrong and Miles Davis also influenced Marsalis. Trumpeter Charles Tolliver points out that Marsalis's approach to the trumpet is also clearly related to that of trumpeter Al Hirt. His adroit musicianship, aided by a recording contract with Columbia Records early in his career, propelled Marsalis into the forefront of the Young Lions movement in the eighties. Whereas other African-American artists had demonstrated deft skill in both African-American and European art music (Arthur Davis, Hubert Laws, Dorothy Donegan, Branford Marsalis, and Keith Jarrett, among others), Marsalis has proved to be more controversial, largely due to his high profile and outspoken disposition.

Wynton Marsalis comes from a musical family. His father is a "jazz" pianist of note. Branford Marsalis (b. 1960), a Tonight Show band leader for several seasons, has become one of the leading saxophonists today. His style crosses traditional "jazz" boundaries into rap and other popular music. He studied with the distinguished New Orleans clarinetist Alvin Batiste at Southern University, and with Frank Foster and Barry Harris while attending the Berklee College of Music in Boston.

Wynton's brother Branford joined the Art Blakey band after the drummer heard him when he visited Wynton in New York. He later worked with Clark Terry and others. In addition to his skill as a "jazz" performer, Branford demonstrated superb command of the soprano saxophone and twentieth-century European repertoire on his 1986 recording *Branford Marsalis: Romances for Saxophone.* Delfeayo Marsalis is a fine trombonist while another brother, Jason, plays the drums. As with Joshua Redman (son of Dewey Redman), drummer Denardo Coleman (Ornette Coleman's son), drummer T. S. Monk (Thelonious Monk's son), and other offspring of professional "jazz" artists, the Marsalis children have benefited from having parents who are professional musicians.

Sharp contrasts between styles and philosophies often exist between family members. In an interview for *Down Beat* magazine with Wynton and Branford Marsalis from 1982, we find such differences. There is also agreement on fundamental issues. Wynton expresses an aversion to the term "jazz" because "it's now taken on the context of being everything. Anything is jazz. Quincy Jones' shit is jazz; David Sanborn . . . that's not to cut down Quincy or David. I love funk, it's hip. No problem to it. The thing is, if it'll sell records to call the stuff jazz, they'll call it jazz. They call Miles' stuff jazz. That stuff is not jazz, man. Just because somebody played jazz at one time doesn't mean they're still playing it."[9]

Branford agrees on that point. "Cats come up to me and say: 'What do you think of Spyro Gyra?' And I say: 'I don't.' That's not an insult to Spyro Gyra. I just don't like it when people call it jazz when it's not." Wynton: "Music goes forward, Music doesn't go backward. Whatever the cats couldn't play before you, you're supposed to play." Branford: "There's a huge movement for the perpetuation of ignorance in jazz."

Regarding music in the concert halls, Wynton feels it hasn't hurt the music because the club scene was already deteriorating. He also thinks, "one of the biggest problems is that nobody wants to do somebody else's song. Everybody thinks that they can write great tunes, and all the public wants is that it sounds different. Music has to be played before it gets old. The music that Ornette Coleman played, that Miles and Trane played in the '60s, some of the stuff that Mingus and Booker Little and Charlie Rouse and these cats were starting to do . . . that music isn't old because nobody else has ever played it."

Wynton's extensive training in European "classical" music led to a special citation as Outstanding Brass Player from the Berkshire Music School in Tanglewood, and to performances under the baton of Seiji Ozawa, Leonard Bernstein, and other distinguished conductors. He began studies at

Juilliard, and was a substitute trumpeter in a Broadway pit orchestra as he began touring with Art Blakey in 1979. "Music has a tradition that you have to understand before you can move to the next step," he says. "But that doesn't mean you have to be a historian."

Currently, many critics and fans consider Wynton Marsalis to be the most influential exponent of "jazz." In 1984 he won Grammy Awards for both a classical recording and a jazz recording, performing primarily in the hard bop and bebop idioms. He was awarded the Pulitzer Prize for his opera *Blood on the Fields* in 1997.

Wynton ventured out as featured soloist with his own band after his extraordinary debuts with Art Blakey and Herbie Hancock at the age of twenty-one. At one time he refused to take seriously the music of Cecil Taylor, Anthony Braxton, the Art Ensemble of Chicago, and other more emancipated styles of "jazz." His position has softened a bit with maturity. Taylor has commented that Marsalis is more respectful in person than his earlier comments might have suggested. Nevertheless, his general attitude about "jazz" aligns with those of his close associate, writer Stanley Crouch: "The jazz musician wields power that is neither melodramatic nor obnoxious, achieving individuality through the collective affirmation of the swinging band, now and again meditating on the moment at the piano keyboard and orchestrating the individual consciousness through the paces of blues and swing."[10]

No single individual's set of perspectives can serve as the basis for defining a music as broad and elusive as "jazz." In the March 1997 issue of *Jazz Times*, saxophonist-composer Henry Threadgill contributed a more equitable analysis: "There are those people who are trying to protect [jazz] or say exactly what it is, and they're destroying it, because it grew from the mere fact that it embraced all the things that were available, from the Caribbean, from Spanish music, everything. It was all these things that allowed [jazz] to happen and it has been those types of ideas that have made it progress."

John McDonough presents another aspect of Wynton's philosophy in an article titled "Original Intent Comes to Jazz" (*Wall Street Journal*, July 21, 1992). One of the most interesting things in the article was the conflict between Gunther Schuller and Wynton Marsalis. Marsalis felt that "jazz" musicians have to play notes their own way, while Schuller's desire was to create jazz "repertory" music. Schuller apparently feels that since people today obviously can't hear a band lead by Louis Armstrong, Duke Ellington, or Count Basie, there's nothing wrong with modern bands performing the old classics for the modern audiences. Schuller claims that "just as every symphony has within it the possibility of individual interpretation without altering a note, . . .so does jazz repertory." Marsalis realizes that "jazz" is not the same as European art music, and so do most other African-American musicians and musicologists. It is as absurd to copy a Louis Armstrong recording note for note in performance and insist on calling the results "jazz." It would be equally inappropriate to improvise on a Mozart symphony and call it European "classical" music. As McDonough points out, "It does not surprise Mr. Schuller that some of the fiercest attacks against [Schuller's desire] have come from black musicologists, who complain that it imposes a Eurocentric view on something that is Afrocentric.

Their conflict is just one aspect of the overall fight going on now over the history of jazz."

On some level, the difference between Schuller's Eurocentric viewpoint and that of most Afrocentric "jazz" innovators is a cultural one that existed throughout "jazz" history. Ben Sidran concludes:

> Whereas white society in America tends to be *conformist*, black culture is collective, or communal. This is due, partially, to its reliance on music as a socializing agent. Black culture did not need *formal* entertainment the way whites did. Rather, it sought an outlet through which Negroes could more or less entertain themselves. The commercial orientation of whites during the twenties was primarily responsible for the subsequent return to segregated (i.e., black jazz for black audiences) music of the thirties and was a major event in the evolution of a self-consciousness within black culture.[11]

Benny Goodman expressed the prevailing Eurocentric "jazz" aesthetic of his day when he said, "I am such a bug on accuracy in performance, about playing in tune, and want just the proper note values . . . in the written parts, I wanted it to sound as exact as the band could possibly make it."[12] Sidran continues:

> Conversely, black musicians, even within the big band context, developed idioms that relied on no written parts.

> Count Basie's band had up to seventeen men playing harmonically and rhythmically advanced music without any music. The black player, even as he was becoming more involved with harmonic exploration, relied on his ear rather than his ability to read music to find his way through the technical maze. In the midst of an increasingly complex environment, the black musician turned to the free-flowing oral modes; hence, he played "off the beat" to avoid the stagnant feel of Goodman's "on the beat" precision; he used increased vocalization, or tone "impurity," to help break through the passive detachment of big band work and to return the emotional honesty to jazz idioms.[13]

In the debates and opinions regarding the impact the "Young Lions" have had on "jazz" music, the spiritual aspect of modern "jazz" receives little mention. Perhaps a conspicuous emphasis on technical mastery replaced spiritual considerations. An important aspect of the "Young Lions" phenomenon, nevertheless, reminds us that the music of the past is not a series of temporary, disposable fads so shallow that we can quickly move from style to style—forgetting or discarding the value of the previous era in a headlong quest for something "different." The so-called "neoclassical" African-American musician realizes that the blues will neither be fully explored, nor its rich set of potentials depleted, for some time. (Perhaps its influence will last as long as the three-hundred-year reign of

European tonal harmony.) From some perspectives, nonetheless, the problem is that "neoclassicists" fail to maintain the high levels of innovation that supply integral and characteristic ingredients to "jazz" evolution. One could spend a lifetime learning the vocabularies that Tatum, Bird, Ellington, Coltrane, Dolphy, Monk, Miles, etc., left for posterity, however. Critics suggest that many good musicians (during the 1980s) got stuck on the "etudes" left by certain earlier "jazz" masters , while others side-stepped the grueling initiation required of past innovators in a rush to popular exposure and validation.

Dewey Redman (b. 1931) collaborated with his son Joshua (b. 1969) on the elder Redman's album *Dewey Redman Featuring Joshua Redman: African Venus* (Evidence Music, 1994). In the liner notes Redman says, "I would like if I'm not categorized, stylized. Like, if someone heard me and said, 'Oh, that's Dewey Redman,' I don't think I'd like that. What I'd like, in whatever context—it may be symphonic, anything—you'd hear me and say, 'That's a good player.' My ambition is not to be a stylist—I think of myself as a student of music, and I study all kinds in order to project myself and make my music better."

The personnel on the recording include Dewey Redman (tenor, alto sax, musette), Joshua Redman (tenor sax), Charles Eubanks (piano), Anthony Cox (bass), Carl Allen (drums), and Danny Sadownnick (percussion). Dewey spent most of the sixties in the Bay Area, where the community was exploring the new freedoms expressed by Coltrane and Ornette Coleman. He went with Keith Jarrett's quartet during the 1970s, moving stylistically from a period of intense concentration to a more languid lyricism. He finally formed his own ensemble, Old and New Dreams.

Joshua's mostly mainstream tenor playing is muscular, exciting, and precise. Understandably, the younger Redman's has not yet fully developed the level of musical flexibility and freedom found in his father's mature style. Dewey's musical depth is evident, incorporating a variety of styles from straight ahead to liberated approaches.

Chico (Earl) Freeman (b. 1949) is the son of notable tenor saxophonist Von Freeman (b. 1922). Von did not release his own album until 1972, but, as Rahsaan Roland Kirk observed, he had influenced the saxophone in Chicago for over a decade. "How he has been overlooked in jazz is a crime," complained Sonny Stitt.[14] The launching of Chico's career was more fortunate. He studied with Muhal Richard Abrams and Joe Daley, and became an AACM member in 1972. After settling in New York in 1976, he worked with Cecil McBee, Sam Rivers, Elvin Jones, Don Pullen, Sun Ra, and others. He also recorded and toured with his father and with an innovative band called The Leaders.

The Age of the Freelance Musician

The 1980s and 1990s present an era dominated by individual leaders and freelance musicians. There are groups of musicians who have replaced the communal training "camps" established by Ellington, Sun Ra, the Modern Jazz Quartet, the Mingus Jazz Workshop, the Art Ensemble of Chicago, and similar ensembles. The interest of most earlier innovators was geared toward creating artistic environments where musical minds could gather to cultivate mutual vocabularies. The musical styles and languages that manifested through such processes provided models often imitated by younger generations of musicians.

Traditional vocabularies allow those who settle into them the opportunity of becoming "lions" at an earlier age. Just as young musicians become impressive performers of European art music, the same is true in "jazz" once the artistic and technical goals become fixed or standardized. There have been rare instances of teenage virtuosi establishing convincing musical languages and styles. Reproducing traditional styles as and end in itself drastically simplified conceptual problems, though the technical challenge remains tremendous.

Innovators created a musical legacy consisting of expressive innovative forms. New generations must continue to explore the world and the inner self in the pioneering spirit of Duke Ellington, Billie Holiday, Mary Lou Williams, Charlie Parker, Charles Mingus, John Coltrane, Eric Dolphy, Cecil Taylor, Sun Ra, and countless others African-American innovators.

As the Young Lions advance in age, prestige, and wisdom, they continue to provoke controversy. Wynton Marsalis's interest in European music seems to have changed directions as he matured. He apparently lost the need to validate himself to mainstream America in that regard. Perhaps a similar transition will occur within neoclassic "jazz" styles as artists continue along a path toward finding unique voices. As artistic director for the Jazz Department at Lincoln Center, Marsalis has done a fine job elevating the status of "jazz." With Dr. Billy Taylor's Jazz at the Kennedy Center, African-American musicians have for the first time held prominent positions at two of America's prestigious cultural centers. Marsalis' presence has caused many European-American critics to lash out at him for an assortment of reasons. Predictably, an African-American outspoken musician such as Marsalis has left Eurocentric critics in an uproar.

The *NYSO Journal* published an article that asked, "Despite his enormous contributions to jazz over the last 10 years, are Wynton Marsalis' notions of the jazz aesthetic limiting the reach of jazz at Lincoln?"[15] The scope of Marsalis' projects augments and blends into the Lincoln Center's structure, which essentially includes European ballet, opera, and symphonic music. Nonetheless, the editor asks, "Though already one of the most sparkling and exciting trumpeters on the scene, is Roy Hargrove properly equipped to tackle a composing commission at Lincoln Center as he did last September?" He suggests that Phil Woods, Steve Lacy, and others would be more appropriate choices for some of Marsalis' concerts. The article admits that

> There can be no quibble with the execution of Lincoln Center jazz presentations. They are well-rehearsed (significant paid rehearsal time is admirably built into each and every Jazz at Lincoln Center presentation), beautifully staged and sound reinforced, . . . finely crafted programming, with an overall emphasis on good taste that often elevates the presentations to event status. Marketing materials have been very extensive, advertising is significant and characteristically high-toned, and

insightful programs are the rule rather
than the exception. The educational
program appears to be impeccable.
Audiences have been eager, alert,
demographically varied, respectful,
sizable, and there is ample evidence of
repeat ticket buyers.

On the basis of the editor's comments, it
seems that the problem is not one of lack of quality
but a disappointment that Wynton has not chosen
other players and composers for his performances.
Other writers (Lincoln Collier, for instance) are less
evasive and make it known that they would like to
see more European-American musicians on-stage.
Marsalis counters that he chooses the best
musicians he can get for the concerts, many of
whom are European Americans (he generally lists
them to refresh memories). Kevin Whitehead took
such a high-handed approach to reviewing one of
Marsalis' concerts that Wynton decided to respond in
print and held no punches.

Whitehead's article claimed that the
"Wyntonians" (as he referred to them) failed to "cut it
technically."[16] He continued to insult Marsalis and
the performers by suggesting, "Patrons paid $35 to
listen to on-the-job training, which raises the larger
issue of why Jazz at Lincoln Center really exists: to
educate the public about and expose it to quality
jazz, or to subsidize Wynton's working groups, whose
members are heavily featured uptown?"

Readers would have to search long and hard
to find similar comments (in print) hurled at
European-American musicians of Marsalis' caliber
and position. The following excerpts are from
Wynton's straightforward and exhaustive reply:

As one reared in a tradition that greatly respects "playing the dozens," I have often enjoyed the twelve or thirteen years of insults posing as aesthetic insight from some segment of what masquerades as the jazz critical community. Normally, I take the position that nothing below me can hurt me, and nothing above me would, but a recent article by Kevin Whitehead in the Voice's jazz supplement—"It's Jazz, Stupid"—was such a mixture of personal attack, · attempted condescension, and disinformation that I have decided, finally, to step down into his arena, where arrogance and ignorance are served up in place of information. This must end. It is not the fact of criticism that disturbs me; criticism can easily lead to enlightenment for the musician and listener. I am disturbed, however, by our neophyte pundit's combination of inaccuracy and disrespect, which proves, under scrutiny, that if he thinks any one is stupid, it must be our audiences, who have enthusiastically supported our efforts for the past seven years with sold-out concerts and standing ovations . . .

My integrity is then impugned by the insinuation that Jazz at Lincoln Center concerts are being used to subsidize my band members. My band members are on my annual payroll. We play about 120 concerts a year. The three or four concerts we play at Lincoln Center have negligible impact on our financial situation. To imply that an old boy system has to be in place for the public to want to hear Marcus Roberts [who won the 1st annual Thelonious Monk competition] or Herlin Riley or Wessel Anderson, is inappropriate and disrespectful.

Marsalis introduces a question that many African-American innovators have often posed privately when confronted with arrogance from Eurocentric critics: "Who has this writer studied with or played with, and what is the source of his authority other than poor editorial decisions?" He continues: "Henceforth, I want to make it clear that I will no longer silently tolerate your willful disrespect of the skills required to play jazz music. I will be responding to inaccuracies in your reporting when I am made aware of it. My intention is not just to expose you for the charlatans that you are, but to supply the public with another opinion."[17]

Wynton Marsalis is a tremendous talent focused on furthering "jazz" tradition. He has gained a great amount of respect from his peers and audiences. He insists that respect be paid to the "jazz" tradition. Regardless of subjective analysis of his style, he has certainly contributed more to the development and perpetuation of African-American music than Whitehead or other self-appointed critics.

Jazz at Lincoln has continued to evolve since 1987, when Alina Bloomgarden, Lincoln Center's director of visitor services, started a concert jazz program to take advantage of the vacant concert halls in August. On December 18, 1995, the Lincoln Center Board awarded the institution's "jazz" department equal status with the New York Philharmonic, the Metropolitan Opera, the New York City Ballet, and the other constituents of the complex. Respect has been slow to arrive in America, but "jazz" evolution continues.

Snapshot: Bay Area "Jazz" in the Early 1980s

The distinction often made to separate East Coast "jazz" during the 1940s and 50s from West Coast variety generally determines that the East Coast variety is more experimental and vibrant. The comparison often weighs the accomplishments and styles of musicians in and around Los Angeles and San Francisco against innovative musicians in New York City. During World War II and in the postwar years, the Bay Area flourished for a while, and San Francisco became a hotbed for "jazz." Miles, Coltrane, and most other important artists of the day came through the Bay Area, performing at "jazz" establishments like the Blackhawk, the Hungry I, Jazz Workshop, Jimbo's Bop City, the Island of Jazz, the Matador, and the Keystone Corner. During the late 1970s and early eighties, the Bay Area was a haven for experimentation involving highly varied, novel, and personal stylistic approaches including multi-ethnic and interdisciplinary presentations.

The Center for World Music at the Fort Mason Cultural Center, a 126-year-old fort that occupies one of the most dramatically beautiful areas on the Bay, is the gateway to the 35,000-acre park called the Golden Gate National Recreation Area on San Francisco's waterfront. Since 1977, Fort Mason has provided performance spaces, exhibitions, workshops, and classes for thousands of people and hundreds of organizations. It became a vibrant arts center, presenting a rich cross-section of various art forms from around the world. New dance presentations, mime, poetry, television and film workshops, feminist theater, children's programs, etc., were a part of Fort Mason's daily schedule of events.

During 1981, for example, Fort Mason presented an array of interesting music and interdisciplinary events. The "Festival of the Sea" was an eclectic presentation featuring the Chinese Instrumental Ensemble, directed by Sek Cheong Siu; Los Travadores, playing Mexican jarocho harp repertoire; and a concert titled "Anglo-Irish Sea Shanties," with Stan Hugill, Jon Bartlett, and Rika Ruebsatt. A North Indian Classical Music Festival with Hariprasad Chaurasia (flute), Malabika Kanan (female vocalist), Zakir Hussain, and others also took place as a part of the festival.

Indian virtuoso Ali Akbar Khan (a virtuoso whose father played over two hundred musical instruments) opened a School of North Indian Music in Marin County during this period. Khan had lived in the Bay Area for thirty years. He performed with his brother-in-law Ravi Shankar, alto saxophonist John Handy, Bola Sete, and violinist L. Subramaniam performed on numerous occasions. These musicians performed a mixture involving "jazz" and North Indian music in various Fort Mason performance spaces.

Malonga Casquelourd and Fua Dia Congo, Viva Brasil, and Klezmorim (a sextet) were other concerts presented at the center. In 1981 the last of these revived the four-centuries-old East European Yiddish musical tradition. There was also music of the Middle East with "Jazayer." The Kearny Street Workshop and Fort Mason presented the First Annual Asian Jazz Festival in the Fort Mason Conference Center. The Asian "jazz" concerts featured Russel Baba (flutist/saxophonist) with drummer Eddie Moore; Mark Izu (bass), with clarinetists Paul Yamazaki and Ray Collins; guitarists Makoto Horiuchi and Peter Fuji with bass guitarist Shido. The tendency toward cross-cultural music activity of this period eventually led to a strong "world beat" movement in the Bay Area.

A group of experimental musicians, sometimes referred to as the "Heralds of California's 'third wave'" by the press, also performed frequently at Fort Mason and a variety of other alternative performance spaces throughout the San Francisco Bay Area. The New College of California presented a series of concerts during 1981–82 featuring Andrew Hill, the Rova Saxophone Quartet, Sonny Simmons and Barbara Donald, the Billy Bang/John Lindberg Dual, solo percussion by Eddie Moore, Paul Stevens and the Eulipian Ensemble, Leon Williams and Impact 77, United Front, Karlton Hester and the Contemporary Jazz Art Movement (CJAM), and many other artists. The performance hall in which the concerts occurred was formerly a funeral chapel, but the festival was very much alive. In 1982 (February through April), CJAM produced a series of eight concerts (featuring a host of musicians, dancers, poets, and visual artists) in another festival at San Francisco's Western Addition Cultural Center. A

review of one of the festivals presented at the New
College printed in *Down Beat* (July 1981) displays
some of the diversity of the programming.

> Trumpeter George Sams organized this
> three-night festival in February at the
> New College of California in celebration
> of Black History Month. . . . It was
> James Newton's first S.F. appearance,
> and his expressive solo flute quickly
> entranced his audience. His original
> compositions were tributes: a lyrical
> portion of *Dream of Freedom* (for Paul
> Robeson) and *Toru* (for Japanese
> composer Toru Takemitsu). Packed
> with overblown notes, multiphonics,
> and cascading colors, *Toru* explored the
> tonal range and spectrum of the flute's
> possibilities.

> . . . Images of a caravan traveling
> through the desert were conjured by
> *Africa 456 According to Herodotus*,[18]
> Karl Hester's composition for the
> Contemporary Jazz Art Movement.[19]
> The group includes some of the Bay
> area's finest . . . Percussion, congas,
> traps, two basses, and piano created a
> textural   rhythmic   undercurrent
> functioning as an open ended drone.
> Oboe, bassoon, bass flute, clarinet, and
> English horn added to the Oriental
> flavor.

At midnight, pianist Horace Tapscott
began his solo set with a sharp,

crashing attack, as if to clear the air. An orchestral collage of sound then emerged from his keyboard; a pleasing shock of richness and variation, contrasting themes woven through several modes, fleeting insights into *Motherless Child, Well You Needn't,* and countless other tunes.[20]

Master saxophonists Joe Henderson, John Handy, and Pharaoh Sanders; pianist Ed Kelly and Andrew Hill; violinist Michael White, bassist James Leary, and drummer Eddie Moore were just a sampling of the world-class artists living and performing around the area. Music was everywhere in the San Francisco Bay Area during this period. An organization called Music by the Bay (in cooperation with Bay Area Music and radio station KJAZ) presented "Jazzmo" in September 1981. Funding from the San Francisco Hotel Tax Fund, and assisted by the Hyatt Regency, radio stations KMEL, KMPX, and KBLX, made "Jazzmo" an entire month of concerts. Over forty performances came under the "Jazzmo" umbrella. Performance spaces throughout the region opened their door to the celebration, featuring the Bishop Norman Williams Quintet; Eddie Moore and Creative Force featuring Eddie Henderson, Mary Watkins, Linda Tillery, Alive, Ed Kelly Quintet, Pee Wee Ellis and the Assembly, Pony Poindexter, Idris Ackamoor, Mel Martin and Listen, Oakland Jazz Complex Orchestra, Rasul Siddik and the Now Artet, Russel Baba, CJAM, and Women in Jazz Seminars.

Music was not restricted to usual venues. The Haight Street Theater and the Charles Turner Gallery presented the George Sams Quartet, Night

Escape with Abdul Waahid, CJAM, and others. Noe Valley Ministry presented Noe Valley Music. The Theater Guild of San Francisco presented Gamelan Sekar Jaya (music and dance of Bali) with I Wayan Suweca, director and dancer I Nyoman Wenten, and French mime in Eliane Walis's *Imagenes* (with CJAM) at the Victoria Theater on 16th Street at Mission. During Black History Month (February 1982), the Oakland Theater of Dance (directed by Jane Brown) presented Duke Ellington's *Such Sweet Thunder* at the Laney College Theater. *Such Sweet Thunder* is a work composed by Ellington and arranged by Billy Strayhorn in 1957. It is a classic suite of twelve thematic portraits dedicated to the peerless Avon poet.

The mix continued to heat up with a host of other experimental and traditional events. The Metropolitan Art Center (Geary at Van Ness) presented a variety of "jazz" combos as well as other solos, duets, and interesting ensembles. An outdoor series at the Golden Gate Park Band Shell held a Conga Drum Festival featuring Batucaje, Babatunde, Kwaku Dadey, Peraza and Flores Percussion Ensemble, and other guest artists. An African Cultural Festival featuring UC Berkeley musicologist C.K. Ladzekpo, Jose Lorenzo, and O.J. Ekemode, took place at the Oakland Auditorium Theater. The Julia Morgan Center on College Avenue in Berkeley invited Batucaje to join them in a concert of folk and ethnic music. The Intertribal Music House presented an "American Indian Music Festival." The People's Cultural Center on Valencia Street (in the Mission District) created a series of performances involving various duets, trios, and quartets. The Communications Center on Sacramento Street funded by the Friends of the San Francisco Public

Library presented a similar series. Kuumba Cultural Center in Santa Cruz presented some of the most interesting concerts in the greater Northern California area, featuring artists such as Sonny Simmons and Barbara Donald, the Art Ensemble of Chicago, Sun Ra, Oliver Lake, CJAM, Anthony Braxton, and many others. Dimension Dance Theater presented African-American dance by director and choreographer Debra Vaughan (with co-founder Elendar Barnes).

There were also "jazz" concerts at the Great American Music Hall that featured Betty Carter, Bobby McFerrin, Ed Kelly, Pharoah Sanders, and others. Keystone Korner, on Vallejo St. in North Beach, had George Cables, Billy Harper, Freddie Hubbard, Tito Puente, McCoy Tyner, Sheila Jordan, Horace Silver, Arthur Blythe, Toots Thielemans, Brazilian musicians Jose Lorenzo and Airto Moreira, and other familiar names on its schedule. Lorenzo's fifteen-member dance, and music company Batucaje (composed of an international group of performers from Brazil, Nicaragua, the Philippines, etc.) also performed at Fort Mason.

The Kronos Quartet, then a young string ensemble serving as artists in residence at Mills College in Oakland, presented a concert in the Museum of Modern Art's Green Room. McCoy Tyner and Cecil Taylor also performed there.

Because the high level of intensity that characterized that period was not sustained sufficiently, many of the Bay Area's creative artists gradually migrated to New York and abroad. For a moment in the early 1980s, however, the San Francisco Bay Area produced innovative "jazz" and world music in a balanced, interdisciplinary setting. The "joint was jumpin'."

This period inspired a subsequent Asian-American "jazz" scene that continues to evolve. Today's seekers of Afro-Asian synthesis, such as Miya Masaoka (a Japanese American koto player who recently recorded an album of Thelonious Monk's music), violinist Jason Huang and baritone saxophonist Fred Ho (both are Chinese Americans), continue to create innovative "jazz" influenced music that affirms their own ancestral identities. The Bay Area remains an exciting place for music.

The Contemporary Midwestern "Jazz" Scene

"Jazz" musicians such as bassists Richard Davis (of Madison, Wisconsin) and Don Mayberry (Farmington Hills, Michigan), pianists Pamela Wise, Teddy Harris, and Harold McKinney, trumpeters Marcus Belgrave and Charles Moore, reedman Wendell Harrison, cellist David Baker, and drummer Leonard King, Jr. (all from Detroit, Michigan), are but a few among the growing number of artists developing a thriving scene in the Midwest. The area includes Illinois, Iowa, Indiana, Michigan, Minnesota, Ohio, Wisconsin, and the Dakotas. Arts Midwest and other arts organizations support cultural and educational programs that stimulate "jazz" activities that have evolved into a vital urban force.

During the 1960s Wendell Harrison (b. 1943) lived in New York and performed with the Joe Henderson-Kenny Dorham Big Band, Betty Carter, Charles Tolliver, Jimmy Owens, Art Pepper, with Jack McDuff and others on the "organ grinder circuit" (Harlem, Newark, Patterson). He played the saxophone much of the time, but eventually fell in love with the clarinet. Harrison performed and recorded with his clarinet ensemble (composed of a variety of soprano, alto, and bass clarinets, with rhythm section). His latest recordings are available on his Wenha label.

In the early 1970s the vibrant Detroit club life of earlier days declined with the downward spiral of the city's industrial base. Detroit musicians soon countered, forming informal collectives and developing community-rooted forums for the presentation of their music. Wendell Harrison was an entrepreneur and "cultural activist" who advanced alternatives to the nightclub circuit and conventional music business channels.

Harrison formed an interdisciplinary organization called Tribe. Tribe began as a performing ensemble with Belgrave, Moore, Harrison, bassist Will Austin, and trombonist Phil Ranelin among its members. It eventually emerged to include a highly topical magazine with a focus on "jazz;" an independent record label; an advertising agency; and a graphic design company. Today Harrison and his wife, Pamela Wise, run Rebirth Inc., which produces concerts featuring Ellis Marsalis, Freddie Hubbard, Jerry Gonzalez, Karlton Hester, Hank Jones, Don Byron, and other artists. Some Rebirth guest artists perform on WDET Radio in Detroit, on the radio show "Destination Out," hosted by Kim Heron.

Geri Allen (b. 1957) is a pianist, teacher, composer, recording, club, and concert artist who is emerging as an innovative force in Detroit. She taught at Howard University before being ranked among the critics' choices in *Down Beat* and winning first place as Talent Deserving Wider Recognition in 1993. After moving to New York, Allen worked with

Oliver Lake, Joseph Jarman, Lester Bowie, Betty Carter, Steve Coleman, and a host of other innovators. Her style reflects her interest in the music of Thelonious Monk and Herbie Nichols, but Allen has developed a unique voice of her own. Her recordings reflect her wide range of interest. She was an early member of the M-Base Collective and appeared on three of their recordings. She has also appeared with Ornette Coleman, Ralph Peterson, Dewey Redman, and Wallace Roney. Allen and pianist Hank Jones (another Michigan native) were the subjects of a January 1994 *Down Beat* cover article , "Me and Mister Jones," by Howard Mandel.

In 1991 Violinist **Regina Carter** moved to New York from her hometown, Detroit. By 1996 she was performing a series of concerts at Sweet Basil in New York with trombonist Steve Turre's ensemble. Although her first recordings were of the smooth-jazz variety, her live performances with Turre, and later with pianist Kenny Barron's (b. 1943) group, display Carter's impeccable musicianship, virtuosity and imagination. While performing Turre's "Blackfoot" (an extremely brisk composition that uses the chords of "Cherokee") at one of her first New York appearances Carter remembers thinking, "Oh my God, they think I can't play, they probably think the only reason Steve hired me was because I'm a woman!" Soon her audiences knew differently. Her natural lyricism is captivating. Carter says:

> "Part of it, I've been told, is an energy that I have when I play, even if I'm really nervous or I'm not quite sure how I'm going to get back to shore. I had a big band teacher who always said if you're going to make a mistake, do it

> loud and do it with vengence. So I just
> give it my all. Maybe I can't play as
> many notes or as many complicated
> phrases as other people play, but it
> really comes from inside."

While touring with Wynton Marsalis' Blood on the Fields production, Carter's finale brought down the house.[21] Her performances with Wynton Marsalis and Cassandra Wilson brought highly favorable reviews from the press, eventually leading to an opportunity to headline her own group at Sweet Basil. Her music and reputation continues to evolve and she has signed a contract with Verve Records at a time when many other artists are being dropped.

Rap and Hip-Hop Culture

Hip-hop culture emerged in Harlem in 1977. Younger Afrocentric musicians began looking for ways around the limitations and trappings of mainstream culture. Denied access to instrumental music programs, mentors, and musical instruments in inner city schools, African-American youth movements created an innovative music that was not a fusion (like "jazz"-rock, third-stream "jazz", acid-jazz, etc.) of musical elements from past traditions. In the spirit of a long-standing legacy of African-American innovation, young African-American students would not have their creativity stifled by economic limitations. Using materials at hand (including the human body as percussion and the rhythmic scratching of LP vinyl records, young musicians created an innovative personal style of music. The music of Flash, Herc, and Bambataa (from the Bronx), along with new uptown sounds from Kurtis Blow, Spoonie G, and The Sugar Hill Gang were distributed by hand on the streets of New York.

Rap is revolutionary and an original style of music that reflects its urban social environment clearly and efficiently. The Sugar Hill Gang released the first rap track in 1979. This unknown group, with "zero street credibility,"[22] called "Rapper's Delight" was a historic novelty release recorded in a small New Jersey studio. It introduced the world to the music that was emerging from the streets of New York.

The progenitors of rap were able to use independent economical means to produce a form of self-expression that was so socially powerful that it soon began to dominate the popular music scene. Equipped with a stack of records, a stereo mixer, a couple of turntables, and speakers, rap pioneers became the new "gangsters," frankly reflecting African-American culture through its poignant blasts of "noise." Equating rap with various "jazz" styles on a purely technical basis is futile. Hip-hop culture shares roots with "jazz" and other innovative Afrocentric music, but direct access to that virtuosic musical tradition was denied. Authors Havelock Nelson and Michael A. Gonzales claim:

> Without a doubt hip-hop culture can be traced back to the tribes of Africa, back to James Brown sliding across the stage at the Apollo, back to the chatter of men-folk inside a barber shop, and yet, much like Futurism, hip-hop/rap began as an avant-garde arts movement for the people on the street who were tired of the same-o, same-o.

Although the hip-hop creators paid homage to past musical influences, this new noise was strictly post-modern: constructed (rather than composed) from sounds, bass lines or guitar riffs scratched from existing texts (other records). The noise found on hip-hop tracks could be anything that bounced off the "walls of sound," from cartoon voices to high-pitched screams. As Tisdall and Bozzolla wrote in their book *Futurism*, "Noise did not mean just din and·cacophony . . . the wealth of sound in the world ignored by the conventions of music ranged from the primary noises of nature to the roar of life and machines in the modern city."[23]

Rap uses intriguing and simple rhythmic phrases, motives, and innovative textures to support its poetry. Nevertheless, rappers did not have the opportunity to absorb the rich knowledge contained within the caldron of "jazz" styles and traditions from Afrocentric elders. Rap, as the name implies, places greater emphasis on the rhythms and messages contained within modern "street" language in poetry.

Rap artists are generally much less interested in sophisticated melodies, harmonies, textures, and other musical elements explored in other Western music. This aspect of the art form bothers many "jazz" artists. Socially conscious Rap is akin to the spirit of innovative African-American music through its tenacity, potency, and universal influence among the members of its generation. It employs a rich verbal vocabulary that involves double entendre messages and the sustained intensity of other African and African-American music. Just as numerous critics predicted the death of "jazz," reggae, rhythm and blues, and other Afrocentric music, others stated that hip-hop was only a fad that would disappear on as quickly as it emerged. Two decades have passed since the earliest prognostications; L. L. Cool J, Public Enemy, Ice-T, Queen Latifah, KRS-One, Salt-n-Pepa, Heavy D, Grandmaster Flash, and other veteran rap artists are still on the scene.

Between 1900 and the 1950s, the "dozens" (also referred to as the "Dirty Dozens," "Signifying," "Cap," "Bad Talk," etc.) was an elaborate African-American verbal rhyming social game traditionally involving boys insulting each other's relatives (especially their mothers) in twelve censures. The object of the game was to test the opponent's emotional strength. We can trace loose ties to "rap" tradition back to African-American religious sermons, the "dozens," and to The Last Poets (considered by many the progenitors of rap) and other revolutionary bards from the late 1960s and early 1970s. The liner notes to the 1997 Mercury Records release "The Last Poets: Time Has Come" tell the listener, "Muthafuckas ran f'cover":

Nobody was ready.

Had 'em, scared o' revolution. Scared o'
the whyte man's god complex. Scared o'
subways. Scared o' each other. Scared
o' themselves. And scared o' that totem
of onanistic worship—the eagle-clawed
Amerikkan greenback!

The rhetoric made you mad. The drums made you pop your fingers. And the poetry made you sail on the cushions of a fine hashish high.

Most importantly, they made you think and kept you "correct" on a revolutionary level.

We all connected. 'Cause it was a Black communal thing. Like the good vibes and paper plate of red-peppered potato salad at a neighborhood barbeque. The words and the rhythms were relevant. We joined together around the peace pipe and the drum. And when it came to the rhythm of the drums, the drums said, "check your tired-ass ideology at the door."

Meanwhile, the "hip-hop generation" who've had to grow up without a clue that life can be about something other than non-stop and mostly futile pursuit of that eagle-clawed greenback, has somehow recognized and claimed The Last Poets as the Godfathers of rap. Savvy young rappers have continued to spin 'em on the air.

Problems of breaks in cultural continuity intensified regarding the appreciation of "jazz" in the rap and hip-hop communities, as popular younger music created wealthy young musicians. When people equate musical value with success, then the "jazz" artist has a harder time convincing younger

African-Americans of the intrinsic value and importance of innovative music of the past traditions. Once directly exposed to substantive art of any kind, however, young people develop curiosity, desire to develop better musical skills, and deepen their levels of appreciation for the process of artistic creation. More European-American students study and learn to play "jazz" because of formal exposure to a variety of music before college. African-American students are also more inclined toward music that reflects today's culture and pace. George thinks this difference in attitude is also due to other cultural factors:

> The black audience's consumerism and restlessness burns out and abandons musical styles, whereas white Americans, in the European tradition of supporting forms and style for the sake of tradition, seem to hold styles dear and long after they have ceased to evolve.

> The most fanatical students of blues history have all been white. These well-intentioned scholars pick through old recordings, interview obscure guitarists, and tramp through the Mississippi Delta with the determination of an Egyptologist. Yet with the exception of Eric Clapton and maybe Johnny Winter, no white blues guitarist has produced a body of work in any way comparable to that of the black giants. Blacks create and then move on. Whites document and then

recycle. In the history of popular music, these truths are self-evident.[24]

Rappers fully realized a fact that has remained a capitalist fiat: profit supersedes racism or any other social motive. The young entrepreneurs who sold early rap records on the streets of New York did not become owners of record companies, distribution networks, and publishing rights to the African-American rap music that later turned unprecedented profit. Sylvia Robinson (Sugarhill Records), Russell Simmons (Def Jam), Andre Harrell (Uptown Enterprises), Luther Campbell (Luke Records), and a few other independent and visionary African-American capitalists were the exceptions. In the tradition of older "jazz" innovators, most rap artists gave their music away to enterprising European American business people, as Public Enemy's "media assassin," Harry Allen discussed in *The City Sun*.[25]

It's extremely rare to see a European American male wearing a T-shirt bearing the image of their favorite living African-American musician. A European-American female celebrating such artists is infinitely rarer. The majority culture has not found many opportunities openly to celebrate African-American heroes or heroines. At the end of the twentieth century people are beginning to show greater respect for African-American artists (albeit, in the case of "jazz," more often than not posthumously). Rap is aiding in the integration of the audience for African-American music without sacrificing Afrocentricity. Rap artists are also beginning to cultivate relationships with older "jazz" artists (like the collaboration between Donald Byrd and Guru). This is an important beginning toward the reunification of the African-American community, reuniting generations of music and people after remaining divided and alienated for a half-century. Brief or superficial unions yield shallow results, nonetheless. Big Daddy Kane was asked about his collaboration with jazz musicians and other rappers on a Quincy Jones album in an interview. He said: "That was cool. Me and Quincy talked and he pointed out that what The Last Poets were doing was similar to rap, and he showed the connection. He showed me a picture of his father with a flattop haircut. You know like evolution, everything just turned back around. I thought that it was cool. So the combination was real cool. It's like it was all there, the first generation and the second generation coming together doing the same music."

When pressed further it became apparent that brief collaborations could not produce miracles. It will take more time to produce greater results. Kane said: "Me personally, I'm not into jazz to tell you the truth. So Quincy was sitting there telling me things like they used to call Sarah Vaughn 'Divine Sassy' and she did this. So I'm just taking notes and putting this in rap form."[26]

Contemporary Politics & Labeling African-American Culture

When people attach labels such as gospel, spiritual, blues, "jazz," soul, or rhythm 'n blues to different pieces of music, one might ask: "Why are the various forms of African-American expression categorized as though they were grossly unrelated to each other?" We have a human need to label our environment in easily definable categories to enhance clarity. Important aspects of Afrocentric styles apply mutually to all categories. African-American music shares African roots. Each generation of African-American musicians produces new art forms with noticeable degrees of independence from earlier forms, yet they evolve from related social environments and social constraints (racism and sexism). We can dissect African-American music into distinct styles, but they all developed from a single tradition.

The oppression of African-American artists is not simply a matter of American racism. The hardship that Bach, Mozart, Beethoven, and contemporary European composers endured during their lifetimes is related to the suffering that African-American innovators have encountered. Beethoven's music in particular received many disparaging comments during his lifetime. Some of these descriptions were ridiculous and belittling in ways akin to those critics used to describe African-American innovators. Rellstab, a "romantically inclined and hero-worshipping" fan,[27] was surprised that Beethoven's "face was much smaller than I had pictured it in accordance with the likeness which has forcibly constrained it to an appearance of powerful, genial savagery."[28] The composer's works received adverse criticism on various occasions during his life, but his letter to the music publisher Breitkopf and Haertel of Leipzig (dated April 22, 1801) demonstrates that he soon arrived at conclusions many serious artists can appreciate: "The outcry at first of your critics against me was so humiliating, that when I began to compare myself with others, I could scarcely blame them; I remained quite quiet, and thought they do not understand it.

And I had all the more reason for being quite quiet when I saw how men were praised up to the skies who here are held of little account by the better musicians *in loco*, and who here are almost forgotten."

Music today remains affected by racial and sexual politics nonetheless. Such proclivities are motivated by social insecurity, quests for economic dominance, and ignorance. Since interracial unions are as old as the human species, there are no "pure" races. J. A. Rogers told us that:

> A great deal of American color prejudice, too, is mere deceit. . . . In private life most of the blatant Negrophobes show no prejudice, and are usually well-liked by the Negroes who know them well. Sometimes such [bigots] go out of the way to aid Negroes, as Cole Blease. The latter, when governor of South Carolina turned out Negro convicts by the thousands saying that they had been put in there unjustly. One of the most violent attackers of the Negro in Congress and on the political stump of his own state had a Negro family. The Negro housekeeper was the real boss of his mansion, and the white wife almost a nonentity.
>
> Of course, no right-thinking individual will admire this type of individual. They are that detestable combination of opportunist and hypocrite.[29]

The transformation of Beethoven's physical image by artists over the years is an interesting footnote. A comparison between early portraits and later ones prompted many Afrocentrists in the 1970s to propose that the composer may have been of mixed African and European heritage. Alessandra Comini, in her book *The Changing Image of Beethoven: A Study in Myth Making*, traces the continuous alterations that visual artists made in representing the composer during and after his lifetime. Comini noted that those who knew Beethoven in his extreme youth tended to all keep an "unswerving line of pure physical description." She mentions that a baker named Gottfried Fischer (c. 1780–1864) was the son of the couple who owned the house that Beethoven grew up in Bonn. His "quite self-conscious"[30] description of the "former physique of Herr Ludwig van Beethoven" was as follows: "Short and thick-set, broad across the shoulders, short neck, large head, rounded nose, dark-brown complexion; always leaned forward a little in walking. When still a boy they used to call him 'der Spanol' in our house."[31] Joseph Neeson's silhouette of Beethoven, as well Louis Letronne's 1814 pencil drawing, supports the Bonn baker's description.

According to Comini, an engraving based on Letronne's drawing pleased Beethoven the most. We know that he presented copies of it to visitors and friends. Anton Felix Schindler (c. 1795–1864),[32] Beethoven's devoted (and unpaid) secretary and factotum, spoke reverently of the composer when he said: "Of all the famous musical geniuses, perhaps Beethoven had the head with the most distinctive features, starting with the thick mass of hair and continuing with the forehead, eyes, mouth, and chin in harmonious proportions, in which the only dissonance was the rather broad nose."[33]

Whether Beethoven was "Black" (as some Afrocentric scholars assert) is not the important issue. More significantly, history apparently performed remarkable surgery on certain aspects of particular iconography and description over the years to create a certain image of Beethoven. The color of a composer's skin should have no bearing on the appreciation of her or his works. It is true, nevertheless, that any such postulations infuriate Eurocentrists. The levels of complexity increase exponentially when we hang veils to disguise obvious bias. David Theo Goldberg has interesting ideas along these lines:

> The claim that racism is nothing more than ideological is confusing or delimiting in a different way. It misleadingly leaves the deleterious effects of racist practices and institutions to be captured by some other term like racialism or racist discrimination. Alternatively, by insisting that the raison d'etre of the racist ideological structure is to hide some underlying form of economic, social, or political oppression, this widely shared claim refuses to acknowledge, and so leaves unexplained, the fact that racist expressions may at times define and promote rather than merely rationalize social arrangements and institutions. Sepulveda's characterization of Mexican Indians as fit only for slavery

enabled their enslavement to be conceived rather than simply serving to rationalize their exploitation ex post facto. I will undertake to incorporate the distinctions between belief structure, aims, practices, institutions, principles, and effects into a coherent characterization of the concepts of racism.[34]

Critics of Afrocentrism attacked claims that Egypt had significant influence on Greece. Mary Lefkowitz, in the name of "rational thought," attacked the scholarship of George G. M. James (*Stolen Legacy*, 1954), Martin Bernal (*Black Athena*, vols. 1–2, 1987–91), and other scholars who propose that many achievements accredited to Greek civilization actually have roots in Egyptian and other African history. Although authors such as James, Bernal, Ivan Van Sertima (*They Came before Columbus*, 1976), and Chief Musamaali Nangoli (*No More Lies about Africa*, 1988) generally research their subject according to traditional Western protocol, they are often systematically dismissed as "persistently imprecise." According to Lefkowitz, in her article "Afrocentrism Poses a Threat to the Rational Tradition,"[35] "the Afrocentrists, . . . not only are assigning credit to African peoples for achievements that properly belong to the Greeks; in the process they are destroying what is perhaps the greatest legacy of Greek philosophy—rational thought." Interestingly, Lefkowitz does not provide a single footnote. John E. Coleman and other scholars have reacted to Bernal (in particular) and Afrocentricity in equally agitated fashions.[36]

The things they encounter in the world influence everyone. The Egyptians they encountered in Africa must, have influenced Socrates, Herodotus, and other Greeks. Egyptians absorbed cultural elements from foreign people with whom they came in contact. After four hundred years of tonal music in the West, the twentieth century ushered in two new approaches: the blues and twelve-tone music. The blues, based largely upon a flexible approach to pitch and melody, operated in alliance with tendencies of tonal harmony. Despite this blending, its true nature remained somewhat elusive because the blues was not a result of simple music fusion. Each chord of the basic blues is dominant.[37] In its modern guise, the tendencies toward total chromaticism (clearly outlined in typical blues walking bass patterns), reveal basic formulas that supply musicians like Coltrane devices with which to devise their own twelve-tone approach to "jazz."

Rock and roll, a derivative form of blues, was cordoned off from other African-American music to enhance its salability among the majority population. Various forms of the blues include rhythm and blues that emerged in the 1940s, which became rock and roll in the 1950s. Perhaps a more precise and honest division of "jazz," blues, and rock could be Eurocentric American "jazz," blues, and rock and Afrocentric American "jazz," blues, and rock. Such labels better reflect the conditions extant in American society reflected in American music.

Labeling people and the art they express can never be a simple task if labels are to have substantive meaning.

African-Americans have never consisted of a perfectly harmonized and totally communal fabric. There is tremendous variety among all groups and cultures. In some regions of the United States, African Americans have grown up in a culture that was more European American (or even Hispanic) than African American. Since it is increasingly more possible for people to align themselves with political, social, or cultural positions at will in America, it is difficult to generalize meaningfully about any sector of the population. Although racism creates predictable paradigms, there will fortunately always be a number of exceptions within a democracy. Human nature tells us that it is futile to expect all African Americans, European Americans, Asian Americans, Hispanic Americans, or any other group of intelligent human beings to restrict their tastes to those things produced by their human subgroup.

Recently, some musicians involved in the creation of music in the European tradition have apparently felt slighted as "jazz" and other African-American music has received an increasing degree of attention. Composer George Walker,[38] in an article in the *New York Times* (November 3, 1991) expressed his feelings that "Black composers are left behind again in the rage for black popular music and jazz." Apparently, according to this statement, Walker does not consider Ellington, Mingus, and Joplin as "Black" composers. He continues: "Folk music, of which jazz is a form, has been assimilated and transformed by composers of all periods. Though many Americans, white and black, began with jazz and moved on to concert music, my background did not include jazz. My exposure to classical music and to European folk music came at an early age. I never listened to jazz until I went to college."

Walker possibly found it necessary to classify "jazz" as folk music to separate his approach to music from other African-American music. Most musicians did not "begin" with jazz and then "move on" to concert music, because most formal instruction musicians received in America this century (privately or in school) was music of European tradition. Jelly Roll Morton, Louis Armstrong, Jimmy Lunceford, Charles Mingus, Dorothy Donegan, Miles Davis, and John Coltrane are examples.

Walker, like earlier African-American church members (who considered "jazz" the "devil's music"), prefers either to distance himself from the negative stereotypes assigned to innovative African-American music or to speak disparagingly about music that is not Eurocentric. Martha Bayles, who also considers "jazz" a folk art, touches on this:

> Of course, the vast majority of people who appreciate jazz do so without any fancy ideas about it one way or the other. Most people don't relate to music, especially popular music, on an intellectual level. But that is precisely why the misconceptions I've been talking about are so influential. The public, whose opinion is registered in dollars, not ideas, offers little resistance.

> Likewise jazz musicians. Along with most artists, jazz musicians accept whatever intellectual acclaim they can get, whether or not it is based on an accurate assessment of their art. In particular, they endorse the Stalinist view of jazz as a folk art corrupted by commerce—largely because it makes room for racial resentment. Too often there *is* a sharp dividing line between the "folk" artist (black) and the "bourgeois" exploiter (white). And too often the memory lingers of the grinning blackface minstrel, bought and sold for the entertainment of whites. What self-respecting jazz musician wouldn't prefer a more heroic image?[39]

Walker is also contemptuous of the notion that "some jazz performers and promoters are trying to redefine the term classical and enshrine jazz as America's classical music. I do wonder what I have been composing for the last 50 years." Walker composed music based upon the European tradition. It cannot be African-American music merely because of the composer's genetic code. Benny Goodman, Stan Getz, Phil Woods, Bill Evans, and other European-American "jazz" artists created music in the African-American tradition (based upon stylistic considerations). For some, such notions are hard to take.

As the world citizens begin to have common experiences that traverse racial classifications, then, and only then, will music eventually be produced that can reflect a generic American experience. As we approach the end of the century, there are signs that Americans are having more shared experiences throughout society. The characteristics Locke described long ago, although reflecting attitudes typical of passed generations, remain features of innovative African-American music:

> The Negro, a musical force, through his own distinct racial characteristics has made an artistic contribution which is racial but not yet national. Rather has the influence of musical stylistic traits termed Negro, spread over many nations wherever the colonies of the New World have become homes of the Negro people. These expressions in melody and rhythm have been a compelling force in American music— tragic and joyful in emotion, pathetic and ludicrous in melody, primitive and barbaric in rhythm. The welding of these expressions has brought about a harmonic effect which is now influencing thoughtful musicians throughout the world. At present there is evidenced a new movement far from academic, which plays an important technical part in the music of this and other lands.[40]

During the long period involving "slave master mentality" in America, Eurocentric claims and stereotypes about Africans or African-Americans went unchallenged. The slave's job was strictly to provide services for the oppressor without ever questioning a request or challenging an opinion, regardless of how ridiculous or demeaning it may have been. These attitudes apparently remain buried deep within the collective unconsciousness of a large portion of American society. Many who have grown accustomed to the delusions and economic advantages of a diabolical system since manumission, are sometimes reluctant to abandon final vestiges.

Some European Americans become aggravated at continual reminders of the legacy of racism in America. Confronting racism on a daily basis is much more enervating. African-American music innovators have confronted such attitudes and responded with the creation of beautiful music. Walton discusses some of the ways race entered into some of the marketing practices in the San Francisco Bay Area:

> Little choice is left for the consumer and aspiring musician since the centralized industry composed of radio, television and recording companies emphasize to a great extent the same type of material; that is, whatever has been contrived by the tastemakers to be the most salable at that particular time. For example, out of thirteen AM and fifteen FM stations in the San Francisco Bay Area, eleven, or close to 40 percent, are rock stations, playing an average of twenty-five minutes of rock music per half hour. A sampling of Chicago radio stations reveals a similar pattern.

There is only one *Jazz* station in the Bay Area. All of the disc jockeys are white, except for one who is an Asian American. Programming, with a few exceptions, leans heavily on the big-band genre. The Dorsey Brothers, Glenn Miller or Stan Kenton are more likely to be heard than "Sonny" Rollins, Horace Silver or Coleman Hawkins. When national Afro-American groups play the one or two "big-time" *Jazz* clubs in the area, there is usually an increase in the frequency of play given to that artist's recordings. Once he or they have gone, the station quickly resumes its previous format. In like fashion, so-called black stations usually exclude Jazz, air time being given mostly to other Afro-American musics.[41]

Sidran points out in *Black Talk*, "The black musician, in taking the process of cultural definition into his own hands, infuriated a vast number of whites."[42] Should the label "jazz" be dropped? Many artists remain disgusted with the label "jazz." Once attached, labels are difficult to remove. Innovators are criticized for abandoning preconceived notions of "jazz."

Summary: Afrocentric Snapshots of a Shrinking Society

I come here to make a speech, to tell you the truth. If the truth is anti-

American, then blame the truth, don't blame me.
                              —Malcolm X[43]

Mary Lou Williams died in 1981. African Americans made many advances during the twentieth century, but racism maintained an economic stranglehold on "Black" socioculture. The absence of African-American record companies, distribution networks, conservatories, and publishing houses show clearly that "Black" music also remained a subject of oppression.

By 1983 South Africa had adopted a new constitution giving limited political rights to "Colored" and "Asian" South Africans, but the privileges were not extended to "Blacks." In November 1984, Israel began a secret airlift of Ethiopian Jews (Falashas) from Sudan in what was called "Operation Moses." Bishop Desmond Tutu, general secretary of the South African Council of Churches, was awarded the Nobel Peace Prize. South Africa launched combined land and air raids against alleged A.N.C. stations in Zambia, Botswana, and Zimbabwe in 1986, ending hopes of truce with the A.N.C. just after a withdrawal from Angola the year before. Mike Tyson (at age twenty) became W.B.C. world heavyweight champion after defeating Trevor Berbick. In 1988, South African "Black" workers staged a three-day strike against a new labor legislation.

The 1990s witnessed the dismantling of apartheid in South Africa and Nelson Mandela was elected its first President. At home in the United States, many sociopolitical issues and problems continued to confront American society as racial divisions increased. In 1989 Charles Stuart, a

"White" businessman in Boston, murdered his pregnant wife to collect the insurance money. He claimed a "Black" man killed his wife and then shot him, thus sending the racist element in that city on a rampage against African-American men. An African-American male with a police record was falsely accused. It was not until Stuart killed himself in January 1990, as his scheme began to fall apart, that the accused man—and Boston's "Black" community (!)—was exonerated.[44]

The bigotry that surrounded the birth of African-American music still remains in contemporary American society. A tearful Susan Smith later claims that a carjacking occurred where a "demonic" African-American male allegedly abducted her two angelic infant sons in Union, South Carolina. Her plea for the return of these children is the subject of national media. Actually, she had drowned the children in a nearby lake. As an article in *Emerge* magazine observed, "Susan Smith knew the powerful grip the image of the dangerous "Black" man has on White American's psyche."[45]

Contemporary American media continually portrays African-American males as criminals. The age of violent criminals in America is becoming much younger than ever before, but they are not of a single race or class.

Stray bursts from eleven-year-old Robert Sandifer's semiautomatic gunfire accidentally killed Shavon Dean, a fourteen-year-old bystander. Chicago police found Sandifer's body four days later. The allegation that the incident was an element of gang warfare in the "mean streets" of the African-American ghetto resounded loudly in the media. A concerted effort seems directed toward accumulating evidence that "implicitly declare the problems of the ghettos a manifestation of 'Blacks' pathological attitudes . . . which has nothing to do with mainstream [White] American society."[46]

Elsewhere, on the same day, a thirteen-year-old European-American boy shot and killed his eleven-year old friend in the blue-collar town of High Bridge, New Jersey. Two twelve-year-old boys, Manuel Sanchez and John Duncan, are also arrested for the unrelated murder of a fifty-year-old man in Wenatchee, Washington. The victim was shot eighteen times because he complained about the boys shooting a gun too close to his home. *Emerge* described another thirteen-year-old boy, Moses Prado, who was charged as an adult on four counts of murder in connection with a grocery store bombing in which four people died in the Bronx. Fourteen-year-old Eric Smith of Bath, New York, was tried and convicted as an adult for strangling and bludgeoning a four-year-old boy. Gerald McCra III, a fifteen-year-old boy, stood accused of murdering his parents and his eleven-year-old sister because he was not allowed to have his girlfriend spend the night. Because none of these boys were African-American there was no media frenzy.

> These are people who, because the assertion of "inferiority" is dressed in pseudo-scientific garb, would pretend that it is not what it really is: The declaration by those of one ethnic group that another ethnic group is "inferior" and therefore has no right to exist except by the super group's permission. They would pretend that *The Bell Curve* —the thesis of which

could be posed only in a climate of
rising intolerance— is not a declaration
of war.

These are people well-skilled in the art
of evading moral responsibility. They
are the spiritual descendants of those
who rationalized the traffic in chattel
slavery, who turned a blind eye to the
declinations of Native-Americans and
who declared that at least Hitler made
the trains run on time while claiming
not to know about the human cargo
and deadly destinations.[47]

During the early 1990s, Michael Jordan, Mike
Tyson, and Michael Jackson all met ill-fated
destinies that are pounced upon by the media. The
"trial of the century" finds O. J. Simpson innocent of
murder in 1995, but the press apparently continued
to assume Simpson guilty. It was one of a few
instances in American history where a jury of
her/his peers tried an African-American defendant,
yet the majority culture suggested that "Black"
people are not capable of trying each other fairly as a
result of the Simpson verdict. Track sensation
Michael Johnson won Olympic gold in both the 200-
meter and 400-meter sprints to make his mark in
sports history. Nonetheless, Johnson was not
considered to have enormous money making
potential (from product endorsements) because the
television industry concluded he "doesn't smile
enough."
      In South Africa, Bishop Desmond Tutu
continues to head the Truth Council that grants
amnesty to those who confess of atrocities

committed under apartheid. As a consequence Africans have heard how their young relatives were "blown to smithereens" or burned alive on a pyre of old tires and wood while their murderers picnicked,[48] much as their American counterparts had done earlier in the United States.

The assassination of Martin Luther King, Malcolm X, along with those claiming the lives of John and Robert Kennedy, signaled the beginning of a quarter-century of ultra-conservative sociopolitical dominance in America. In earlier African-American communities, such as Harlem, drugs were largely confined to musicians and their associates. Now drugs began their malignant infestation, consuming unprecedented numbers of people of all ages in inner city neighborhoods. Conditions eventually became so severe, and suspicions ran so high, that a representative from the CIA attended a town meeting in Los Angeles in the fall of 1996 to defend the agency against claims that the CIA planted drugs in African-American neighborhoods allegedly to destabilize them.

Is the recent appreciation of retrospective Afrocentric music evidence of a natural tendency to reclaim the past before embracing the uncertainties of a complex future? Should we expect retrospection in large dosages as a jam-packed millennium comes to an end? Courtney Pine (b. 1964), a young multi-reedman and composer who makes no compromises, summed things up this way in the liner notes to his album *Courtney Pine: Underground* (Antilles, 1997):

> I truly believe that jazz music should reflect the social climate of the current times. It does this by being influenced by the part which enables the user (the

musician) to see the future with a clear insight. Sometimes external influences, i.e., critics or negative entities, do not, due to the lack of research, understand the mix of certain elements, and will run down a concept because it does not fit into their vision of a jazz artist. I have been fortunate enough to have met enough people (and critics) around the world that have expressed their understanding of this mixture of the traditional (blues, bebop, soul, jazz, avant-garde, etc.) and modern day musical communication (hip-hop, drum and bass, acid jazz, trip-hop, etc.) forms of music. This record is for you as I watched you become at one with the music (whilst on stage), you inspired me to piece this record together. Some may say that I am playing for the audience. What about musical content? Have I lost the battle between backbeat and swing? Well, I have never had a desire to climb that lonely staircase up into that ivory tower. . . there is nothing that we jazz warriors can do to change your minds (c'est la vie) but this will not stop me on my quest to find like-minded warriors, swing as hard, long and purposeful as possible.

So how can we produce a unified genre of music in the United States? America today wants to claim "jazz" as America's classical music. If this desire becomes strong enough to eliminate the racism that results in segregated American sociocultures, and if it manages to bring a fragmented society together, then we can expect to produce a strong, vibrant, and unified American music in the next millennium. A truly unified culture cannot tolerate government leadership that tolerates or contributes to economic and social inequities, that plants drugs and nuclear waste in "minority" neighborhoods that incarcerates the majority of young African-American males as political prisoners, or that limits employment and educational opportunities for underprivileged youth. The long-standing Western imperialist tradition of confiscating art, land, and knowledge from around the world and claiming ownership of them cannot continue to happen.

African-American "jazz," admired, celebrated, and analyzed for the abundance of musical joy, direction, and knowledge it yields, is also a part of the African-American musical legacy chronicling the cultural, psychological, emotional, spiritual, and intellectual history of Africans in the "New World." The music's evolutionary path stands as a reminder of the strength, knowledge, wisdom, durability, and genius of a sector of the American population said to have contributed little to American culture.

The African World

A SURVEY OF AFRICAN KINGDOMS

The story of humanity may be richer than that we know,
We must examine all of it to know that this is so.

HAM AND NOAH'S OTHER SONS THEN CREATED
ALL HAMITIC AND SEMITIC LEVELS
THESE SONS LED AFRICAN & ASIAN CANAANITE
TRIBES FROM THE TOWER OF BABEL
THESE TRIBES WERE CALLED PHOENICIANS BY
GREEKS WHO ADORED THEIR PALM TREES
COULD THIS HAVE ALSO BEEN THE OLD
EGYPTIAN BIRD FROM WHOSE ASHES HE OR SHE
LEAVES
SOME SETTLED IN THE LAND OF CANAAN, NAMED
AFTER THE YOUNGEST SON OF HAM IN FACT
NOW IT'S CALLED ISRAEL BUT BIBLICAL LEPROSY
LAWS CONFIRM THESE PEOPLE WERE BLACK

Kush (Nubia)

The Kushite kingdom lasted over a thousand years
They used elephants in combat evoking all kinds of
fears.
King Piankhy was the first Kushite king to rule Egypt
we see
He ruled these people fairly during the twenty-fifth
Dynasty.
They conquered the Egyptians in 730 B.C. remaining
for a century,
They were then defeated by Assyrians with superior
iron weaponry.
The Kushites fled to Nubia moving their capital to
Meroe in the south,
Soon it was the iron capital of Ancient Africa and
strong once again.
It was King Natashien who reigned from 328 B.C.
and he was no slouch;
With his firm rule, Nubian hieroglyphics, alphabet
and script began.

Trade exploits to Arabia, India and China caused
their fame to expand.
After the crucifixion, many Kushites became
Christians as times changed;
And by 320 A.D. King Malequereliar became the last
king that reigned.
The Axum Empire was eventually the new trade
center, and after 1200 years,
Christian Nubia fell to Moslem rule despite all the
struggling and tears.

Goddesses became gods when the pagan temples
were destroyed,
Her story became his-story as sacerdotal egos
became annoyed.
Time can erase the memory of a soul,
Then the mind becomes tired and old,

Ancient Ghana

Ancient Ghana should not be confused with today's
Ghana at all.
It was the gold capital of the world, then to the Arabs
it did fall.
Koumbi, its famous capital was divided into two
great & powerful African cities
Where miners found nuggets for the king while
placing gold dust into their own kitties
The king & Soninke tribe lived in one area, Moslems
& foreigners in the other
The latter group taxed all goods entering into or
passing through the city.
A strong army kept the Trans-Saharan trade routes
open & under cover
Until 1054, when Almoravids invaded the region for
14 years, finally conquering it, what a pity.

How many mothers, sisters and daughters achieved
their arcane aspirations,
Yet the names of their sons, brothers and fathers are
preserved within the nation.
I know sield an easy way to be,
The universe is creative if you take the time to see,

WE KNOW THE SUMERIANS AND HAMURABI'S
BABYLONIAN KINGDOM OF CIRCA 2150 B.C.
IT TAKES MUCH MORE THAN RACIST CANALS TO
CHANGE A HISTORY FROM SEA TO SHINING SEA
MESOPOTAMIA WAS INHABITED BY ETHIOPIANS
AND SOME CANAANITES WERE CARTHAGINIANS
AFRICANS WERE CERTAINLY AFRICAN FROM
NORTH TO SOUTH & SO WERE INDIA'S
DRUVIDIANS
JUST AS ALL MAYAS, AZTECS, INCAS, CHOCTAW,
SIOUX, APACHE, AND ESKIMOS ARE ALL
MISNAMED "INDIAN"

Mali (not the Republic of Mali)

Out of the ruins of the Moslem state of Ancient
Ghana around 1230 A.D.
Grew Niani, the capital of the Mandingo Empire, and
strong it was to be.
Sundiata captured rich salt and gold mining areas
then sent his men away,
So his generals became his governors & counsel was
held with local chiefs each day.
By 1312 King Mansa Musa kept desert raiders away
with his 90,000 men,
This infantry was backed by 10,000 more on camels
and Arabian horses.

Soon peace came & warriors became farmers and
didn't have to fight again,
Their fair king became known as a lover of music,
poetry and created new resources.
Mali's empire spread to Tazhaza & the gold areas
Galam & Bure to the south
Numeruos gold, copper, silver & leather craftsmen
put food in every mouth.
Timbuktu & Djenne became centers knowledge,
commerce and culture we hear,
But in 1324 Mali's economy became inflated and
remained so for 25 years.
A devout Moslems that led a pilgrimage to Mecca
took 60,000 men and such,
And although they forced no one to convert the gold
they left there was too much
Good king Mansa Musa died in 1337, but his empire
improved continually until its time was through;
Many Greek, Roman and Indian scholars came to
study there in Sankore at University in Timbuktu.

So the great queen Isis is dethroned from the trinity,
And once great folk become indentured for eternity.
The weak, not the meek then inherit the earth . . . for
a while,
But insecurity and insanity can be measured in the
absence of a smile.

Songhay

It is the largest Ancient African kingdoms we've
examined thus far,
Its people came from the region of Dendi on the Niger
River bar.
This occurred before the 9th century and by the 11th
century or so,

Songhay expanded quickly well beyond the bend (at
Niger) to Gao.   Before long this capital city became
the Moslem center of learning & trade
So when Sunni Ali came to power prosperity had
already been made.
That was 1464, then beginning in 1468, this warrior
king attacked Timbuktu,
Defeating the Tuaregs and Djenne (in the south),
subjugating the whole
slew.
The war took 7 years, later King Askia Mohammed
continued the proliferation of this plight . . .
The empire now created farmers, merchants and
miners (who were traditionally out of sight).
Soon every member of the community held roles
such as keepers of cattle, miners, & fishmen.
Until the Portugese took over the rich African trade
and brought things
to a bitter end.

But how does the Queen of Sheba fit into his-story?
Can Queen Nefertiti find her place in all this
masculine glory?
Time can erase the memory of a soul,
Then the mind becomes tired, the mind becomes old,
So the great queen Isis is dethroned from the trinity,
And once great folk become indentured for eternity.

THEN CAME INVASIONS; INDO GERMANIC AND
GERMANIC INVASIONS OF ASIA
GREEK INVASIONS OF THE MIDDLE EAST; ROMAN
INVASIONS OF THE MIDDLE EAST & NORTHERN
AFRICA; JEWS AND ARABS BECAME INVOLVED IN
THE "WHITE" SLAVE TRADE . . . THE WORLD WAS
BECOMING MORE COMPLEX AND SO WERE ITS
COMPLEXIONS.

ALTHOUGH THESE EARLIER SOCIETIES HAD
AMPLE PREJUDICES,
THEY WEREN'T BASED STRICTLY ON COLOR -
READING HERODOTUS PROVES THE POINT - YET
WE'RE ASTONISHED TO REALIZE THAT SOCRATES
WAS A BROTHER
BEFORE TRUTH OF MOSES, ABRAHAM,
CLEOPATRA, AESOP, HANNIBAL AND OTHERS WAS
TOLD
OUR WESTERN HISTORY SEPARATED THE LAND
FROM ITS PEOPLE; WAS THAT DUMB OR BOLD?

AN EGYPTIAN WAS AN EGYPTIAN; A GREEK A
GREEK; A HOTTENTOT WAS A HOTTENTOT
THE LAND OF THE FREE; HOME OF THE BRAVE -
ARE WE MOVING
BACKWARDS OR WHAT?

Kanem - Bornu

These twin kingdoms lasted over a thousand years;
Idris Alomia was its greatest king.
The dominions were located on either side of Lake
Chad; its mighty military controlled everything.
It traded nuts, leather, ivory, and ostrich feathers for
salt and European goods.
Their warriors were famed for horsemanship so the
Lake Chad Region was free of robbing hoods.
Thus the trade and commerce was usually not
impeded; consequently, its economy could not help
but flourish.
To sustain both Kanem & Bornu for so many
centuries most certainly took strength, wisdom and
courage.

How many mothers, sisters and daughters achieved
their arcane aspirations,
Yet it's the names of sons, brothers and fathers that
remain preserved within the nation.
I know destructive force yield an easy way to be,
Yet the universe remains creative if you have the
eyes to see,

Benin

The trading center for large sections of West Africa,
and a culture rich in communal commitment from
people harboring pride within every heart . . .
Was the forest kingdom of Benin in what is now
Southern Nigeria from whence wood and bronze
artifacts sprang forth as African art.
These dignified people used Manillas (or metal rings)
& cowrie shells as money, while making daily
shopping & bartering a casual affair;
The Oba or chiefs allowed various officials to manage
the kingdom, while a few miles away the "Queen
Mother" groomed the king's heir.
Ewuare the Great (who ruled from 1440 to 1473), a
somewhat eccentric chief, was known as a magician,
doctor, warrior and wise man;
The city had long, broad, and straight streets with
many houses, complex temples, and law-abiding
citizens (you must understand).
At first the Portugese tried to steal Benin's many
riches, but they changed their approach after being
forcefully and repeatedly driven away.
Then they and other Europeans trade partners
learned that dealing with shrewd African merchants
took 8 to 10 entire days.

Before making important decisions the custom was
to eat, drink and be festive for a significant period of
time.
After all, the people of Benin reserved a day each
month for celebrating -
as diametrically opposed to plotting crime.

---

[1] *Emerge*, January 1999, pp. 70–72.
[2] Ed Enright, *Down Beat*, February 1999, pp. 20–26.
[3] Richard M. Sudhalter, *New York Times*, January 3,
1999.
[4] John McDonough, *Wall Street Journal*, January 27,
1999.
[5] *Down Beat*, January 2000, p. 35.
[6] Listen to *Jumping in the Sugarbowl* (1984) and
other Myers albums from this period.
[7] Peter Watrous, *The New York Times*, June 16,
1991, p. 22.
[8] *Down Beat*, January 2000, p. 33.
[9] A. James Liska, "A Common Understanding:
Wynton and Branford Marsalis," *Down Beat* 61, no. 2
(February 1994); originally issued December 1982.
[10] As cited in *NYSO Journal* 5, no.1: 1 (a National
Jazz Service Organization Organization publication).
[11] Ben Sidran, *Black Talk* (New York: Da Capo,
1981), p. 76.
[12] Benny Goodman and Irving Kolodin, *The Kingdom
of Swing*, p. 241.
[13] Sidran, *Black Talk*, p. 90.
[14] Liner notes in *Fathers and Sons*, Columbia
Records FC37972 (1982).
[15] "Editorial commentary: Jazz at Lincoln Center,"
NYSO Journal 4, no. 4

[16] Kevin Whitehead, *Village Voice*, November 23, 1993, jazz supplement.

[17] Wynton Marsalis, "Wynton Speaks: 'Who Actually Is Stupid,'" *NYSO Journal* 5, no. 1.

[18] The actual title is *Africa, According to Herodotus—456 B.C.*

[19] Karlton Hester organized the Contemporary Jazz Art Movement (CJAM) in 1978. Many of the members of the Contemporary Jazz Art Movement also led their own groups.

[20] *Down Beat*, July 1981, p. 56.

[21] John Janowiak, *Down Beat*, June 1999, p. 22.

[22] Havelock Nelson and Michael A. Gonzales, *Bring the Noise: A Guide to Rap Music and Hip-Hop Culture* (New York: Harmony Books, 1991), p. xix.

[23] Ibid., p. xviii.

[24] Nelson George, *The Death of Rhythm and Blues* (New York: Pantheon Books, 1988), p. 108.

[25] Nelson and Gonzales, *Bring the Noise*, p. xx.

[26] Joseph D. Eure and James G. Spady, eds., *Nation Conscious Rap* (New York: PC International, 1991), p. 29.

[27] Rellstab first met the composer in person in 1825 when Beethoven was internationally acclaimed.

[28] Alessandra Comini, *The Changing Image of Beethoven: A Study in Myth Making*, p. 22.

[29] J. A. Rogers, *Sex and Race* (St. Petersburg, Fla.: Helga M. Rogers, 1972), 3:85.

[30] Fischer knew that he was describing a famous man.

[31] Comini, *Changing Image of Beethoven*, p. 30.

[32] Schindler became Beethoven's first major biographer.

[33] Comini, *Changing Image of Beethoven*, p. 27.

[34] Goldberg, *Racist Culture* (Oxford: Blackwell, 1994) p. 95.

[35] *Chronicle of Higher Education*, May 6, 1992.

[36] Coleman wrote an article, "Did Egypt Shape the Glory That Was Greece?" that takes a position similar to that of Lefkowitz.

[37] A major or minor tonic is never established in accordance with Western tonal harmony in authentic blue forms.

[38] Walker is African-American .

[39] Martha Bayles, *Hole in Our Soul: The Loss of Beauty and Meaning in American Popular Music* (New York: Free Press 1994), p. 85.

[40] Alain Locke, preface to *The Negro and His Music* (Port Washington, N.Y.: Kennikat, 1968).

[41] *Music: Black, White, and Blue*, p. 137.

[42] Sidran, *Black Talk*, p. 97.

[43] As cited in *Emerge: Black America's News Magazine*, February 1995.

[44] Ibid., p. 60.

[45] Ibid., p. 62.

[46] Ibid.

[47] Ibid., p. 64

[48] From a radio broadcast of live confessions on National Public Radio, December 12, 1996.

INDEX

Karlton E. Hester

"Jazz" FINAL EXAM

Name: _____

*[**Part 1** - class "active" listening = 30 points] Give the title and name of the leader (or group) for each of the following recordings:*

1.
2.
3.
4.
5.
6.
7.
8.
9.
10.
11.
12.
13.
14.
15.

*[**Part 2** - Text = 55.5 points (1.5 each)] Give name, phrase or word that matches the apppropriate answer.*

1940 - 1950

1. _____vocalized in combination with the bass lines he played creating a stronger presence. It also made the bass player think in a melodic

fashion rather than limiting its fuction to the outlining of basic chords.

2. Drums came to the U.S. as components from all over the world. _____ made these individual percussion instruments into the drum set in America. Baby Dodds evolved the set to a higher level in early "jazz."

3. When Charlie Parker met _____ in 1941, they became the catalyst for the bop revolution and brought this improvisational style to its peak.

4. Resistance to bop was so great during the 1940s that an attempt was made to revive _____ as the "authentic" jazz music of America.

5. In bebop, _____ was much faster and more complex than any other music in the Western tonal tradition. The use of clever dissonances is heightened by chord extensions and substitutions. New scales are applied to a harmonic framework that most ears had grown to consider traditional.

6. The impact of this pianist's music on modern jazz history was enormous. The incredibly fast improvised lines and added chords tones of _____ inventive improvisations were absorbed by Charlie Parker and other early progenitors of be-bop.

7. _____ had tutored Powell when the latter pianist was a teen. Powell's mentor's composition "In Walked Bud" is a tribute to his younger

comrade. Powell premiered his tutor's composition "'Round Midnight" on a recording with Cootie Williams.

8. During the bebop era vocalist ⸱_____ performed four-hand piano pieces with Earl "Fatha" Hines in 1943, and in 1945 pianist Vivian Glasby played at the Rhumboogie in Chicago with The Fletcher Henderson Band for an engagement.

1950 - 1960

9. This pioneering stylist would lead a series of innovative groups that included many illustrious innovators of the "jazz" world. Later collaborations with Gil Evans produced such albums as "Porgy and Bess" and "Sketches of Spain," expanding the "Birth of the Cool" idea into a full orchestral setting. _____ 1959 Kind of Blue popularized modal improvisation in the 1960's, but in his later life he turned more to electronic music, mixing in elements of rock, funk, salsa, and modal jazz into his works which set the style for fusion and jazz rock.

10._____ led a string of Big Bands throughout the 1940's and '50's, and was heavily influenced by Claude Thornhill, sometimes referred to as the father of the cool style big band. This band leader became one of the best known jazz arrangers ever because of his work on college campuses accross America.

11._____ music from his last stylistic period often bore religious titles: "A Love Supreme,"

"Ascension," "Om," "Crescent," "The Father and the Son, and the Holy Ghost," "Ogunde," "Meditations," "Amen," "Ascent,"and others. His thinking, like Sun Ra's, also focused on outer space: "Infinity," "Interstellar Space," Sun Ship," "Cosmos," "Out of This World," etc.

12. Chic Webb featured Louis Jordan as both a vocalist and saxophone soloist between 1936 and 1938. The _____ was a small swing band that developed in the late1930s and early 1950s and was later advanced by Jordan's group, the Timpani Five. It generally featured two or three soloist in front of a swinging rhythm section. In was appealing to the African American cabaret audiences because it retained the sexual and nuptial humor of the music from old "black" vaudeville shows.

13. _____ made important recordings with Miles Davis in 1954. His composition "Oleo," recorded during this period, became a "jazz" standard. After this productive musical phase, and during the height of a battle between critics over wheter he or Coltrane was the "best" tenor player of the day, this innovator took the first of many long sabbaticals from public performance.

14. _____ experimentation with collective improvisation involved a significant advancement in liberating the melody from preset chord changes. Many hard bop performers aligned their melodic improvisations closely to preset chord structures, while this innovator devised a conceptual methodology that allowed musicians more autonomy. This freedon applied whether in

constructing solo improvisations or in playing accompaniment.

15. Although this iconoclastic pianist always drew an audience, it was often not the type or size a clientele clubowners desired. His unconventional style was conducive to neither selling drinks or for sexual advancements because people listened and didn't want to be disturbed. This was not background music. He did not come from the type of blues-based backgroud that Bird, Coltrane or Ornette Coleman came from. _____ produced percussive music that fit a musical void that had not yet been filled.

16. _____ added to the musical controversity started by Taylor and Coleman, and soon influential musicians like Coltrane and Dolphy evolved in the direction of free experimentation. The atmosphere was often hostile and the musicians were ostracized from many mainstream musical venues. John Gilmore was among this leader's most loyal bandmembers. Gilmore had been offered a position in Miles Davis's and other prestigious bands, but remained with this innovator's Arkestra through the years despite his towering status on tenor saxophone.

1960 -1970

17. Trombonist/ arranger _____ conducted her own arrangements on Randy Weston's *Uhuru Africa* session and the Swahili language was used to demonstrate the beauty of African languages. The album was recorded in early 1960

and was also intended to show "how the African language is also part of the African rhythms."

18. In 1969, bassist _____ and cellist Earl Madison brought suit against Leonard Bernstein and the New York Philharmonic for racial discrinination.   ˙

19. This alto saxophonist, bass clarinetist, and flutist, like Coltrane, continued to maintain ties between his hard bop roots and his more radical experimentation. While Coltrane's stylistic development evolved gradually from traditional hard bop to a freer musical approach in a highly methodical fashion, _____ continued to oscillate between the two opposing stylistic poles. He participated as co-leader in the 1960 *Free Jazz* recording with Ornette Coleman, then recorded with Oliver Nelson and Booker Little a year later in sessions that were decisively hard bop oriented.

20. _____recorded his first album on his own Debut label as he celebrated his 39th birthday (1951). This bassist/composer was at the height of his musical development during the early part of the 1960s, then fell into obscurity. His 1959 recording of his bitterly comical composition *Original Faubus Fables* and his disagreement with Columbia over the sales figures for his recordings left them unable to renew their contract. The lyrics for his composition did not sit well with some listeners.

21. In May 1965 the _____was formed by pianists Abrams and Jodie Christian, drummer

Steve McCall, and trumpeter Phil Cohran. Its original member were from several groups that had been playing around Chicago. Their goals were to create a situation where they could produce the brand of music of their own choice and maintain self-reliance and control over their music.

22. The _____ was one or the first groups to place a heavy degree of emphasis on silence in "jazz." This ensembles approach helped us to realize that silence can become animated it eventually becomes apparent that music contains more than length, width, and depth. Through their music it became increasingly more clear that music contains immeasurable elements that registers strongly upon our senses but are difficult to define emperically.

23. _____ secured a job with Art Blakey and the Jazz Messengers by 1969 and remained with the band until 1972. She was the only woman to play with the Messengers for a significant period of time. The innovative pianist played with saxophonist Joe Henderson's group from 1972 to 1975 and then joined saxophonist Stan Getz until 1977.

24. _____ felt that "When there is chaos, which is now [December 18, 1966], only a relatively few people can listen to the music that tells of what will be. You see, everyone is screaming 'Freedom' now, but mentally, most are under a great strain. But now the truth is marching in, as it once marched back in New Orleans."

25._____ toured throughout the
sixties. By the end of the decade, the
harpist/composer became increasingly involved
with writing and presenting musicals that dealt
with African American concerns.   She wrote
scores, lyrics and performed with the shows, as
her husband (the drummer) established an
African American theater company in Detroit.

26._____ debuted as composer and leader at
Town Hall in New York in a concert that included
original solo, trio and big-band compositions in
1967. She then began to set the foundation for
her own unique orchestra, which would enter
maturity during the following decade. In 1969
she married saxophonist-flutist Lew Tabackin
and formed a quartet with him.

27.By the 1960s _____had made its way to
New York City bringing with its rituals the music
of the bata drums. Many of the "free" players were
eager to incorporate these new rhythmic sounds
into their universe bringing the evolution of
African American music full circle, back (so to
speak) to its point of origin - African music.

1970 - 1980

28.A small sampling of the diverse spectrum of
musical styles presented during the 1970's was
preserved on the limited issue of the five record
set _____. The record set was recorded
live in 1977 and was produced by Alan Douglas
and Michael Cuscuna in association with Sam

Rivers. Over 60 musicians performed on the 22 performances that were released.

29. Virtuoso pianist and composer _____ (b.1940), had absorbed the new experimental formulas he encountered with Miles and exposed this musical influence on his album *Crossings* in 1972. This direction continued, and began to display a heavy funk influence on subsequent albums such as *Headhunters* (1973), *Sextant* (1973), and *Thrust* (1974).

30. Pianist Ramsey Lewis, traditionally a hard bop style pianist, collaborated with the popular ensemble Earth, Wind & Fire in 1974 to produce a "cross-over" album entitled _____.

31. _____ was not the first to focus on the flute as a front-line jazz instrument (Wayman Carver, Herbie Mann, and others played flute exclusively earlier), but his contribution invoved taking flute technique to a new level of virtuosity that emphasize an expanded array of the inherent qualities of the instrument.

32. _____ is a remarkable vocal recitalists who was living in London when the American "jazz" influence strongly affected singers abroad creating a fresh new vocal approach. Her unusually wide range found a new stylistic function within a musical approach that found popularity on her 1973 album *I Am a Song* .

33. Trumpeter _____ came through the hard bop school to establish another type of fusion in

the seventies with his highly successful group, the Blackbyrds.

34. Woodwind multi-instrumentalist and composer _____ (b.1945) has been a major figure in contemporary instrumental music since the midseventies. He took part in the experimental music of the Association for the Advancement of Creative Musicians, went on to resists categorization and to explore non-conventional conceptions of tone color, solo construction, and other unique ideas. His techinal proficiency extends to such rarely seen horns as the sopranino and contrabass saxes. He is a composer whose works form a bridge between jazz and the classical avant-garde idioms, is becoming increasingly more widespread.

35. _____ was formed by three saxophonists from the Black Artists Group (formed in St. Louis in 1968) who became prominent during the 1970s and a younger Bay Area born saxophonist. Oliver Lake (b. 1942), Julius Hemphill (1940-1995), and Hamiet Bluiett (b. 1940) were the members of BAG who founded the ensemble in 1976 with saxophonist David Murray (b. 1955).

36. _____ performed with Mongo Santamaria, Willie Bobo, Herbie Mann, Blue Mitchell, and Stan Getz before recording his first solo album, *Tones for Joan's Bones* (later retitled *Inner Space*). His Latin rhythms and melodies during the seventies on albums like *Light as a Feather* (Polydor PD 5525) and the jazz-rock oriented *Musicmagic* won him a popular following.

37._____is an Indian virtuoso whose father played over 200 musical instruments. He opened a School of North Indian Music in Marin County in the San Francisco Bay Area.

[**Part 3** - Essay = 15 points]

In the space provided, discuss ways in which modern "jazz" reflects the world in which the music was created. Be brief but cite a few concrete examples.